**Science, Sin, and
Scholarship**

Science, Sin, and Scholarship
The Politics of Reverend Moon and the Unification Church

Edited by
Irving Louis Horowitz

The MIT Press
Cambridge, Massachusetts,
and London, England

This book was set in Baskerville by
dnh typesetting, inc. and was
printed and bound by Alpine Press in
the United States of America.

Library of Congress Cataloging in
Publication Data
Main entry under title:

Science, sin, and scholarship.

Includes index.
1. Moon, Sun Myung—Addresses,
essays, lectures. 2. Segye Kidokkyo
T'ongil Sillyŏng Hyŏphoe—Addresses,
essays, lectures. I. Horowitz, Irving
Louis.
BX9750.S4S35   289'.9   78-9021
ISBN 0-262-08100-8

Contents

Preface   ix

Acknowledgments   xii

Sun Myung Moon: Irving Louis Horowitz
Missionary to Western
Civilization   xiii

I Theory and Theology of
Sun Myung Moon:
Documents

1 God's Hope for America   Sun Myung Moon
Keynote Speech at
Yankee Stadium
June 1, 1976   2

2 The Search for Absolute   Sun Myung Moon
Values: Harmony among
the Sciences
Founder's Address,
Fifth International
Conference on the
Unity of the Sciences,
November 26, 1976,
Washington, D.C.   12

3 Sun Myung Moon and   Frederick Sontag
the Unification Church:
Charges and Responses   20

II The Metaphysics of Moon

4 The Last Civil Religion: Reverend Moon and the Unification Church 46

Thomas Robbins
Dick Anthony
Madeline Doucas
Thomas Curtis

5 Jews and Judaism in Reverend Moon's *Divine Principle* 74

A. James Rudin

Addendum 84

Marc H. Tanenbaum

6 Some Thoughts about the Unification Movement and the Churches 86

Barbara W. Hargrove

7 Critique of the Theology of the Unification Church as Set Forth in *Divine Principle* 102

Agnes Cunningham
J. Robert Nelson
William L. Hendricks
Jorge Lara-Braud

III The Politics of Moon

8 The Activities of the Korean Central Intelligence Agency in the United States 120

Jai Hyon Lee

9 Profits, Politics, Power: The Heart of the Controversy 148 Marianne Lester

10 The Korea Lobby 160 Frank Baldwin

11 Moon's Sect Pushes Pro-Seoul Activities 176 Ann Crittenden

12 On the Civil Liberties of Sect Members 192

Part 1 193 Charles C. Marson
    Margaret C. Crosby
    Alan L. Schlosser

Part 2 198 S. Lee Vavuris

Part 3 208 John J. Leahy

IV The Psychology and Sociology of Sun Myung Moon

13 Moon Madness: Greed or Creed? 218 C. Daniel Batson

14 The Pull of Sun Moon 226 Berkeley Rice

15 The Eclipse of   Chris Welles
Sun Myung Moon   242

16 Science, Sin, and   Irving Louis Horowitz
Sponsorship   260

Contributors   283

Name Index   285

Subject Index   289

Preface

For some years a large portion of my intellectual work has been devoted to the study of ethical issues that emerge in concrete social settings. To use Anselm Strauss's felicitous phrase, I have used "grounded theory" to discuss abstract, large-scale value considerations. In part, like the character in Molière's *The Would-Be Gentleman* who discovered that he was using prose all of his life but didn't know it, I have found that moral considerations inevitably structure American society in much the same way as organizational effort and ideological belief.

In *The Rise and Fall of Project Camelot,* what began as a case study of a specific counterinsurgency undertaking considered for Latin America ended as a large-scale analysis of the policy distinction between those who believe that the mission of social science includes saving the world *for* the American system and those who believe that social science should be used to save the world *from* that system. Of course, there are a series of continuities that modulate these extreme positions, but the fact remains that even these continuities represent specific ethical persuasions as to the nature of social science performance.

In an examination of the rifts that developed among members of the Institute for Advanced Study at Princeton, again what started out as an analysis of different points of view on the permanent appointment of one sociologist finally ended as an examination of whether social science can be considered a scientific discipline on the same level with the physical sciences and mathematics. In the course of this study I rediscovered the significance of Robert Merton's distinction between latent and manifest functions; so often pedestrian organizational or fiscal considerations disguise the profound moral and valuational differences among different strata within American society.

Science, Sin, and Scholarship evolved in much the same way as my other works. It was begun as a discussion of a specific meeting, the Fifth International Conference on the Unity of the Sciences, but it turned into an examination of the relationship of funding to commitment and belief. Long-standing, simmering issues concerning the relation between science and religion were thrust to the forefront of analysis in the act of discussing a single conference and its procedures and participants. Once again, almost through accident, I rediscovered the obvious: that a decision to attend a particular event may well involve a series of wide-ranging antecedent concerns about the essential worth of an organization or a theology. In this sense the collective enterprise contained in this anthology attests to the ongoing power of symbolic politics, no less than civil religions, in American society.

Because my own position is clearly etched in both the introduction and the conclusion to this volume, not to mention a shared vision with many selections herein contained, it would be unwise to burden this preface with any elaborate discussion of issues. It is nonetheless evident that real issues are involved. These range from the nature of social movements to the character of established religions; they embrace the cries of the young for salvation and the whispers of the old for rewards. This volume attempts to put the Unification church movement into the perspective of American social history as well as the international political future.

This work contains a hidden set of heroes and heroines who require mention, namely, the contributors; specifically the social scientists, historians, and journalists who were quick to respond to the larger meanings and moorings of the Unification church and its founder and leader, the Reverend Sun Myung Moon. There was a time, not long ago, when movements such as this one would require a decent burial before being addressed by the research community. There was, for example, a precedent, probably a consequence of the norms in diplomatic history, that nothing under twenty-five years of age can be researched in a scholarly manner — this is such obvious nonsense that the belief itself deserves investigation. Still, it is my hope that this kind of collective endeavor provides the sort of in-depth analysis that makes possible a public scholarship that goes beyond the popular media. To each of the contributors goes my genuine appreciation.

Irving Louis Horowitz
Rutgers University
September 25, 1977

Acknowledgments

Grateful acknowledgment is made to the following authors, publishers, and agencies for permission to reprint copyrighted material in *Science, Sin, and Scholarship*. All other materials in this volume are either original and prepared for the volume or were issued as reports, testimony, or source documents. In a number of instances the materials in this volume are greatly expanded or revised, and the listings are acknowledgment for original publication purposes only.

Frank Baldwin, "The Korea Lobby," *Christianity and Crisis*, Vol. 36, No. 12 (July 19, 1976): 162–168.

C. Daniel Batson, "Moon Madness: Greed or Creed?," *APA Monitor*, Vol. 1 (June 1976): 32–35

Ann Crittenden, "Moon's Sect Pushes Pro-Seoul Activities," *The New York Times*, May 25, 1976.

Irving Louis Horowitz, "Science, Sin, and Sponsorship," *The Atlantic*, March 1977.

Marianne Lester, "Profits, Politics, Power: The Heart of the Controversy," *The Times Magazine:* July 25, 1977: 13–16. Used with permission of the Army Times Publishing Company.

Berkeley Rice, "The Pull of Sun Moon," *The New York Times Magazine*, May 30, 1976.

Thomas Robbins, Dick Anthony, Madeline Doucas, and Thomas Curtis, "The Last Civil Religion: Reverend Moon and the Unification Church," *Sociological Analysis*, Vol. 37, No. 2 (1976): 111–125.

A. James Rudin, "Jews and Judaism in Reverend Moon's *Divine Principle*," December 1976. Used with permission of the American Jewish Committee.

Frederick Sontag, "Sun Myung Moon and the Unification Church: Charges and Responses," from *Sun Myung Moon and the Unification Church*. Abingdon, 1977.

Chris Welles, "The Eclipse of Sun Myung Moon," *New York Magazine*, September 27, 1976. Used with permission of International Creative Management.

Sun Myung Moon: Missionary to Western Civilization

Irving Louis Horowitz

In attempting to develop a balanced perspective on the Reverend Moon and his Unification church, one comes upon a point raised by Thomas Robbins, and before him, Robert Bellah, on civil religion in America. The very fusion of a notion of civics and religion portends a breakdown of the classical Western dichotomy between Caesar and God, between the secular and the sacred, and between the empirical and the supernatural. This dualism has served Western society well. It has permitted the relationship of religion to society to coexist without victory or surrender for either party and has carved our realms of being with boundaries that are invisible but real.

The great ubiquity of the Unification church is that like other Eastern-origin cults, it renders helpless, if not entirely useless, this Western dualism. It is a movement without boundaries, expressing belief systems at once political and theological, outlining premises for political action and religious realignment. Western Christendom has endured and survived a variety and host of economic and political systems so that it is able to cope with the present moment in political time far easier than with a movement like the Unification church.

Here we come to the primary reason why the Unification church has elicited such enormous concern and consternation: the movement articulates a classical anticommunist standpoint and at the same time reasserts the need for traditional, theological verities. The Reverend Moon is a fundamentalist with a vengeance: he has a belief system that admits of no boundaries or limits, an all-embracing truth. His writings exhibit a holistic concern for the person, society, nature, and all things embraced by the human vision. In this sense the concept underwriting the Unification church is apt, for its primary drive and appeal is unity, urging a paradigm of essence in an overly complicated world of existence. It is a ready-made doctrine for impatient young people and all those for whom the pursuit of the complex has become a tiresome and fruitless venture. If there is any message in Moon's own statements and in those of his articulate interpreters, like Frederick Sontag, it is simply the need for a vision that somehow restores meaning to events. It is a rearguard attack on a positivist tradition of truth without meaning, existence without essence, and facts without interpretation.

The metaphysical appeal provides a direct assault upon the Judeo-Christian tradition; indeed that tradition accepted limits to the role of religion in society. For the purposes of its own sur-vival it put some distance between the everyday events of the world and the transcendental meaning of life reserved for sab-bath. The institutionalization of most Western religions depends heavily on this maintenance of boundaries between the sacred and profane, divine experience and daily activities.

In the past most conventional Western religions have been able to turn back without entirely suppressing mystical challenges. Indeed the fact that most challenges were mystic made them vulnerable to the rationalistic religions of the West. But because the Unification church and the Reverend Moon come forth as both a social movement and a civic movement, they are able to translate its theological mysticism into events, or at least par-ticipation in those events. And for that reason the Unification church enters world history as neither rationalistic nor mystic but rather as some strange conglomeration of the two fused by the sensuous events of world politics.

In some odd way, what was once said of postwar Germany has become true of a place like the two Koreas, where confrontation and schism exist within the bowels of the society itself: where East meets West, where communism takes on democracy, where all the visible symbols of modern conflict continue and exist in uneasy stasis. The peculiar genius of the Reverend Moon and his movement is that they have tapped this strange truth: that there are places in the world where geography meets symbolism and where confrontation is a matter of both land and ideology. In this sense the Korean source of the Moon movement should not be viewed as a simple accident of time and place but is the very essence of the movement and its efforts to inculcate new meaning into old struggles.

The Moon movement is also a social movement. The very momentum from East to West changes the conventional pattern of messianic and missionary activity. The entire history of Western Christendom, indeed the entire history of Christianity under capitalist aegis, has been to colonize the heathen, convert the barbarian. It has always been a movement of white people converting colored people, advanced nations instructing backward nations. And here comes the Reverend Moon and his movement, indisputably Oriental, unquestionably nonwhite, and beyond the pale of Christianity, representing a small state but making his biggest impact on the center of world civilization itself, the United States. That this irony has been lost on interpreters is of small wonder. It is, to begin with, inconceivable in theory and unacceptable in practice, for the conclusion must be that the heathens are Western and white and that the truly devout are Eastern and colored. Who is to educate the educators? Apparently the Reverend Moon has been sent by God to answer that question.

Under the circumstances, it is little wonder that questions of civil liberties would become central, and that in a rage to prove the Reverend Moon wrong, there would be debriefing ceremonies, just as there are briefing rituals: that parents would seek the return of children even to the point of kidnapping them. One is forced to wonder if African parents of children converted to Christianity had similar feelings or accepted the white religion as a sanguine truth. Of course in a civilized nation, the question of rights becomes a judicial matter, and at this level, whatever the metaphysical standpoint of the Reverend Moon, rights to proselytize, to convert, to change take on their own transcendental meaning and throw into a state of disrepair the judicial mechanisms that work so well as long as there is a recognized separation of power between church and state.

In a sense the Reverend Moon and his church have only followed a classical model of institutionalization, the natural history of which is, first, to recruit acolytes in the alien world, second, to have such a following secure funds, third, by a division of labor based on the rights to disperse those funds, fourth, institutionalization of the faith through mass mobilization and membership drives, and fifth, rationalization of the faith through ideology and theology. This is really nothing more than the course of action Saint Paul outlined in the Second Letter to the Corinthians. But when it is done today it somehow shocks—as if the early followers of Christ did not proceed in precisely the same manner to secure an economically viable foundation for the Christian church. This is not to suggest that the Reverend Moon has a testament equal to those already revealed or that the staying power of his church will rival that of Western religions. Indeed the likelihood is the reverse: the very linkages of secular and civic problems to a living deity probably have done more to doom this church than theological shortcomings.

It is one thing for masses of alienated, disaffected students or young people to link up with such a movement, but it is quite another for such a movement to generate a response among a large portion of the Western intelligentsia. Of course at one level, the mandarin class, the intelligentsia itself, is without a focus. Under such circumstances, quasi-religious movements with a strong dose of social movement concerns are bound to generate a response. It is wrong to think that the intelligentsia is somehow different from those who presume to serve. They are cut from the same marrow and suffer the same pangs of uncertainty. The difference between intellectuals and young novices is not their value systems but their capacity, or lack thereof, to articulate that value system.

That the Reverend Moon and his Unification church have understood both the importance of articulation and the relationship of ideology to theology is a brilliant stroke, a recognition that vast, simplified concepts based on religious zealotry and anticommunism require a mass battering ram at one end and intellectual justifications at the other. The question of the linkages between the Reverend Moon and his Unification church and the Korean regime still exist, even though they have become increasingly muddled over time. Just as there is no doubt of the past connections and linkages, institutional and individual, so too there is no doubt that there has been a falling out among the various overseas activities of the Korea lobby. While it is extremely important to distinguish the politics of the Moon religion from the Korean regime, it is also important to understand that were this simply an extension of the Korean CIA, the Moon movement would have long since ceased to have any importance.

Reverend Moon and his church are a long, low cry from the past: a demand for a return to a simplified, unified world over and against what must appear to many to be a complicated and fragmented present-day world, growing more so daily. It is also a cry of the heart for a Western civilization that has no menaces and no communists: the last crusade, the final roundup, the assertion of antihistory, a demand that compromises yield to principle and that religion replace realpolitik.

There have been many evangelical movements in the past. In fact their value lies precisely in forcing each of us to reexamine premises of what we consider to be progressive and forward looking. That we cannot dismiss the Reverend Moon and his church is made amply plain by the final series of essays in this collection. We have yet to cope with a religion that turns political, although we have had less trouble with political movements that turn religious. We understand fanaticism when it progresses from politics to theology. We have less familiarity with absolutist theologies that drift into authoritarian politics.

I hope this volume will provide information rather than ammunition to those for whom social movements are always problematic and who appreciate the fact that irony and history is not a one-way trek. Whatever the fate of the Moon movement—whether it goes into rapid decline or slow eclipse—we have entered a period in human history where fragmentation is so thorough and alienation so deep that movements of this type have a compelling power for vast numbers, to the point where the foundations and premises of Western civilization must themselves be reexamined.

I

Theory and Theology of
Sun Myung Moon:
Documents

1

God's Hope for America
Keynote Speech at
Yankee Stadium,
June 1, 1976

Sun Myung Moon

Distinguished Citizens of the United States and Honorable Delegates of the world, I would like to speak to you tonight on the subject "God's Hope for America." But first of all I would like to express my heartfelt thanks and appreciation to all of you for coming today. Here in grand Yankee Stadium we have gathered to celebrate America's two-hundredth birthday. Among this year's many celebrations, our festival at Yankee Stadium is unique for the following reasons: first, we have gathered together in the name of God, and, second, we are having an international celebration. Representatives from all over the world are here for this joyous celebration.

God's Goal in History
Today we are living in an age when we must look at every individual and every nation as vital components of the world. In our world there are basically two ways of life. One is the selfish way of life, and the other is the unselfish way of life where one thinks beyond oneself and family and lives for the greater purpose of the nation and the world. Throughout history, whether in the East or West, those who played important roles were public-minded or selfless persons.

The well-being of the family should come before that of the individual; the nation should come before the family; and the world before the nation and God before the world. This is the philosophy of the selfless way of life. The righteous men and women and saints in history were those people who selflessly sacrificed themselves for God and mankind. Jesus Christ was indeed the supreme example of such a righteous man. It is truly God, however, who is supremely selfless, supremely public minded. When mankind rebelled against him, God did not take revenge; he forgave. And God has been working tirelessly to raise sinful men up out of sin into salvation. To do this, God sent his only son Jesus Christ. Even at the cost of sacrificing his son, God wanted to save the world. And God raised up Christianity for the same purpose—to save the world.

The Bible says in John 3:16, "God so loved the world, that he gave his only son, that whoever believes in him should not perish but have eternal life." Remember, the world is God's goal. And just as Jesus willingly gave his life so that the world might live, God wanted all Christians to be willing to give themselves for the salvation of the world. However today Christians of the world are not even close to realizing this heart of God. God seeks to build one family of man. Therefore the family, church, and nation that God desires transcend all barriers of race and nationality. The people who are a unified blending of all colors of skin and who transcend race and nationality are most beautiful in the sight of God and most pleasing to him.

The Meaning of America

Let us look at America. It is most important that we know whether the United States of America was conceived by God. Ladies and gentlemen, it is my firm belief that the United States of America was indeed conceived by God.

There were, however, two kinds of people among your forefathers. One kind came to this land seeking wealth. The others came to this land seeking God and freedom. They dreamed of building a new nation centered upon God. If the former had become the mainstream of America, there would have been far greater strife, division, and struggle among the different races and national groups. The United States would have been filled with unrighteousness and injustice. From the beginning, however, God intervened. Therefore of all the immigrants, the righteous men of God were to find their proper place as leaders in America. All the different races and nationalities of the world harmonized upon this land to create God-centered families, churches, and the nation of America. The beautiful tradition of America was set by your forefathers.

Look at your own families. Most families have the virtue of a distinct international character. If your lineage has been in America for some time, it probably united many different nationalities. In your bloodstream many kinds of blood are blended together. Nations who used to be enemies have united in your blood. When the individuals and the families that transcend racial and national barriers gather together to create a church, that nation will become God's ideal nation for all peoples. There is only one nation like this in all of history—the United States of America. It is apparent that the unique nation of America is the creation of God. The people of America have come from every corner of the world. To be an American does not depend upon what race you are, what belief you have, or what cultural background you are from. It is only in this nation that no matter where you are from, you can say this is my country. That is America.

America is a microcosm of the world. Transcending nationality and race, America has created a model for the ideal world. God himself had purposely hidden this land of America from civilization until his time was full, and then upon it God raised up this model nation. In his providence God anointed America with oil; he poured out abundant blessing upon this land. In a short two hundred years, God raised this nation to be the mightiest on earth.

America Today

But blessing never comes alone; it comes with responsibility. If one forsakes the responsibility, one also forsakes God's blessing. Inevitably the blessing of God will leave, and the nation doing this will decline. Is it not true that the signs of such decline are already apparent in America today?

Beloved American people, the time has come that we must repent. We must fear the wrath of God. In the truest sense, who are the true Americans? True Americans are those who have a universal mind. True Americans are those who believe in the one family of man, transcendent of color, and nationality as willed by God. True Americans are those who are proud of such international families, churches, and the nation that consists of all peoples. In the sight of God there is no black; there is no white; there is no yellow. We must look at the human race as God sees it. America must return to the true founding spirit of the nation, to the ideals that its ancestors sought to establish with sweat and blood. America must return to Godism, an absolutely God-centered ideology.

God is the motivation, the cause, and the foundation of the independence of America. America was born through the providence of God. If we are centered upon God, we will remain united and enjoy prosperity. However as soon as we turn away from God, we will be divided. Ladies and gentlemen, if America wants to keep the blessing of God as the leading nation of the world, it must form a partnership with God. Do you have God in your homes? Do you truly have God in your church? Do you have God in your society and nation? God is the cement. With God America will stay together like concrete. But if God leaves, it will be like sand. When the flood comes, all will be washed away.

America's greatness and pride stem from God. With him America deserves the blessing and can remain the mightiest nation. With God you can preserve your dignity and the leadership of the world. If you allow God to leave America, however, this nation will decline; it will be subjugated by satanic hands. When this happens, the future of America will be dismal, tragic. America will become a living hell.

When God's blessing is great, and one forsakes God's will, God's punishment is equally great. In the early 1960s America seemed to be the only hope of the world, and the symbol of America was the city of New York. Today, however, the world has lost faith in America, and New York has become a jungle of immorality and depravity. It has been transformed into a city under the attack of evil. Chicago is no different, nor is Los Angeles. Throughout all of America, Satan is becoming the master. God has been forgotten in this country, and if forgotten, God can only leave America. Now is the very moment that this is taking place. When the unifying force of God leaves America, nothing will be able to hold America together. The family will break down, churches will divide, and America will become mortally ill because the cells of its body are decaying. This will be the perfect opportunity for the evil of communism to overtake America. This state of emergency is here now. Someone must do something!

The Work of Reverend Moon

There are critics who say, "Why is Reverend Moon so involved in America's bicentennial? It is none of his business." Ladies and gentlemen, if there is illness in your home, do you not need a doctor from outside? If your home catches on fire, do you not need firefighters from outside? God has sent me to America in the role of a doctor, in the role of a firefighter. That is why I have come to America. Good medicine may taste bitter and an operation may involve some pain, but the treatment must begin at once. Should a patient complain and push away the doctor's hand when he touches the infected part?

For the last three years, with my entire heart and soul I have been teaching American youth a new revelation from God. They now have a clear concept of what the God-centered family, church, and nation should be like. They also know the dark reality of America. Thus they have become determined fighters to bring new life and salvation to America before it is too late. They know the critical state of the nation. They know the grieving heart of God. And they are absolutely determined to turn the tide back to God. Their enthusiasm is beautiful to behold. Your dedicated sons and daughters are champions of God, crusading for the victory of God's will. At God's front line, they are declaring war against evil. They are courageously fighting this noble battle. We must overcome evil. It is our mission to build the kingdom of God here on earth. Therefore we must build a model of the kingdom of God right here in America, which God loves and has prepared the most.

Ladies and gentlemen, remember, these young people are working tirelessly. Their hearts are filled with tears and sighs in order to create a world free of tears and sighs. These young people are struggling, agonizing over their mission to create a world free of struggle and agony. Our battle is God's battle against Satan. For the sake of God, we will never retreat but will win, whatever the sacrifice may be.

It is not important whether I am persecuted. I am only concerned with the will of God and the mission God gave me. I am concerned that your rejection of me could result in the rejection of God. I am concerned that without knowing the situation clearly, you may be found opposing God's will. If what I am doing is not the will of God, it will not go too far anyway. If, however, what I am doing is the will of God, then no matter how much some people reject and persecute us and try to block the way, this mission will succeed.

Why has Reverend Moon come to America where he has encountered such tribulation? Am I pursuing my own honor? Is money my goal, or power? No. Never! I came to America because this is the country that God, our Heavenly Father, has chosen. I came to America because I know the heart of God. I know that in spite of America's rebellion against him, God will not abandon this country. His will is to make America an example of a godly nation that the nations of the world can follow. I know God's will is to save the world, and to do this America must lead the way. This is why I came to America. With God you can win; with Satan you will fall.

Three Great Tests
Ladies and gentlemen, two hundred years ago your brave ancestors in the Continental Army fought the Revolution, the War of Independence, with faith in God. George Washington

knelt down at Valley Forge asking divine intervention, and he and his army were able to win over the British army. Only through divine intervention could he win the war and America's independence. At that moment God laid the "Foundation of Law" for America.

Approximately one hundred years later when, contrary to God's will, slavery and segregation were rampant here in America, God raised up Abraham Lincoln as his champion and brought about the victory of the Civil War, liberating the slaves and affirming equality for all people. By doing so, God laid the "Foundation of People" for America, transcending race and nationality. Yet this was an external test. Today, two hundred years later, America is undergoing another test. This time the test is an internal or spiritual one. It is a religious test, a historical, ideological test. On the other side of the world, the God-denying ideology of communism has risen up and is ready to undertake an all-out offensive against the free world. Destroying America is the communists' final and ultimate goal. They know America is God's final bulwark on earth. More than anything else, this is a test of whether America will stand as God's nation or fall.

America cannot win this battle alone. It needs God. In this test you cannot win without God, who is the foundation of all truth and all true ideology. A confrontation is inevitable between the two worlds—the God-affirming world and the God-denying world. This is a confrontation of ideology. Therefore as a champion of God, America must win ideologically over atheistic communism on the worldwide scale, with the unity of all races and nationalities. Our faith in God must be stronger than their faith in communism. America must win in the name of God. Thus God would establish the "Foundation of the New World Ideology" in a higher dimension.

One World under God
The American forefathers fled from religious persecution in Europe, came to the New World, and in the spirit of building one nation under God they brought about a new nation here in

America, which is now at the threshold of its third century. In a similar way today people are fleeing from the communist world of slavery to the free world. Many were persecuted for their religious beliefs and ideological differences. The time has come to unite them to build a new world centered upon God. United, the free world must liberate the enslaved communist world. This time our task is to build one world under God.

To do this, Christianity of the world must unite. The church must liberate itself from sectarianism. It must undergo a drastic reform and achieve an ecumenical and an interreligious unity. For this we need a spiritual revolution. We need a new ideology, and this new ideology must incorporate Oriental philosophy, uniting the cultures of the East and the West. This new ideology will also be capable of unifying all the existing religions and ideologies of the world. Therefore it has come in the form of a new religious or spiritual movement. The Unification church movement has been created by God to fulfill that mission. This spiritual movement must first succeed here in America in order to spread throughout the world. The new ideology that the Unification church brings is "Godism," an absolutely God-centered ideology. It has the power to awaken America, and it has the power to raise up the model of the ideal nation of God upon this land.

With that done the rest of the world will follow America's example and will build the kingdom of God upon their respective lands. Then we shall all truly become brothers and sisters under one Father, God. This will be a world of love, a world of happiness. Our planet will be one home, and mankind will be one family. God's will, his long-cherished desire from the beginning of time, will finally be fulfilled. This will be the eternal, ideal world of God. Indeed it will be the kingdom of God on earth. We will build it with our hands.

This is our supreme mission. It is truly our God-given, sacred mission. God is crying out to the world, and we are his instruments. The world must respond to his call. Listen to God's commandment. Initiate a courageous march toward the kingdom of

God on earth. Whatever the difficulty, let it not stop us. Our
march is God's, and it will go on to the end.

My beloved citizens of America, today let us pledge to God
Almighty our loyalty and dedication to the fulfillment of this
divine mission. Ladies and gentlemen, in the name of God, let us
unite, and together build the kingdom of God on earth! Let us
together give our united thanks to God. In the name of the people
of the world, may I congratulate you on the two hundredth birthday of the great nation of America. May God bless you, and may
God bless America and its third century. Thank you very much.

2

**The Search for Absolute
Values: Harmony among
the Sciences
Founder's Address,
Fifth International
Conference on the
Unity of the Sciences,
November 26, 1976,
Washington, D.C.**

Sun Myung Moon

Honorable Chairman, Distinguished Scholars and Scientists: I would like to extend my sincere welcome to all of you on this occasion of the Fifth International Conference on the Unity of the Sciences. And I would especially like to welcome those of you who have continuously participated in these conferences. For the past years the participants of these conferences have been discussing the subject of absolute values, and this year you will deal with the specific topic of "The Search for Absolute Values: Harmony Among the Sciences." Please let me share with you a few ideas on this subject.

To discover absolute value, one must clarify the origin of the existence of man and the universe. Here we come across the question of whether the origin of the universe was from something in existence or from nothingness. As you well know, neither natural science, social science, philosophy, nor religion has searched for truth in the world of nonexistence. Instead they have tried to locate a causal being in the world of existence and to discover the principle of the existence and operation of the universe including man, all proceeding from the origin itself. Ultimately they wanted to discover the reason for and value of any existence by clarifying its contents or nature and by understanding the relationships between different existences.

We may call the smallest unit necessary to constitute matter an "atom" and define it as coming from something in existence. If so, it is logical to say that the origin of the atom was definitely from something in existence, not from nothingness. Modern science views that the origin of the atom is a certain energy, which again must have had an origin. Then we can draw the conclusion that this energy also is derived from some ultimate existence.

If we view the vast universe as the expansion of the infinitesimal atom, and therefore also as a result derived from an ultimate cause, we can clearly come to know that man also is a resultant being and not the causal existence. Then there must also be a causal existence for man. It is reasonable to set up a system of logic whereby all things were generated from an absolute causal existence and developed into more complex and higher beings. This system would need to refute the systems of those scholars who insist that existence was generated from nonexistence.

Thus we can say that a certain absolute being existed in the first place as the cause of the universe resulting in all things from the smallest to the largest, connecting them and causing them to interrelate organically and initiating various actions. From this viewpoint the established theory of evolution must be reexamined. In order for anything to progress to a higher level of being, some activity must occur; and activity always requires energy. Can extra energy be created in the process of this activity? No, because during activity energy is consumed. Therefore it would be absolutely impossible for more energy to be generated that could be used to give birth to a being of higher level. If, theoretically, energy is consumed in the process of activity, then why have things been directed toward the development of things into more valuable and higher dimensions? This is the question.

The theory of evolution seems to be logical, but the process of the stage-by-stage progression of all things can never convincingly be explained through the theory of random mutation. Without outside energy added, this progression into more valuable and higher dimensions is absolutely impossible. The evolution of all animals has culminated in man, and we can say that man is the ultimate purpose of the first causal being.

Here again we can establish the logic that the first causal being existed from the beginning. Next comes the question of which was first, existence or energy? No being can maintain its existence or activities without energy. There is an energy that operates within an individual being and an energy that enables the interaction between different beings. The question now is how this kind of energy is produced. Without there first being a subject and object pair, it is impossible to produce energy. That is to say, the relationship of a subject and object is indispensible as in the case of an atom where the proton (which is the subject) and the electron (which is the object) must both be present before beginning to interact.

There can be no flow of energy until there is the purpose of uniting the subject and the object. Therefore if a question is raised whether "energy" or the "subject and object pair" comes first, the answer is clearly the "subject and object pair." Energy is the phenomenon resulting from the process of the two becoming one. According to the variety of subject and object relationships, the energy generated differs in degree, intensity, direction, and objective. This results in the variety of beings in the universe. The reason why the particular actions of subjects and objects have directions and objectives is that in the first causal being, there exist a fundamental subject and object that act with a certain direction and objective.

In order for a being that has attained a perfect oneness between the subject and object within its individual self to form a relationship with another being, it must take either the subject or object position to and be united with that other being, thereby progressing into a greater form of being with the direction and objective of higher dimension. When a being in subject position wants to interact with a being in object position, they must find a common interest; then by interacting they can progress into the higher form of being.

The formation of this vast universe is the common purpose shared by all subject and object pairs. Thus the universe protects itself, and at the same time it protects and promotes beings that have attained oneness. Furthermore it causes repulsion in beings that lack harmony and repels those that try to invade the existences that have attained oneness. This is how perpetuity becomes possible. One may call the protecting force the *correspondence force* and the other the *rejection force*, or *action* and *antiaction*, respectively. This is true in both the material world and the human world. When our mind and body are united into one, we receive the protecting power of the universe and therefore experience happiness; but when mind and body are not one, the repulsion causes suffering.

The suffering experienced in illness is similarly caused. When the subject and object elements in our body fail to attain unity and harmony, they lose the protective force of the universe, and the repelling force causes suffering. The medicine administered after a doctor's diagnosis helps the harmonious unity between the subject and object to be restored. The same rule governs the individual and family. For instance before marriage, a man and woman enjoy being with friends of their own sex. After marriage as subject and object they will eventually attain perfect unity and form a family, and thus receive protecting or helping power from the universe and become happy. At this point as soon as a third party, either a man or a woman, comes, potentially interfering with their marriage relationship, some repelling force starts to take action lest the perfection of the relationship should be hindered.

The repelling power is not necessarily harmful to such third parties because it serves to suggest that they too can act positively to find subjects or objects and attain unity and thereby receive the protecting power of the universe and become happy. In other words the repelling power also serves as a stimulant toward attaining perfection. One finds that electric current completes its circuit when a paired subject (+) and object (−) attain unity and function well; however a (+) and another (+) or a (−) and another (−) will repel each other. When all beings find their counterpart and form a proper relationship, they experience stability and happiness under the same law. When a paired subject and object become one as a result of give-and-take action, according to the theory mentioned above, they come under the protection of the universe. Since all the actions we see in this universe are the resultant actions derived from the first causal being, we can state that there exists a central being that is both causal and active. Just as children take after their parents, results take after the cause.

Now let us look into the seed of a plant. We find that there are two complementary parts in perfect oneness within one shell. They interact only with each other by their give-and-take action through the embryo, and by doing this alone can they multiply and give birth to another life. Eggs are the same. They each have a yolk and a white with the embryo in between, yet they are all united in one shell. The human fetus also develops in a similar manner. When a subject and object of any species of living beings becomes one through give-and-take action, whether man, plant or animal, they multiply beings who take after the form of their cause and who eventually return to that original form. If we admit that all these take after the ultimate first cause, we come to the conclusion that the first causal being is the basic model for all of them, having the perfectly united subject and object within itself. Then the first causal being takes the subject position to all the rest of the beings.

The objective of the progressive creation of all things in the universe is man. Man is the fruit, the microcosm, and the model of the existing world. Man is the highest being and contains all elements of the minerals, the vegetables, and the animals. Yet since man is also a resultant being, one must conclude that he was made to take after the image of the first causal being. In other words there must be an absolute subject being that takes man as an object. Since men are beings of personality with intellect, emotion, and will, to relate with them that absolute subject must also be a being of personality. That absolute being is called "existence" in philosophy and "God" in religion.

Today the world is filled with confusion and contradiction in regard to evolution, dialectical materialism, epistemologies, idealism, materialism, and so forth. Our immediate historical task is to reexamine all of these and to find and establish a new, absolute truth. Only then will we be able to form a world of absolute value. The being of absolute value is eternal, unchanging, and unique. Then what principle in the universe is eternal, unchanging, and absolute? It is the cause-and-effect relationship and the subject-and-object relationship. When you apply these to human society, the heart of the matter is the "parent-child" relationship, which is horizontal. The unity of the subject and object on the vertical plane plays the role of greater subject to the object made up of the unity of the subject and object on the horizontal plane. They conduct perfect give-and-take action to create a harmonious spherical movement. This is the model of the ideal love-centered family, which is the smallest unit of human society.

In this sense one cannot help but recognize love as the most valuable thing. Since the ultimate source of love does not come from man but from an absolute, unchanging, and causal subject, the family of love centered around the causal being is the basic unit for realizing the ideal in human society.

To realize an ideal of absolute value, we must begin with this family of love and expand to the scope of the nation and the world to reach the ideal world of unity where eternal happiness of absolute value is promised. I sincerely hope that this conference will contribute to providing solutions for the various problems present in human society and to straightening the path to the future. I urge all of you, no matter what your religion, nationality, or academic point of view, freely and fully to bring the results of your research to these meetings and discussions so that the general welfare of mankind might be better served. May your efforts become a decisive, contributing factor toward the realization of an ideal world of peace, happiness, and love. Thank you.

3

**Sun Myung Moon and
the Unification Church:
Charges and Responses**

Frederick Sontag

Because the charges most often made against the Unification church tread on every sensitive area in society today, they have a tendency, merely upon mention, to inflame the hearer. There is no chance to debate the issue; the statement of a charge is sufficient to convict. Emotion concludes the matter, while reason need not bother about it. No solution I uncovered lies on the surface; rather each requires some consideration in depth. What are the charges?

The Unification church separates children from their families, creating an alienation of natural affection, particularly with the doctrine of True Parents. This is the most inflammatory issue for the press. The stories of parental anguish spur the anti-Moon movement. A multitude of factors are involved.

1. As the church has expanded in each country, the pattern of family disruption has been universal, although perhaps it varies in severity. It is also true that most new religious movements create the same disruption at their beginning, and it is a phenomenon predicted for an eschatological time.

2. Family disruption tends to subside after the initial missionizing thrust and the church becomes established as a known part of life.

3. The doctrine of True Parents is hard to explain because it is both central to the movement and much misunderstood popularly. Because of the Fall, all human beings live under original

From *Sun Myung Moon and the Unification Church* by Frederick Sontag. Copyright © 1977 by Abingdon. Used by permission of the publisher.

sin; thus no one now lives an ideal life. The Unification doctrine of the plan for restoration calls for beginning a pure line in which families can give and take love without disharmony. The True Parent is the founder of this new line, although that involves no rejection of biological parenthood. It should create a wider sphere of loyalty and affection, but it does turn the convert away from his own family centeredness to a world-family ideal.

4. Perhaps the greatest irony of the movement is that it announces itself as bringing peace, love, and unity but begins by arousing hostility and creating family alienation. One could claim that members of the Unification church preach one thing and act out its opposite, but that does not explain the puzzle adequately. First is the long-range versus the short-range goal. The disciple is at first torn away from his or her family, but the long-range goal is to unite. This program is long, carefully worked out, and involves many prior conditions. Thus in the short run, the disciple must sacrifice the family and other comforts. Of course those who do not believe in the program or the goal see only the immediate disruption.

5. Undoubtedly it is true that some children have been held from their parents and contact denied. Church officials go further and admit many mistakes in handling family relations. However the interesting and sad fact is that often it is the convert who wants to avoid family contact. He or she chooses to do so for a wide variety of reasons, and then the church serves as an excuse or buffer when parents turn hostile. The unfortunate tendency is for the child to draw away from the family just when coming together is what is needed. Perhaps the greatest subtlety in the problem is brought out if we ask, Did the church cause the family breach or simply bring into public view what had been a private fact? One member claims that family relations can remain close if they were close before. But if they were bad before, the abrupt change brings every problem to an unavoidable head. This probably is too simple an answer.

In interviews many members said that their parents mistakenly thought they were close to or understood their children. Often the new member reports involvement in a restless search before meeting the Unification church. Family and friends did not know about this because, until the point of conversion, it was an inner search and a private alienation. If difficulties and a lack of communication exist, parents can accept alienation as long as the child stays on an accepted societal track. But if the child claims to have solved his or her problems and is happy in the church, most parents have trouble accepting the new goals and life-style because they are so foreign. We have grown used to accepting certain external forms as a sign of happiness. When these are absent or altered, it is hard to recognize happiness in this strange dress.

6. Parents report that they cannot talk to their children and are startled by the change in demeanor. After intensive training the child has a new world view and mission, which according to doctrine, cannot be blurted out abruptly. A convert who meets hostility or unbelief is driven to silence, a phenomenon familiar to all parents in dealing with children between the ages of eighteen and twenty-five. The child who possesses a "truth" becomes the teacher and feels in a way privileged, or perhaps superior, as a result of what he or she has now learned, creating a reversal of roles that is difficult for parents to accept. The change is often exaggerated by the young who have so long been held in the role of the one instructed.

7. Because of their belief in the existence of a spirit world with good and evil forces, new members may interpret the negativism of their parents as indicating that they are under the sway of Satan. This creates a barrier, even when the ultimate aim is to overcome the opposition with love. The church may advise the convert to separate from parents until a "more propitious time" arrives. As a Westerner who believes in open confrontation, I find this indirect technique hard to accept. Yet the new member bides time until the conditions are right for parental contact. Belief in a spirit world can be exaggerated and overdone, but it is also true that confronting hostility directly in an emotionally charged setting does not lead to more understanding unless careful preparation is made.

8. Despite the rash of angry-parent stories, not all parents are hostile, and not all members have bad relations with their parents. Some parents are positive, supportive, and even appreciative. The difficult ones tend to get the headlines since their stories are much more interesting. Numbers are hard to estimate, but perhaps the largest share of parents are silent and reluctantly accepting. If all parents were hostile and no member communicated with his or her family, the generation gap would be an easy problem to solve. But there is a spectrum of reactions, all the way from hostile to skeptical to openly accepting. Of course, in some cases (particularly in the Orient), whole families may join the church, or children may draw their parents into membership.

The Unification church severely damages the convert's personality and often is the source of long-term psychological problems.

1. All religions attract people in trouble, including some with severe emotional difficulties. The question is not whether some are lost but whether the cure rate is sufficient to justify the difficulties involved. Numbers are hard to pin down. Those touched by the movement number in thousands. The real question is, "Did the experience in the movement, its training methods and life-style, of itself cause or induce the psychological difficulty, or did the experience simply expose it?"

2. Some members assert they have been helped and changed in beneficial ways. We must note that it is the parents, slightly more than their children, who claim that harm is done by the church. This charge often means that the person in question has changed dramatically; thus the question of whether alteration is for good or ill is left open. Unless one rejects totally the phenomenon of religious conversion, we are at best dealing with a mixed result. This leads to the conclusion that the harm or benefit depends on the individual situation and cannot be generalized. Of course such a conclusion will not hold for those who reject the movement's doctrine and on that basis alone deny that it can produce any good. But this turns the issue into a theological, not a psychological, one.

3. One confusing factor is the introduction of forcible

deprogramming techniques. The point to note is that in the case of those deprogrammed, it is hard to tell which psychological symptoms are the result of the shock technique necessary to extract the child and which are the result of the movement's training methods. Psychiatrists say that a year's recovery period is usually needed before the person is normal again. But how much of the disorientation results from the forced detachment of the person from the idealistic cause and the Unification family support? The forces that lead to human deterioration are hard to isolate.

4. One psychiatric social worker commented that the devoted member's idealistic exaggeration of life in the church family is matched by the overly negative exaggeration of the ex-member, once he or she is deconverted. When the glamour of devotion to an ideal is gone for the ex-member, his or her personal importance depends on swapping horror stories. What once was devotion to a cause becomes a crusade against the cause. Both require total absorption of the individual and encourage the human tendency to exaggerate.

5. Can we explain some, but not all, of the problems that the press reports (for example, families denied access to children) as a discrepancy between theory and practice? I have indicated how the theory legitimizes many practices that others question (such as fund raising and Moon's life-style). In this case their practice does not represent a violation of professed ideals but rather is an embodiment of a goal. Yet in other cases, which are more the source of general anguish, leaders deny that these reflect intentions such as separation of child and family. Just as Marxism has often been most objectionable not in theory but in practice, so the Moon hierarchy will have to "clean up its own house" if it is not to allow aberrant practices to make its professed ideals appear as a sham.

The training and conversion techniques amount to brainwashing or mind control and rob the individual of free will so that any supposed voluntary acceptance is somehow false.

1. This charge is perhaps the most difficult to deal with. First,

no member interviewed agreed with the brainwashing charge, and most laughed at it. One cannot judge all members, but some certainly engage in intelligent and natural discussion and seem well in charge of their faculties. The term *brainwashing* is probably misleading, and the discussion of the issue would be enhanced if it were omitted. Its use indicates that offensive and violent tactics were employed, and I discovered no hint of a prison mentality in any training center.

2. There is no question that pressure is applied, but is it so severe and subtle and hidden that it robs a person of free will? Let us bypass that question now and note that persuasive techniques are a fact of life and one had best learn to deal with them rather than think there is some safe place where no one applies any pressure to gain support. Given this situation, the training sessions of the Moonies have some distinctive features, but essentially they seem to be little different from retreat settings that have been the stock-in-trade of quite acceptable religions for centuries. Is it the religion, then, more than the technique that really is being questioned?

3. If the charge of mind control comes from ex-members, we have to ask how much of it is self-justification to explain away their once-ardent commitment to a cause they now reject. If it comes from parents, how much of the charge is made to cover the hurt of facing the fact that a child might have voluntarily turned away from his or her inherited life-style and opted for something different?

4. The concept of free will has baffled philosophers for years. We cannot settle the issue, but we should be careful of any assumed definition that seems to take itself as the only alternative. If free will is taken to mean lack of commitment, if it disapproves most of all of total commitment, and if it requires a cautious suspension of judgment, then by this definition most religious conversions will fail the test. We should be careful of assuming without question that the world is such that, rationally, it never permits a total commitment. That assumption rests on a particular metaphysical view of the basic uncertainty in the

world, and it is not an obvious fact about all experience. If free will means an absence of all persuasive influences, some laboratory experiments might meet this criterion but most important life issues are decided in the "heat of the kitchen," to borrow Harry Truman's phrase.

One psychiatrist defined free will as "a capacity to take in data, sort out and compare, deal with ambiguities, come to a conclusion to act without referring to a source of truth. Behavior should be occasionally idiosyncratic and should deal with ambiguities, recognize that they are there and act without needing to be certain." This definition involves a nest of assumptions. Almost any Moonie could accept these criteria, except perhaps "without referring to a source of truth," "occasionally idiosyncratic," and "act without needing to be certain." In some cases new-member behavior might even fit these, but more in practical matters than in doctrine. Individualism, a lack of any truth, and the impossibility of certainty should not be assumed as desirable when in fact these involve great questions. Some quite rational men and women still think certainty is possible.

5. A psychiatrist who is knowledgeable on brainwashing techniques said that the church clearly uses some aspects of the classical techniques, such as control of the environment, but it does not employ the whole set of conditions that constitute mind control. Every movement that seeks to change people employs some instruments to control thought (for example, the narrowing of perspective). These become pernicious only at some critical point when the mind is coerced beyond possible self-control. One issue is whether totalism ever produces a good result. It can, but of course it also has the potential to become destructive. When asked about deprogramming by way of contrast, the psychiatrist replied, "I'm opposed to coercion of the mind in any form." This summarizes the dichotomy succinctly.

Are abnormal conversion techniques used? Constant attention and affection is paid to the guest, and members cite this display of love as one of the attractions that pulled them in. The doctrine is progressively revealed ("deception" is a separate issue). The novice is urged to consider and explore further. The individual, chances are, is in a transitional phase, but that applies to most in this age bracket and to almost all who explore religious solutions. Is withdrawal made difficult? Like the peer pressure on any college campus to try marijuana and sex, many young people find the invitations flattering. Yet of the thousands who attend training sessions, only a handful eventually join. Such a low conversion rate would disappoint most professional recruiters.

The Reverend Moon has esoteric and exoteric teachings. He preaches love and unity publicly, but privately he urges questionable techniques and more ego-centered goals.

1. Does the Reverend Moon teach anything in private to his followers different from what he admits in his public proclamations? I asked this question of members around the world and got every answer but "yes." You can say I ought not to trust their answers; they were given to an outsider, to one uninitiated into the mysteries. Still, in reading Unification church materials, although I did learn many subtleties about the necessity for "slow revelation," I never uncovered or stumbled across private teachings that were in blatant contradiction to public doctrines.

2. What I did learn is that their doctrine of the active spiritual world that invades human life makes them feel that everyone needs careful preparation before he or she is capable of hearing and absorbing the full truth. Both slow induction and right circumstances are important, and Moonies believe that a novice cannot be expected to understand on the same level as a seasoned member. Trial and suffering and the paying of indemnity are necessary foundations too. Finding the truth is not an easy matter but a long trail. Most people outside the church miss the fact that those inside are under constant pressure to continue to "grow spiritually." Thus there is no single level of truth but rather progressive revelation. It is hard to reveal the truth of the inner life to someone outside who has not gone through these spiritually maturing experiences.

3. It is the series of talks by the Reverend Moon, "Master Speaks," that most people have in mind when they report on

hidden teachings of an explosive nature. It should be noted that these are "family conversations," and we might expect them to be somewhat different from official utterances. The question is whether contradictions are involved. The Reverend Moon is speaking to his followers, in Sunday service or on special occasions, and the enthusiasm generated by this situation might leave the words open to misunderstanding. At the least we must admit that we are dealing with doctrine open to a variety of interpretations and also one that is easily slanted.

4. Are the private claims stronger and more blatant than the printed *Divine Principle*? For now, I can say that there does seem to be a rising sense of urgency as the timetable (of forecasts) comes closer to its predicated date of completion. The growth and success of the movement do seem to generate a kind of euphoria, exhilaration, and pressure. Most of the time, however, the pronouncements are quite consistent with the *Divine Principle*. The suspicion of secret teachings stems more from either a failure to understand the public (and understanding it is no easy task) or a total rejection of it. This takes the form of suspecting sinister hidden teachings.

Mobile fund-raising teams use fraudulent means to collect donations and purposefully conceal their relation to the Reverend Moon and the movement.

1. This is a difficult charge, which in my estimation does not allow a single answer. On the one hand enough instances have been reported to make it certain that deception sometimes occurs. On the other hand the sales technique clearly is designed to establish a personal relationship first and not to barrage the people they approach with the church name immediately. Some teams operate legally and do identify their connection when questioned. It is clear that top-level official church advice is for honesty and legality. To anyone who insists on immediate labeling, their fund-raising techniques will always seem "dishonest," no matter how legal they are.

2. Given the furor in America over fund raising, two factors are overlooked. First is that in countries where public fund raising is prohibited, the church earns its money in other ways. The

openness of Americans to direct charitable appeal is unique on the international scene. Second, as the church becomes more established, its money raising will assume more orthodox forms (such as industries, newspapers, services, and fishing). There is already a shift to more conventional enterprises in America. The great fund-raising effort on the streets was an emergency measure undertaken to establish the movement in America and to fund its elaborate public programs. Whatever one thinks of these objectives, one has to admit their amazing success.

3. "Heavenly deception" is the controversial term that many object to, and it is slippery to pin down. For the purpose of a good cause, is it acceptable to lure a subject by half-truths or statements that deceive because your intention is not and cannot be understood by the "victim"? Members joke about "heavenly deception" among themselves, a term that to them seems to mean something like "effective public relations" or "good sales techniques." They deny that open, conscious deception is approved, although they admit that zealous members overstep bounds of propriety in their eagerness to succeed and to keep up their fundraising quotas. The issue is whether these are individual mistakes or a practical technique of the church.

The programs of the Unification church do not fit the standard church-charity stereotype. I suspect it is the use of the funds collected that bothers most people, not so much any real knowledge of illegal or fraudulent means. The detractors are sure that the fund raising is largely deceptive; the church members treat it as work with a high spiritual aim. Money goes into centers, real estate, and academic conferences. This is a far cry from the relief of economically deprived people, which most churches espouse as their mission. The Unification movement, I think, believes their "public influence" programs are the way to bring the kingdom of God on earth. Few outside accept this program and so cannot accept the fund raising as legitimate either.

4. If deception is practiced in fund raising—and there is some—still it is surprising to learn the attitude of practicing

members toward what we take as an unpleasant task. The ex-members are disgruntled, of course, but the active members speak of their fund-raising days with a nostalgia that surprises the outsider. Why? The answer is connected with the strong pioneering spirit in the church and also with the members' belief in the necessity to suffer and struggle in order to lay the foundation for spiritual success. Some members may have had bad experiences with their teams and leaders. Others speak of it as a time of closeness, struggle, and a way of carrying their witness out into the streets. Fund raising has for them a spiritual dimension, which few outside can see.

The church forms and uses a constantly shifting series of front organizations to disguise its activities and to lure support under false labels.

1. One thing is obvious to anyone who follows the history, growth, and international scale of the movement: the members have an almost infinite variety of activities. Shifts in projects come with a rapidity that members joke about and find hard to keep pace with themselves. Antichurch groups have compiled lists of organizational titles, and probably they have found only half of them. Indeed it is doubtful that anyone in the church hierarchy could list all the activities that the church has had going in every country in its history. They move too fast to keep long records and are too interested in new ventures.

The church does use many organizational names, but is it either accurate or helpful in understanding church procedure to call them front organizations? The issue is not whether the church sponsors a multitude of organizations but whether it is open about its connection to each group. Is the Pilgrim Fellowship at my Congregational church a front organization? No; my own church sponsors it as a special activity for youth. Is the Unification church equally open about its various sponsored activities?

2. First we have to note the human failing of not noticing very carefully the sponsorship of many activities we join. Many people really do not read their mail. Only later when some question arises do we inquire. In my travels I crossed paths with more

Unification church activities than I cared to keep track of. But with the one exception the connection to the church never seemed consciously hidden. On the contrary, leaders all over the world were excited and proud to outline the hundreds of forms that their activity took. The doctrine prescribes that energy must be poured out on many fronts simultaneously.

3. The exception is the Creative Community Projects Foundation in San Francisco/Berkeley founded primarily by church members, who prefer to maintain the image that the group is not a direct church operation. Most stories of church deception center around this special Bay Area operation. Leaders explain by saying that Berkeley of the 1960s would not respond to any organized church, and they wanted to be free to involve non-members in their projects without commitment. Whether this answer justifies the situation or not, I think the lack of clear church identification is a mistake even in this case, and it is also the origin of much generalized allegation. But if sponsorship is designated, then "front organization" is not a helpful term. That should be reserved for clandestine, secret operations—a situation that does not describe this movement's activity accurately.

The church raises great amounts of money, which go illicitly to support the leaders' ostentatious style of living.

1. The church and the Reverend Moon lived in poverty for years; thus the movement's present opulence is a new phenomenon. The other fact difficult for outsiders to understand is that the movement never intended to live constantly in poverty. In fact the doctrine predicts material success and aims for it on religious grounds. Sincere believers have, of course, been agonizing for a long time over the question of whether vows of poverty should be required from all full-time religious people. Some adopt this style, but there has been no universal agreement about the virtue of poverty among the religious. Many religions control great resources.

2. As we deal with the problem of wealth and its use, we face a most interesting and controversial aspect of Unification doctrine: the financial world is to be "restored" too. The way to do this is

to plunge into the middle, to secure financial power, to gain financial allies, and to demonstrate in practice the ideal that material means can and must be bent to the service of God's work. This is the only way the kingdom can come on earth. If we view this concept as a counterpart of Marxist goals, it offers a capitalist alternative. The means of production must be controlled for the benefit of all, but the proposal is to do this through capitalist economics now bound to Christian ideals. To one of a socialist or political left leaning, this avenue does not seem to be the way to go. In fact it is contrary to any religious view that combines Christianity and a Marxist social program. All one can do is to note the issue at stake and also recognize that Moon is not alone in this alliance of economics and religion, even though it is out of fashion in some church circles. Many cannot even consider this as an acceptable alternative religious program, so feelings do run high. The use of wealth by established churches is, was, and will remain a prime religious issue.

3. The basic underlying dilemma is whether any one person or any group of the leadership profits personally from the accumulated wealth. Of course the leaders enjoy certain privileges of control, as any executive does. This favoritism is not only acceptable to them but is part of their religious program. They categorically deny that anyone, Moon included, uses these resources for his personal gain. Diversion of funds to personal control would be false to the doctrine. Active members express their approval and trust of the way the hierarchy exercises its stewardship. One knowledgeable secular editor expressed his doubts on the matter, even though he did not question the sincerity of the religious intention. It remains a difficult issue, and it is not apt to go away.

4. Does the movement have a sufficient emphasis on helping the poor, the downcast, the neglected of the world? In this instance the evangelical stress on missions, on securing converts, and on the salvation of souls is the best model for our understanding. We live in an age of extreme consciousness about social programs, and we often stress outreach programs to the neglect of winning souls and the care of our spiritual life. Nevertheless the

Moon movement probably overemphasizes the need to win support from intellectuals and prominent leaders, which leads them to spend a disproportionate amount of time and money on schemes of influence. Of course their doctrine links winning this support with the way of salvation. However if their day of restoration is postponed, perhaps their attention will turn to ministering to souls in need on a nonprestige basis rather than service in return for potential influence.

The church invests vast sums in industry and in real estate and is building a financial empire, not a church.

1. This, of course, is a continuation of the previous issue. The movement is buying prominent pieces of real estate and controls various industries around the world. For them this ownership is not a denial of their religious goal. It is a confirmation of the truth of their revelation that the aim of restoration includes physical and economic restoration. Thus they take great pride in the way they purchase, renovate, improve, and use decaying physical monuments (for example, the New Yorker Hotel).

Since its origin the church has engaged in various business enterprises as a church family. They were not terribly successful in the early years, but their entry into the commercial field was an original announced goal. The success and expansion of the Japanese church really triggered the Korean development and financed the missionary movement abroad. Just as the pattern of members' living in centers as a family group developed in Japan and spread, so Japanese economic success set a place for the rest of the church's development. It aims to control vast sums so that it can fulfill God's will and thus establish the physical kingdom on earth. The aim is unselfish. The issue is whether it can be carried out without corrupting its ideals by its very success.

2. What about the way the movement uses the money that the members collect and the industries produce? Their doctrine makes plain why they expend effort on congressional and U.N. relations and why they spend large sums on academic conferences. They are free to do so if they want, and I find little but enthusiasm for these projects among the members. Other

churches spend money on physical plants, music, and so forth, which bear little relationship to the relief of human suffering either, and few object to that. Personally, however, I do not think the restoration of mankind will come through influencing academicians or politicians. I do not share Moon's hope for these social avenues of reform. On the other hand, I see nothing sinister in the motivation, only a lack of understanding that intellectuals usually tend to undercut the roots of religious practice and life.

The movement is unchristian and anti-Semitic, spreading hatred and division, not unity and love.

1. The Unification church raises once again the question of what it means to be Christian and who has a right to claim the title. Although many standards are offered and some are more or less widely accepted, all who call themselves Christian still have no universal agreement on a creed. There is no single authoritative, established church in America. Over the centuries we have witnessed many proposals to settle this argument definitively, but we are no nearer to a final answer than we ever have been. In fact I suspect that final agreement about Christianity is impossible. Perhaps it is not even desirable, given our record of using dogmatic formula as an excuse to bludgeon those whom we oppose. Judgment depends on what standard is set for Christianity. The Moonies are Christian according to some definitions but not others. But most important—and also most complicating—they claim Christianity for themselves and so cannot be dismissed without a hearing. Given the record of the various councils we have called to settle these doctrinal matters, we should not be too optimistic about a final settlement of this question. However raising the question of who is a Christian ought to shock us into new awareness. Challenges to orthodoxy from outside should startle us into reexamining the adequacy of our own responses to the question, Who is Jesus? The Moonies have a clear answer; do we? Individually, maybe yes. Organizationally, probably no.

The interpretation given in the *Divine Principle* of Jesus's role is not the orthodox one, but it does not lie at some opposite extreme; actually it is very close to tradition on many major points. The real difference lies in the question of the Second Coming and how the final kingdom is to be established. Quoting New Testament solutions on this matter misses the major point: the Moonies claim new revelation in the *Divine Principle*, which provides a key to clear up previously misunderstood, biblical questions—a not too unusual claim of new groups. If you accept this new revelation as being "of Christ," the Moonies are Christians. If you do not, you are left with doctrinal differences as old as New Testament days.

2. The charge of anti-Semitism is more difficult to pin down. Movement officials deny the charge, so at least there is no acknowledged anti-Semitism. But who is anti-Semitic? The question should perhaps be left open with the ironic note that it is unlikely that all Jews will agree on one definition either. However, the movement draws an unusually large percentage of Jewish converts (many of whom occupy leadership roles) who obviously do not see it as anti-Semitic. Why it does so is an unanswered question in my own mind, and it adds a subtle complexity to the hostile charges from official Jewish sources. The Moonies are a new messianic movement like many others in the history of Judaism that arose during particularly troubled times.

Moon is blasphemous in claiming to be the new messiah now on earth to usher in a new age, usurping a role reserved for Jesus.

1. Few outsiders accept the subtlety of the question involved or have the patience to try to unravel it. To my knowledge, there is no recorded claim by the Reverend Moon, "I am the messiah." His followers vary in their assertions, although those who make strong claims for him have some grounds to do so. The *Divine Principle* certainly "reveals" that the time is again right for God to try to establish his kingdom on earth, that the Lord of the Second Advent will come from the East and probably from Korea, that the Reverend Moon has been called to announce this and to play a central role.

2. We also face the complication of the messianic secret. Perhaps the followers know and believe Moon to be the expected

Lord of the Second Advent, but they do not disclose this belief to outsiders because the time is not right and the people are not prepared. This would be a simple answer if it were not for the complexity of the *Principle*'s assertion that even this new attempt will not necessarily succeed. God is man-and-nation-dependent, so the attempt could fail again. Jesus carried the mission part way (which is an orthodox point), and he succeeded spiritually more than any other man. But the final resolution is not entirely in God's hands (theologically this is the most debatable point in the Unification doctrine). No success is predictable in advance, but they are again calling on us to make the effort, and the time is propitious.

3. Since his followers do vary in their own private response to the question, Who is the Reverend Moon to you? we know that no dogmatic formula is enjoined as the price of membership. The effort to establish God's kingdom on earth takes precedence, and there is no question about Moon's leadership in that campaign. Success depends on the loyalty of the followers, and by himself Moon cannot fulfill the messiah's role. Jesus was unable to carry the mission to full fruition not through his own fault but because of the failure of those around him. The shortcomings of people account for the intensity of discipleship in the movement, but it also means that Moon could fail in his leadership. Nothing is guaranteed to him except a call to the attempt at this time.

4. The Second Coming of Jesus is today the least sharply defined traditional Christian doctrine in most Christian minds. Some even dismiss the expected event as nonessential. How do we, then, expect God's kingdom to be fulfilled if we agree that the record of established Christian institutions to date leaves the question in doubt as to whether we have progressed toward the kingdom since Jesus's time? That is, are the destructive and evil forces loose in the world any more in God's control now than earlier? And how will God accomplish his decisive victory if it now exists only on an individual level and not as a worldwide accomplished fact?

5. One reason it is difficult for us to deal with Moon's supposed

claims to be a messiah is that we look at this issue from a post-Christian perspective rather than a pre-Christian one. That is, the early church changed the role of messiah as they assigned it to Jesus, thus cutting themselves off from their Jewish roots. Moon represents a return to the pre-Christian notions of messiah, before it was spiritualized by the early church to explain Jesus's failure to fulfill the role of messiah as the people at the time expected. The Christians later made Jesus into an incarnation of God, "fully God." This is not what *messiah* means in the Old Testament, and Moon feels that the early church changed its definition to account for its own failure to support Jesus and to explain why the expected kingdom had not been inaugurated. Messiahship is not a claim to be Jesus-as-the-Christ (to use Tillich's term). It is a return to the Jewish expectation of a human leader elected by God who will guide his chosen people in the restoration of the lost kingdom.

The Unification church is subject to the same tendency to reinterpret pronouncements if plans do not go as expected. I am sure they would respond well to success and public acceptance and prestige, since they seek it. When attack and persecution come, their response is to say, "This is what we expected." Religiously we all seem to demand too much in the early days. This attracts followers, but, when the plan runs into trouble, we "spiritualize" the failure of the overt success we expected but which was not forthcoming. Messiahs demand a great deal. Our task is to explain our failure to live up to their expectation.

The Unification church is a bogus religious institution using spiritual doctrine to mask political and economic ambitions.

1. In my travels, study, and interviews, I come to only two firm conclusions: the movement is genuinely spiritual in its origins, at least as much so an any other new religious movement, and it probably will establish itself as a long-term movement of some solidity. I could, perhaps, have been "sold a bill of goods," but all the testimony in Korea points to the church's authentic origin in an intensely spiritual and religiously prolific time. The Reverend Moon's authenticity as a religious leader is clouded by his later

success and the general lack of acceptance of his program. The movement may develop new paths or go astray, but there seems to reason to question its origin in a time of religious ferment. Certainly Koreans see it this way. Even those who oppose it violently accept it as a competing religion.

2. A cloud comes over this question because of the unabashed political aims of the movement. Whether one accepts the goals or not, we should understand why a religious movement thinks it must enter the political and economic realm with its own programs in order to bring God's kingdom on earth. It is not the first religion with a political platform, and it is not likely to be the last. The United States was founded in an argument over theocracy.

Has the movement committed grievous political and financial sins that mark it as unacceptable and not a creditable religion? There are many complex questions concerning acts of impropriety to which I do not know the answer, but I have no reason to convict anyone in advance of the evidence. I understand why the movement finds political and economic involvement crucial to its task, and I think this path is full of risks and pitfalls. They know that too, but it is their way. I am sure errors have been made. The issue is whether those were intentional and whether they involve any cover-up operations. I tend to doubt it, but gaining a definitive answer involves detective talents far more sophisticated than mine.

3. Are "infiltration tactics" unacceptable, or are they a necessary religious practice? According to the Moonies, Jesus lacked an effective "battle plan," but they have one. The conspiratorial air about the Moon movement that bothers many stems largely from the battle-strategy mentality the *Principle* encourages. Because Satan's spiritual forces are real and subtle, we must be as astute in our maneuvers as Satan is in his. This marshaling of human, godly forces requires an uncanny use of power and skill. We recognize this as either necessary or legitimate in business and in politics, but is it offensive when it appears in religion? Or is the one who will not take up a battle

stance simply condemning himself to be ineffective and thus conceding the victory to Satan by default?

The movement is totalitarian, authoritarian, and even fascist, resembling in its structure the Hitler Youth movement and is a threat to democracy.

1. The movement's literature frequently mentions democracy in laudatory terms. It opposes Marxist dictatorship and claims to oppose communism because it would destroy democracy. Of course Marxists claim democracy for themselves too, so everything depends on how the term is used. Members indicate that the movement is authoritarian in the sense that they have sought and now accept a source of authority and willingly bind themselves to it. However their loyalty is as much to the *Principle* as to the man, a fact hard for any outsider to determine.

2. The charge of similarity to the Hitler Youth is more difficult to deal with, because it involves both understanding the origins of the youth movement and predicting changes in the direction the Unification movement might yet undergo. Hitler Youth, too, began as an idealized and almost spiritual search for new ethics in the midst of degeneration. It turned militant later. The Unification church, on the other hand, is international, not nationalistic, and it is antimilitaristic. The lurking question is whether it might change if its ambitions or timetable were thwarted. Would it then become less peaceful? One member states, "I think the church will disband before it becomes militant."

3. In assessing the right of the Unification church to claim to support democracy as we know it in America, one must remember the theme of the Reverend Moon's bicentennial campaign and city tours. America is faltering morally and spiritually, and Moon has come to call us back to our task, to seek regeneration before it is too late. Democracy was given to America as God's gift; it was a holy experiment, a trust we hold in store for all mankind. Given the grossly self-seeking view most citizens have of what democracy means today, there is something in this religious view to make us stop and think.

The Reverend Moon supports the Park regime in Korea and is in league with the Korean CIA in illicit schemes.

1. This charge opens a large can of worms. In watching the emotional reactions involved, one is led to reflect on the dubious human quality of liking to believe dirt about one's opponents. Our human frailty accepts the charges it wants to believe even when evidence is lacking. We do experience an ancient human, perhaps unconscious, desire to believe the worst about those of whom we don't approve.

2. First, church officials (Colonel Pak Bo Hi in particular) have denied the charges of the church's KCIA connection and demanded that evidence of it be produced. But because the maker of an accusation traditionally has the advantage of being believed first, over the defender (a built-in inequity in the world, which a democratic legal system is supposed to counterbalance), it may be that such charges cannot be substantiated. Personally I think it would take numerous Justice Department agents numerous hours to get solid evidence. But let the investigation be carried out. We know that the church is not averse to entering the political arena. If it does, though its motives be pure, it is likely to be stained with guilt by association, as every politician knows. The church's program invites antagonism and reprisal, but it does not shun dubious associations. Rather the church hopes to league them to God's cause.

3. A short explanatory trip to Korea does not qualify me as an expert on politics in the Orient, but it did teach me that the situation is more complex than most Americans realize. Rewards look a little different standing on a tiny peninsula, one that has been overrun and conquered during much of its history, than they do looking out from America. There is repression of civil liberties in Korea, and there is undoubtedly religious as well as general surveillance. As for dubious activities beyond this, I do not feel competent to answer. Clearly the Reverend Moon supports President Park as the preferable alternative to communism. Civil libertarians not only disagree with him but condemn his associations

and are suspicious of his motives if Moon does not speak out against Park.

4. Business is not conducted in Korea without government sanction; thus the church carries on its industrial affairs under government approval. It appears to be a marriage of convenience, which is enough to convict the church on the spot for those whose views on religion and politics differ. I found that all religions are somewhat suspect in Korea as potential sources of political disruption. The Unification church was not only out of favor in its early years but was subjected to some persecution. As it succeeded financially, however, government cooperation increased. Now, with the church's rising negative press in the United States, the Park government has pushed it to arm's length again. Church members have trouble getting visas to leave the country now, they say, and they talk darkly of expected repression. Recently some of the church's leaders in Korea were arrested on charges of income-tax evasion. It is hard to see the church as joining the Park government in secret schemes at the same time its leaders are being arrested.

The Reverend Moon himself came from a shady past involving sex scandal, multiple legal and illegal marriages, and several arrests on various charges. The first thing to note here is a historical oddity: every strong religious leader has been charged with sexual irregularities. Such stories surround Jesus too and survive in the early literature. Even if the charges are proved, it is not quite certain what these sins tell us about present legitimacy; but there seems to be a feeling that this would invalidate the doctrine or disestablish the credibility of the teaching. When I asked followers what it would mean to them if the stories of early scandal should prove true, some replied it would make no difference; they maintain their loyalty on different grounds.

Many charges are published by religious competitors in Korea, but little evidence seems forthcoming. We confront the unseemly business of one religion discrediting another. I confess I draw back from this as the sin of self-righteousness and the lack of charity that has plagued Christianity and all religions throughout history. There is no question that the Reverend Moon was arrested several times in the early days, in the north first and later in Seoul. These arrests are not only admitted but celebrated as persecution, which the leader must go through and overcome to pay the indemnity necessary to found the movement. It would seem best to evaluate the movement as it stands today if we lack concrete evidence of a legal quality concerning its past.

The morality of the whole movement is questionable because of its tactics and deceptive practices. Fund raising and so-called front organizations are the main concern, but the question of moral principle needs to be faced directly. There have been cases of deception or lack of honesty in fund raising, and the issue is whether the ends justify the means. Of course there is the official denial that deception is condoned or advocated, but the deeper issue buried here involves the meeting of East and West. Is the principle of loyalty to the leader the chief ethical goal above all others, and is it that by which the follower ultimately will be judged? In the West we do not tend to think this way and are more individualistic in our ethics. But Unification doctrine puts the blame for the failure to complete Jesus's mission to bring the kingdom of God to earth on the disloyalty of his disciples and those around him. Thus dedication to the leader and the cause become the chief ethical norms by which the individual expects to be judged. We must recognize a possible conflict in Eastern and Western ethical priorities. God, according to this theology, will not save us individually but only through a leader whose salvation plan depends for its effectiveness on the pledged loyalty of those who join him. Here is the core of Unification church's Eastern ethics and also the source of conflict for those with different priorities and a predilection for Western directness.

II

The Metaphysics of Moon

4

**The Last Civil Religion:
Reverend Moon and the
Unification Church**

Thomas Robbins
Dick Anthony
Madeline Doucas
Thomas Curtis

The increasing domination of the economy by corporate and governmental bureaucracies with concomitant structural differentiation and pluralism has undermined consensual civil religion. In the resulting mass society the nuclear family is increasingly isolated because of a lack of secondary groups linking it to the larger polity. Religions of the youth culture can function as secondary groups and supply legitimations locating young people within the larger society. Some movements do this through tolerant partial ideologies. Others, such as the Unification church, attempt to reconstitute an overarching synthesis of threatened patriotic and theistic values within an authoritarian and totalistic organization—in short, within a civil religious sect. The existence of authoritarian civil religious sects provides some evidence for Bellah's (1970) thesis that without a revolutionary reconstruction of civil religion, either societal disintegration will increase or the nation will relapse into authoritarianism.

Bryan Wilson (1966) has analyzed sectarianism as a response to secularization that compels persons committed to supernaturalistic belief systems to isolate themselves and create homogeneous spiritual communities (sects) serving as plausibility structures for hard-pressed belief systems. It is our view that Wilson's thesis holds not only for purely supernatural meaning systems but also for civil religion. A decline in the plausibility of

From Thomas Robbins, Dick Anthony, Madeline Doucas, Thomas Curtis, "The Last Civil Religion: Reverend Moon and the Unification Church," *Sociological Analysis* 976, 37, 2:111–125.

civil religion will produce divisive and disciplined civil religious sects. The context of secularization will exert pressure on those who remain faithful and on those who vehemently oppose traditional civil religious orthodoxy (those who still care about civil religion) to organize themselves communally in militant, sectarian fashion. A secularizing civic milieu may produce mass apathy and privatization, but on the fringes of this apathy will be strident sects of civil religion, which will discipline and organize cognitive minorities against a hostile or unconcerned environment.

Decline of the American Civil Religion

The American civil religion has been defined by Bellah (1970) as the common, public dimension of religious orientation that Americans share and that has imparted a religious significance to the whole fabric of American life. Although the content of the civil religion "has suffered various deformations and demonic distortions" over time, it has generally involved a qualified sacralization of American political existence and an assumption that America is or should be an instrument of divine providence. According to John Coleman (1970), who has formalized Bellah's concept of civil religion, there are three central characteristics: the nation is the primary agent of God's meaningful activity in history; the nation is the primary society in which the individual American discovers personal and group identity; and the nation also assumes a churchly feature as the community of righteousness.[1]

"Today," however, "the American civil religion is an empty and broken shell" (Bellah, 1975, p. 142). A sense of collective identity as a unitary people seems to be declining, while political cynicism and apathy are increasing. Szymanski (1974) reports that electoral participation is significantly down since 1960, while army desertion rates were substantially higher in the Vietnamese war than in the Korean war. A Gallup opinion index for April 1972 reports that younger citizens (32 percent between ages eighteen and twenty) are more likely than older citizens to express a wish to move to another country. In summarizing this evidence, Szymanski (1974, p. 11) comments, "On the political, cultural, familial, economic, legal and personal levels, virtually all indicators point to the increasing alienation of the American people from American values and institutions and to the general decay of the moral fabric of American society."

Analysts have focused upon Vietnam, Watergate, and détente in accounting for this deterioration in civil religiosity. Longer-range trends also underlie this decline. Proponents of the end-of-ideology thesis argue that increasing structural differentiation and the growth of cultural pluralism have made a consensual civil religion supplying cultural integration for the total society both impossible and unnecessary (Bell, 1960; Fenn, 1972). As a result, "There is no dominant set of interests, values or meanings in our society today" (Douglas, 1974, p. 95). The related tendency toward "privatization" of religion has also been seen as undermining civil religion and entailing a permanent withdrawal of supernaturalist sanctions from political institutions (Luckmann, 1966; Fenn, 1972).

The secularizing factors that have undermined symbolic integration have also created a crisis of community associated with the onset of mass society (Kornhauser, 1959). Enhanced structural differentiation has resulted in the extreme isolation of the nuclear family, which can no longer meet the expressive and communal needs of its members. The bureaucratization in work and educational milieux, the increase in geographical mobility, and other trends have diminished the communal viability of secondary groups, which are no longer capable of linking the individual to the total society. A need has arisen for new kinds of collectivities intermediate between atomized individuals or primary groups and the total society. Such collectivities would provide contexts for diffuse communal intimacy and would resocialize the individual away from exclusive dependence on the nuclear family toward broader societal and universal values. The current communal breakdown naturally impinges most heavily on young persons who have left their family of origin but have not yet created their own families and are therefore most susceptible to communal deprivation and anomie. Groups catering to the resulting communal deprivation, then, will recruit most heavily from among young people.

Two different resolutions are possible. One is a reconstitution of pluralism through new groups and communities. The emergence of new "social inventions" (such as communes or encounter groups) has recently been interpreted in these terms (J.S. Coleman, 1970; Marx and Ellison, 1975). Religions of the youth culture may also be viewed as such secondary groups providing loci of community (Anthony and Robbins, 1974). They supply tolerant "partial ideologies" legitimating the movements without imposing such solutions on others. In Fenn's (1972) view religious movements in contemporary society will increasingly have this character. Christian sects, moreover, will tend to be introversionist to quietist but not revolutionary or conversionist. These movements would in effect be privatized and lack a civil dimension that would orient individuals to broader societal values and issues.

A second response would involve the emergence of civil religion sects. Some would likely be iconoclastically "anti-civil religion," perhaps typified by the New Left movements of the 1960s, or by the growing National Caucus of Labor Committee (NCLC) or the underground Weathermen. Other groups, perhaps only a few in the context of general disillusionment, may uphold the traditional civil religion orthodoxy, which has now become a minority, sectarian orientation. In the sectarianization of the civil religion, supernatural aspects of traditional civil religion up to now implicit in American political consciousness may be overtly articulated, and the supernatural sanction for American political institutions may become explicit in some ideologies.

Because of secularizing pressures, however, attempts to uphold orthodox civil religion are likely to involve a totalistic reconstruction, which may point to the creation of Kornhauser's (1959) "totalitarian society" in which the whole nation becomes a solidary community based on standardized conceptions of the national purpose. In such an event secondary groups are controlled by political elites and so coordinated as to impose a uniform ideology and mobilize the populace in support of national goals. Privatized goals and activities are suppressed in behalf of imposed civic priorities. Bellah (1974) describes this "relapse into authoritarianism" as a possible outcome of a breakdown in the modernization syndrome, were a utopian reconstruction of the civil religion not to occur. He states that right-wing Protestant fundamentalism is the most likely system of legitimation for such a regime but suggests that one of the more doctrinaire of the Asian religions might also be used for this purpose. From this perspective it is interesting that the Moon movement provides a dogmatic synthesis of Protestant Christianity with themes from Oriental religions.

Reverend Moon's movement can be interpreted as an attempt at a totalitarian response to the cultural fragmentation of mass society. Unlike other current religious youth movements, the Unification church is stridently collectively oriented, its concerns transcend individual redemption and focus on the reformation of the broader collectivity. The Unification church and its allied organizations represent an attempt, in the context of growing political apathy and privatism among young Americans, to redirect community and transcendence toward the civic realm and to revitalize and standardize the civil religion.

We are reporting a pilot study based on our attendance at Unification church functions in New York City, Washington, D.C., and Berkeley, California, from the fall of 1974 through the fall of 1975 and at residential workshops held at Barrytown, New York. Through our interaction with members we have sought to assimilate the meaning and linguistic systems of the movement. We have tape recorded formal interviews with members in order to confirm and elaborate impressions obtained through participant observation.

Some Jesus groups tend to define American political institutions as sacred entities that should not be tampered with (Richardson, 1973); others tend toward political conservatism

(Nolan, 1970) and sometimes even acquire ties to local Republican party organizations (Mauss and Petersen, 1974). However the Unification church is the youth-oriented spiritual movement most conspicuous in expressing a revived civil religion. Its founder, Reverend Sun Myung Moon, has declared "America must be God's champion. I know clearly that the will of God is centered upon America" (Moon, 1974a, p. 65).

Reverend Moon is a Korean evangelist who suffered imprisonment by the communists in North Korea in 1947 and was subsequently liberated by the Americans during the Korean War. He sees himself as the new messiah or "Lord of the Second Advent," although he does not announce this publicly.[2] He has also received a divine revelation, which is embodied in the *Divine Principle* (1974), written by followers on the basis of Moon's talks. The Unification church is envisioned as a vital instrument in spreading Moon's word and in uniting Christianity and the world around the Divine Principle, which is essential to the establishment of the kingdom of heaven on earth. A key element of the mission is winning people's hearts from the "false ideology" of communism, which embodies Satan's plan to unify mankind in subjugation to himself.

The Unification church was founded in 1954 in Korea and since has developed followings in Japan and Taiwan, as well as in Europe and America. Reverend Moon first visited the United States in 1965; however until the early 1970s there were only small numbers of American converts around the country.[3] The church currently claims 30,000 followers in the United States and operates 120 communal centers throughout the country (Rice, 1976). The movement is thus growing rapidly and has attracted widespread but generally unfavorable attention from the media. It is particularly strong in New York State, where Reverend Moon has acquired over a hundred acres of land in Westchester County. A number of converts have been made at Queens College. Among the organizations developed by the Unification church is the Collegiate Association for Research on Principles (CARP), "The One World Students Community," which is dedicated to working on college campuses to revive "Judaeo-Christian foundations of democracy," revitalize education, and combat communism.[4] Most of the Queens College converts to Divine Principle have been recruited through CARP.

Most Unification church members in America are between eighteen and thirty-five and usually in their twenties. About a fourth of the members appear to be of Oriental (usually Japanese) descent, and there seem to be more men than women. It also appears that many members are from lower middle-class or upper working-class backgrounds. Although they are overwhelmingly college educated, they do not appear to be the culturally sophisticated upper-middle-class elite one usually finds in Eastern mystical cults. Many seem to have had a strict religious upbringing.

Lifestyle and Social Process

Among converts all energies are bent on spreading the Unification principles, which combine "religious and scientific truths—a powerful and workable ideology that can bring about world unity." The primary aim of street proselytization (or "witnessing") seems to be to persuade the potential convert to attend introductory lectures on Divine Principle (Unification principles). They are given in various contexts, including campuses, communal Unification centers, Unification church offices, and urban headquarters and during special weekend and week-long workshops set up in rural enclaves on land purchased by the church.

Before one is accepted as a full "family member," one will generally have attended at least one workshop in which intense indoctrination is combined with films, group discussions, sports, entertainment, prayer, and meditation. (Parents of members have charged that young people are brainwashed at these workshops.) During the highly regimented workshops participants live in dormitories, sleep on small cots for five or six hours, and are awakened at 7:30 A.M. for calisthenics. They listen to four or five hours of lectures each day, which are interspersed with sports, communal meals, group discussion, prayers, clean-up chores, and the preparation of songs and skits for evening entertainments. All participants at the workshops are divided into small groups that function as teams in workshop activities. Church members are designated as leader and assistant leader for each team. The atmosphere at the workshops is illustrated in the following impression formed by a researcher after participating in the workshop at Barrytown.

The general atmosphere is one of conscientious benevolence and managed congeniality. Team leaders deliberately contrive to include every person in discussion, query each person's reaction to lectures, etc., and find out each dubious person's (e.g. my) motivation. This results in some persons who are retiring, passive and inarticulate gradually "coming out," as it were. Members take great pride in helping shy people to "flower," as two experienced members expressed it, and in noting the change in a person over the period. (Robbins, 1974)

Communal Life-Style

When one "joins the family," one generally gives up one's other instrumental and expressive involvements and takes up residence in a communal "Unification center," henceforth devoting most of one's energies to the movement.[5] There are exceptions—nonresidential members (usually older married couples)—but they seem to be the minority. Communal centers are coeducational, but living quarters are segregated by sex, and strict premarital celibacy is the rule. Life in a communal center is disciplined, and most of the day is devoted to activities such as witnessing on the street, giving and listening to lectures, and attending other functions. The center director is appointed by the central regional office and supervises activities. Authority is hierarchical and flows downward from Reverend Moon. Unification centers are centrally financed; members receive free medical care plus money for clothes.

A close-knit solidarity develops among Unification converts. Reverend and Mrs. Moon are referred to as "our true parents," and Reverend Moon is frequently called "father." According to

Divine Principle, familial relations can be harmonious only if they are "God centered"; non–God centered familial and conjugal relations are spiritually harmful. Thus it is fairly common for members to sever relationships with parents and spouses to join the movement.[6]

Many of the more committed members serve as members of fund-raising groups, which travel across America selling flowers, cookies, ginseng tea, and other articles to raise money for the movement. The Unification church also owns its own business (a ginseng tea company), and Reverend Moon himself is the proprietor of various businesses and factories in Korea and Japan. The movement currently takes in about $10 million a year.

In addition to witnessing, lectures, and money-raising ventures, various political activities are sponsored by the movement. On November 21, 1974, Unification members conducted a six-day fast in protest against the North Korean treatment of Japanese women who are married to Koreans. The protest also included demonstrations at the United Nations, and members believed that their activities helped turn the tide against North Korea's recent effort to be admitted to the United Nations. In July 1974, the Unification church participated in a three-day prayer and fast program organized by Reverend Moon's National Prayer and Fast Committee in cooperation with Rabbi Baruch Korff's Citizen's Congress for Fairness to the Presidency. After Reverend Moon issued a statement on Watergate on November 30, 1973, rallies in support of Nixon were held in several cities. Rallies against pornography have been held in New York City and San Francisco.

Sources of Appeal

We have been impressed with the communal dimension of the movement and its appeal to young persons. As one member stated while discussing his initial contacts in a communal center, "There were about sixty people living together there. It completely amazed me, the cleanliness of the people, the warmheartedness of the people and togetherness of heart and not just in the geographical sense and actually in heart, really like a family!" (Robbins, 1975). Other current youth culture religious movements—among them, the Guru Maharaj-ji, Meher Baba, and the Jesus movement—have frequently been depicted as appealing to young persons by providing expressive milieux in an impersonal bureaucratic society (Robbins and Anthony, 1972; Petersen and Mauss, 1972). However the communal factor cannot by itself explain why persons would be attracted to this particular movement in the context of so many competing groups, especially with the proliferation of Eastern cults. There are indications, however, that the Unification church appeals to a kind of person to whom Eastern movements do not.

Eastern cults, particularly those that emphasize meditation, do not generally have explicit rules and philosophies for structuring social relations and facilitating moral evaluations (Anthony and Robbins, 1975; Messer, 1976). Instead it is assumed that the experience of meditation, which is ineffable, will subtly transform one's consciousness and automatically harmonize one's interpersonal relationships without the necessity of a conscious application of social ideology. In contrast Unification principles contain an explicit social or interpersonal ideology that addresses itself to the harmonizing of social relationships and the achievement of communal unity.

The Unification philosophy can be briefly summarized. God originally intended that Adam and Eve breed perfect progeny, who would form the basis of a perfect God-centered family, which would ramify into a perfect nation, perfect society, and perfect world. Eve, however, was seduced by Lucifer and then entered a non-God-centered conjugal relationship with Adam, resulting in their and their progeny's becoming "fallen beings," separate from God, and incapable of truly harmonious interpersonal relationships. The goal of Reverend Moon's ministry is to enable people to overcome their fallen nature and to reunite humanity into God's family, all of which is possible if enough persons internalize Unification principles. A truly united and harmonious family consists of both "vertical" (such as man-God, father-son) and "horizontal" relations (brother-sister, husband-wife, relations among friends), which must be mutually supportive. Harmonious "give and take" (a key term) must prevail among family members, peers, social classes, and nations and between God and man so that man will fulfill his true purpose of constituting God's perfect creation. This philosophy has an operational dimension that specifies a complex system of rules governing all dimensions of interpersonal behavior. Those Unification principles govern even seemingly casual social interation, which normally would be structured only by social etiquette or left to the vagaries of individual impulse. As a result the social behavior of Moon followers has a somewhat mechanical and stereotypical quality, which may seem repellent to outsiders. Nevertheless these guidelines produce reassuringly structured settings for social interaction, which are attractive to Moon converts. As a follower stated during a lecture:

We need to know the principles of right relationship, the means by which we can establish the unity of feeling and thought within us and the unity of feeling and thought between us. We take for granted the physical law by which we can gain a certain harmony and grace in our physical body with the world. We find in our principles that there is an exactly correspondent set of moral and spiritual laws. To understand these moral laws is to be able to establish harmony in relationship to other people. (Robbins, 1974)

Thus persons who are very concerned with social relationships may prefer social movements that devote such explicit ideological attention to interpersonal issues. As one devotee reported, "I really wanted to develop my relationships with people to where I could really perfect my way of being with people, of loving people, of getting along with people. That was the most important thing to me" (Robbins, 1975).

In addition to perceiving Eastern cults as lacking an ideology for structuring relationships, converts view the individualistic approach of such groups as selfish. They perceive members of such movements as tuning into their own inner vibrations, but not caring about others or about the problems of the society. According to a student in a new religions honors seminar at Queens College, who wrote a term paper on the cult of Guru Maharaj-ji but eventually decided that she was more drawn to the Unification church,

I don't like the idea of only looking inside yourself to see God. I feel we should look to see God in each other rather than in ourselves. This seems so much less self-centered and so much more loving. I, therefore, think the Unification Church has more validity than the cult of Guru Maharaj-ji because they believe in finding God in others. (Gezurian, 1974, p. 21)

Or as another member expressed it, "People sit on top of a mountain and meditate, maybe finding Nirvana by themselves but they aren't doing anything to help out the world."[7] Later this respondent described her motives for joining the Unification church: "I had the feeling that I had to get involved in something where I was really doing something substantial for the good of people in general" (Robbins, 1975).[8]

Thus many Unification converts, particularly converts made through CARP, are idealistic young people who are strongly collectivity-oriented and are not attracted by what seems to them exclusively privatized or noncivil religions. At Queens College CARP makes a conscious attempt to point up the relevance of the philosophy of Divine Principle to world problems such as war and poverty and to project an image of intense and compassionate concern with these problems. CARP presents a program of activities that includes films and discussions dealing with such topics as starvation and famine in Africa, the life of Gandhi, and harmony in interpersonal relationships. The leader of CARP at Queens College reported that serious social idealism was one basic quality he looked for in seeking potential recruits; even atheists could be led into the movement through fervent social idealism: "A person who is seeking to change the world, you know, anyone who just wants to change it, even though he doesn't believe in God, if he thinks that religion is terrible, you know . . .

as long as that person wants to change the world . . . that person is open to Divine Principle" (Robbins, 1975).

Thus the ideology of the Unification church, and in particular of CARP, appeals to young persons' desire for humanistic involvement in alleviating pervasive misery and strife. Unification converts perceive Eastern mystical cults as too privatized and self-oriented to satisfy this desire. They are also not attracted to apolitical neofundamentalist and pentecostal groups, which sometimes seem to have given up on a world doomed to destruction and to be restricting salvation to an elite of saints. In addition most of the surviving Left political groups appear to these young people as shrill and negativistic sects. Secular conservative groups such as Young Americans for Freedom seem estranged from counterculture love and peace rhetoric and less able than CARP to relate to humanistic and spiritual concerns. In the current atmosphere of apathy and cynicism, the number of conventional and social idealists may be dwindling, but they do exist, and the Unification church attracts them by combining upbeat social idealism with familial solidarity.

Civil Religion Themes

The Moon movement represents an attempt to legitimate a secondary group ministering to communal deprivation in collectivist terms. It does so by appealing to the ideology traditionally used for legitimating social integration: the American civil religion. Because of secularization stemming from increased structural differentiation, however, that ideology has lost plausibility. As with the sectarian response in noncivil religion (Wilson, 1966), the Moon movement must formulate its version of the traditional faith in a dogmatic and totalistic manner in order to counteract secularizing pressures. In the process chauvinistic and theistic elements that were implicit in traditional civil religion become overt and explicit.

According to Reverend Moon America has a special role in God's providence and a special spiritual destiny:

During most of history America has not been involved in God's providence, God kept it in reserve. European Christianity went steadily downward. The Pilgrims came to America to serve God. This was parallel to Abraham leaving the security of his business and children to follow God's command to wander. European colonists in North America came to find God, while colonists in South America came to find gold. God is mentioned on American coins, which is true nowhere else. This shows that we view these coins as God's money rather than ours. God is central to our constitution, which is also very unique. Thus, America is blessed and has accomplished great things. The 200 years of American history is a replay of the 2000 years of Christian history. (Robbins, 1974)

Fenn (1972) argues that with a decline in the plausibility of civil religion, questions of equity become paramount in ensuring adequate social integration. The political rhetoric and social action programs of the 1960s may be viewed from this point of view as a last fervent attempt to justify the war in Vietnam, though democratic and anticommunist rhetoric may similarly be viewed as a failed attempt to justify pragmatic and self-interested political conflict by reference to the disintegrating civil religion. One follower's awareness that America's providential status as it was conceived in the 1960s is under attack prompted a reaffirmation of that role:

America . . . the reason it was started some people had a new idea and something different and they had the courage to break away and say, "listen we know this is right and we're going to do something about it." . . . America is a kind of country where people can speak out. . . . So many people are saying, "Oh, America isn't really a democracy, we're not really doing anything." But if you look at other countries our degree of democracy is certainly much higher. And this is why we feel we're proud of our country . . . because it has this opportunity for people to really get involved and to say something, because we have so many resources, we can do so much for the world to help out. (Robbins, 1975)

Celebratory and chauvinist elements in the Reverend Moon movement are fairly straightforward.[9] Bellah has warned against the "dangers of distortion" inherent in civil religiosity when America's providential status is used to justify particular foreign or domestic policies; thus "the theme of the American Israel was used, almost from the beginning, as a justification for the shameful treatment of the Indians so characteristic of our history" (Bellah, 1970, p. 182). Moon's view is different: "America's existence was according to God's providence. God needed to build one powerful Christian nation on earth for His future work. After all, America belonged to God first, and only after that to the Indians. This is the only interpretation that can justify the position of the Pilgrim settlers" (Moon, 1974a, p. 55).

And his stand on Watergate:

This nation is God's nation. The office of the President of the United States is, therefore, sacred. God inspired a man and confirms him as President through the will of the people. He lays his hand on the Word of God and is sworn into office. At this time in history God has chosen Richard Nixon to be President of the United States of America. Therefore, God alone has the power and authority to dismiss him. (Moon, 1973b)

Reverend Moon's speeches in America are also full of prophetic warnings, however. America is forsaking God, and God is about to abandon America:

But today America is retreating. It's not just an accident that great tragedy is constantly striking America and the world, such as the assassination of President Kennedy and the sudden death of Secretary-General Hammarskjold of the United Nations, both in the same decade. The spirit of America has declined since then. Unless their nation, unless the leadership of the nation, lives up to the mission ordained by God, many troubles will plague you. God is beginning to leave America. This is God's warning. (Moon, 1974b, p. 62)

Specifically he is accusing America of relapsing into selfishness. America is alleged to be on the verge of decline because it has withdrawn its compassion from the poor nations and the nations menaced by communism. According to one respondent:

All the time when we went to help out, when we went in World War One to help out overseas . . . we prospered afterwards. But during the twenties we started closing in to ourselves again and the whole bit of "Zenophobia" I think . . . and things went down—zoom!—right into depression in the thirties. . . . so each time when America gives out herself to help out in the world and to give of herself to help other nations, every time things come back to us . . . if America stops giving now . . . things are going to stop going along in America. (Robbins, 1975)

A number of followers have explicitly interpreted this sacrificial imperative as America's moral obligation to feed the starving peoples of the world and help the underdeveloped nations. As Reverend Moon has stated, "We must think to raise living standards for all" (Moon, 1973b, p. 66). America must become God's sacrificial nation: "God proposed the United States to fulfill the mission of the sacrificial nation" (Moon, 1973b, p. 63). Of course another aspect of this sacrificial role is America's obligation to defend the "free world" against communism. From this perspective America's enterprise in Vietnam was "sacrificial," and America's diminishing willingness to support embattled anticommunist regimes in such areas as Cambodia and South Vietnam is considered selfish.

According to Arthur Vidich (1975, p. 72) American capitalism has been insufficiently legitimated since the 1930s: "It was only World War II and the cold war that rescued capitalism from its ideological poverty. The ending of the cold war once again reopens this issue for the capitalist countries and their political systems." Since World War II a Manichean orthodoxy has prevailed, which has been elaborated around the duality of democratic and God-fearing America versus totalitarian "Godless communism." This dominant "cold war" version of the American civil religion is currently disintegrating because of the immediate impact of Vietnam, Watergate, and détente and because of the longer-range problem of accelerated structural differentiation. Reverend Moon's militant movement represents a sectarianization of this former orthodoxy, now embodied in an authoritarian movement.

In the process of sectarianization, the linkage between patriotic religiosity and transcendental theism, largely implicit in the cold war ideology, has been made overwhelmingly explicit as Moon's revelation puts the United States into a precise and detailed providential position. In a speech given in Washington, D.C., Moon discussed the origin of the political categories Left and Right. When Jesus was crucified, two thieves were crucified with him, one on either side of him. The thief on Jesus's left reviled and taunted Jesus while the thief on his right defended him.

At this moment the seed was sown by the left-hand side thief that the God-denying world would come into being—the communist world today. And the seed for the existence of a God-fearing world was sown by the thief on the right-hand side. The free world is in the position of the right-hand side thief. And America is the center of those God-fearing free world nations. America has been chosen as the defender of God, whereas communism says to the world, "there is no God." (Moon 1974a, p. 61)

Interestingly it is the atheism rather than the collectivism of communism that Unification converts object to. According to Moon communism represents a premature, non-God-centered satanic socialism, for "Satan, always trying to realize God's providence in advance, is steering his way toward the world of communism by advocating so-called "scientific socialism" based on materialism" (*Divine Principle*, p. 445). Nevertheless Moon states, "there will ultimately have to come a socialistic society centering on God" (*Divine Principle*, p. 444).

Reverend Moon views his current movement as the prototype for a coming worldwide collectivist society. God had intended that such a society result from the advent of the first Messiah, Jesus Christ. But Christ failed in this mission because, among other things, he failed to marry and establish a model family, which would have been the cornerstone of the new society. Moon, though, is the "Lord of the Second Advent" who will avoid the mistakes of Jesus and usher in the millennium when "atheistic" communism is completely defeated and the world is united into a benevolent theocracy (with Moon at its head). At that time the world will be run in the authoritarian but loving fashion in which he now runs his church.

Moon envisions America as playing a major role in this

program.[10] According to *Divine Principle* (pp. 516–530) Korea has replaced Israel as the "land of the Messiah." In numerous speeches in the United States, however, Moon assigns to America a special providential role in leading the free world against satanic communism. Moreover *Divine Principle* (pp. 458–497) depicts an apocalyptic struggle between atheist-totalitarian "Cain-type democracies" (communist nations) and God-fearing "Abel-type democracies" epitomized by the United States and Great Britain. In an address on September 18, 1974, Moon argued that Jesus originally intended to utilize the economic and political might of the Roman Empire to establish the kingdom of heaven in the world (John the Baptist failed to lend his anticipated support, and so Jesus failed and was crucified). The implication is that America is really the New Rome providentially designed to provide the material strength to exalt the new messiah and establish the new kingdom. If America unites behind Moon and aids him in the destruction of satanic communism, then the benevolent totalitarian theocracy he envisages will be established on a worldwide basis.

Moon foresees these events as occurring rapidly, and he and his followers share an apocalyptic vision. They expect communism to peak in the period 1976–1977 and thereafter either conquer or decline. The president of CARP at Queens College explained:

Each person, each nation must fulfill . . . its responsibility in the world. . . . If America, if Reverend Moon's ministry in the world is successful for the next few years, then communism will very soon cease to exist on the earth. . . . 1977 is the 60th anniversary of the birth of communism in Russia. . . . The year 60 is a very symbolic number in Divine Principle and it symbolizes the most crucial point in its existence. If it, communism, can go over that line, it can take over the world. But . . . if the world can unite with Reverend Moon at that time, then the world can be brought back to God. (Robbins, 1975)

Reverend Moon's "Americanism" clearly has a tactical dimension; he is more concerned with South Korea than with America. However seeking to influence anticommunist power centers is an essential characteristic of his ministry; hence his ties to the Park regime in South Korea, his support of Nixon, and his attempts to influence congressmen (*New York Times*, December 21, 1975). Despite the tactical nature of Reverend Moon's ministry to America, the dynamic growth of his movement in the United States represents a totalistic response to the problem of mass society, as well as a militant sectarianization of American civil religion. Thus, communism is considered a greater menace on college campuses today than it was in the strident heyday of the New Left. According to another member:

It's just that very quietly on campus communism is taking over. And America is still a free country, but it's not going to be for long, if this keeps happening. . . . It just never fails. That's the way it goes with communism. . . . Our movement is growing quietly in some places, not so quietly in others. . . . And when it comes right down to it, it is going to come to a point where either one or the other has to be on top. (Robbins, 1975)

Fulfilling America's sacrificial purpose in combatting communism will require a substantial change in American life-styles and substantial sacrifices on the part of individual Americans. If Americans are unwilling to make these sacrifices, then dark prophecies will be fulfilled. As a lecturer at a workshop warned: "We in the USA have relative economic security and welfare, but God may abandon America in a few years unless we reform and create a spiritual revolution. If we can't give up our little things: our privacy, our apartments, our record players, all the big things will go" (Robbins, 1974). Thus there are certain liberal elements in the Unification ideology (aid for the poor, for example). But even the conservative elements (such as anticommunism) have challenging prophetic implications. A strident call for stronger resistance to world communism represents a prophetic condemnation of the status quo of détente. Moon's warnings about the imminent decline of an unreformed selfish America have a prophetic tone. It is these challenging and idealistic elements that are significant for explaining the appeal of the movement to articulate young idealists. Particularly important in this respect is the challenging call to self-sacrifice and service: "The church must find individuals that will sacrifice themselves for their families, sacrifice their families for the American nation, and sacrifice the United States for the world. The ideal that can lead the whole world must come from the spirit of sacrifice for the greater cause. For the benefit of the whole world, one nation must really give herself to pursue the one ideal world" (Moon, 1973b, p. 64). Reverend Moon's vision is liberal, then, in demanding an identification of the individual with the broader collectivity and a dedication to collective goals identified with the welfare of humanity. The movement repudiates social apathy, alienation, and consumerist hedonism and calls for a rededication to an American mission. Manichean and right-wing distortions not-withstanding, Moon's call for individuals who will sacrifice themselves for the nation and for a universal ideal recalls the dictum of President John Kennedy: "Ask then not what your country can do for you. Ask rather what you can do for your country."

Conclusion

The need for communal solidarity and expressive warmth in an impersonal bureaucratic society has frequently been cited as an explanation for the current upsurge of relatively nonpolitical mystical, occult, and pentecostal groups. There is an impetus toward new communal forms in a milieu in which the nuclear family is becoming increasingly isolated from other institutions while other communal collectivities, such as extended kinship units or homogeneous neighborhoods, are losing viability. The marginal status of youth, who have developed contacts and con-cerns beyond the nuclear family but are not well integrated into the occupational sphere, intensifies the communal needs of young persons. It was probably inevitable that movements would develop that attempt to project these needs on to the state and to seek transcendence in the civic realm.

The trend toward secularization of the civil religion has produced the sectarianization of God and country. As political apathy and disenchantment have grown, civil religion has lost its plausibility. Still viable are civil religious *sects* that manifest communal solidarity organized to carry their message to an essentially unconcerned if not actively hostile environment. This sectarian fringe includes negativistic radical groups such as the National Caucus of Labor Committees, as well as Moon's umbrella of anticommunist movements, right-wing Jesus groups, the John Birch Society, and the Wallace movement. What is peculiarly ironic is that political movements that seek to reconstruct and give overt articulation to traditional America-as-an-instrument-of-divine-providence civil religion now seem to occupy almost the same militant sectarian fringe position vis-à-vis mainstream political (or rather apolitical) currents as do revolutionary Marxist movements.

The Unification church can thus be viewed as a revitalization movement that attempts to reconstitute and recombine declining theistic and anticommunist patriotic values in a context of pervasive politico-moral secularization. As an embodiment to threatened and increasingly problematic values, the movement tends toward an authoritarian and totalistic sectarian pattern, which in turn further exacerbates tensions between the movement and the society. It seems likely that most social movements attempting a renewal of civil religious themes in an over-whelmingly secular and privatized liberal environment will tend toward authoritarian totalism.

Fenn (1972) suggests that introversionist or quietist Christian sects are compatible with structural differentiation and pluralism because they avoid confrontations with secular institutions by preaching indifference to worldly concerns. He argues, therefore, that Christian sects in contemporary society will increasingly be of this form. By their very nature, however, civil religious sects such as the Moon movement may maintain their plausibility only by actively attempting to control secular institutions.

Moon and his followers believe that their authoritarian recon-stitution of the civil religion will communalize the whole society. Their attempt to reunite all factions of the population against a satanic communist outgroup will probably not succeed. That failure could be taken as evidence that Fenn is right when he argues that consensual civil religion is impossible in a highly differentiated society. On the other hand the rapid growth of the movement could be viewed as evidence that Fenn is wrong when he argues that an overarching value synthesis is unnecessary. Certainly the growth of the Unification church is evidence that widespread hunger exists for such a synthesis. The growth of the movement contradicts Fenn's prediction that revolutionary and conversionist sects cannot flourish in the contemporary secular milieu. Moreover the rapid increase in indexes of alienation, such as divorce, crime, and juvenile suicide, (Bronfenbrenner, 1974), suggests that an increase in social disintegration may be a possible outcome of a failure to provide a viable civil religion.

Fenn argues that in a highly differentiated society, social integration will be maintained by the achievement of equity with respect to the pragmatic interests of all segments of the population. He maintains that civil religion is no longer necessary, then, because the primary function of civil religion has been to motivate participation in inequitable economic institutions. It is possible that during periods of relative affluence—as in the 1960s— aggressive expansion of the economy and social welfare programs may convince large segments of the population that satisfactory levels of equity may soon be achieved. In such a climate a civil religion that provides rationales for sacrificing individual interests in favor of the common good may appear superfluous. The enhanced expectations of individual prosperity produced by such an environment, however, inevitably create a "revolution of rising expectations." It is unlikely that any society can indefinitely sustain this society's rate of growth in the 1960s. The ensuing economic recession of the 1970s has predictably resulted in widespread disillusionment as the materialistic new Jerusalem predicted in the 1960s has not materialized.

Without an overarching value synthesis capable of ensuring commitment to economic and political institutions—in spite of their apparent defects—social disintegration may result from such disillusionment. Thus, the rise of indexes of alienation may be related to the decline in symbolic integration of the society. A case can be made, moreover, that pluralistic interests, unrestrained by rationales for self-sacrifice in behalf of the common good, may generate inflationary pressures, which in turn produce economic recessions such as the current one. Without a viable civil religion to legitimate restraint, a representative government sensitive to the demands of special interest groups may be unable to follow orthodox Keynesian theory and increase taxes during periods of rapid expansion. Such a failure apparently occurred in the 1960s, thus contributing to the current recession. This cycle seems likely to become a recurrent feature of American society unless some substitute for the declining civil religion is found.

Bellah (1974) agrees with Fenn that secularizing factors make the attainment of an overarching value synthesis difficult, if not impossible. He argues, however, that American society will either continue to disintegrate (the "liberal scenario") or relapse into authoritarianism (possibly along the lines planned by Moon) if a revolutionary reconstruction of the civil religion does not occur. Walzer (1975) argues that given the present unappeased hunger for communal solidarity legitimated by civil religion, a national crisis could result in the assumption of power by a demagogue preaching authoritarian civil religiosity. Nixon's "silent majority" was for some time remarkably tolerant of his use of state power to suppress dissent, and the current recession has been accompanied by the continued growth of civil religious sects. The national crisis envisioned in Walzer's authoritarian situation could occur if indexes of social disintegration continue to rise and if pluralistic pressures generate increasingly severe swings between inflation and recession—eventually resulting in a full-blown depression.

The growth of the Unification church at least demonstrates the continued existence of a widespread hunger for a religion with a pronounced civil dimension. In this respect it provides some evidence for Bellah's view that without a viable politico-religious value synthesis, modern society will suffer a crisis of legimation."

Notes

1. According to Bellah (1974) the American civil religion has traditionally involved conceptions of Americans as the chosen people who are fulfilling a providential purpose in history. Bellah sometimes writes as if the civil religion has been explicit in American culture. One does not, however, write an article to establish the existence of Catholicism or Presbyterianism. In general assumptions of America-as-an-instrument-of-divine-providence have been implicit in American political consciousness and have not been routinely articulated in the twentieth century to legitimate particular national policies and institutions.

2. At gatherings of disciples Reverend Moon is capable of making his messianic status quite explicit (referring to his wife as the "bride of Christ" and pointing out how all contemporary history is centered on him). Such references are avoided in public meetings and speaking engagements and in street level proselytization, presumably to avoid alienating other religious leaders and political figures who have given Reverend Moon's mission qualified support. It is worth noting in this connection that the Christology of the Unification church identifies both Jesus Christ, the original Messiah, and the second messiah or "Lord of the Second Advent," as perfect men used by God to lead mankind to redemption. Trinitarian doctrines are rejected. The first Messiah, Jesus Christ, was betrayed by John the Baptist and hence was not accepted by the people of Israel; he thus could not establish the kingdom of heaven on earth, which awaits the Lord of the Second Advent.

3. It is little known among sociologists of religion that the well-known volume by Lofland (1966) and the article on conversion by Lofland and Stark (1965) represent early studies of Reverend Moon's movement. It is our conjecture that at the time of the research, Reverend Moon's American following was so small that the researchers apparently felt obligated to protect its identity.

4. Reverend Moon has developed a number of organizations, in addition to CARP, to supplement the work of the Unification church. One is the Freedom Leadership Foundation (FLF), which is "dedicated to developing the standards of leadership necessary to advance the cause of freedom in the struggle against communism." The FLF, the American affiliate of Reverend Moon's International Federation for Victory over Communism (IFVC), publishes *Rising Tide*, "America's fastest growing freedom newspaper." Another organization, the International One World Crusade (IOWC), publicizes Reverend Moon's speaking tours and sends mobile teams of young enthusiasts from country to country to hold rallies, give lectures, and put up posters announcing Reverend Moon's appearances.

5. This is less true of CARP, which is a student organization, although some members take light class schedules in order to devote more time to movement activities.

6. This has provoked strong resentment on the part of deserted kinfolk, who are also concerned with the tendency for young people who join the movement to drop out of school to work full time for the movement. In New York State a "concerned citizens" group has emerged under the leadership of a Jewish rabbi, who has denounced Reverend Moon as a "charlatan manipulator" and charged

that young people are being "brainwashed" at Unification workshops. Young converts have been forcibly abducted by persons hired by their parents and deprogrammed.

7. It should be reemphasized that followers of Guru Maharaj-ji and others involved in meditation and Eastern groups do not, from their own standpoint, "ignore other human beings." Rather they perceive an enhanced "loving" quality of their interpersonal relationships as emanating automatically from the deepening of their inner spiritual awareness. Thus Eastern movements tend to view improvement in interpersonal relations as resulting from improved spiritual "intuition" rather than the reasoned application of invariant moral principles. The Unification church, on the other hand, views such improvement as resulting primarily from an intellectual conviction in an application of its system of moral absolutes. It thus appeals to young people whose approach to life is more ideological than experiential.

8. This particular subject had been getting interested in socialism (the Young Socialist Alliance) at the time she was converted to Unification principles: "I had been interested in socialism because I felt the workers had, you know, to do something for each other. But there was a lot of things I didn't realize about it. Anyhow, he [YSA worker] talked to me and said 'We really have to do something, something has to be done. Look at the mess the world is in!' And I said, 'Yeah, that's true!' And I said I really should do something" (Robbins, 1975). Our interviews with these subjects indicate that young people who are looking for a rational solution to the problem of evil may be attracted simultaneously to groups with radically conflicting ideologies (such as the Unification church and the Young Socialist Alliance). It may be the absolutist character rather than the content of these ideologies that generates initial interest in potential converts.

9. Stauffer (1974) has recently distinguished between "celebratory" and "prophetic" variations of American civil religiosity. "Celebratory" versions are "patriotic reaffirmations of the status-quo" which tend to assume that the ideals of American Freedom have already been fulfilled and need only to be defended. "Prophetic" orientations regard American ideals as unfulfilled and impose the challenge of "renewed commitment to struggle for the attainment of these ideals." It is arguable that Stauffer has distorted the meaning of *prophetic* by transforming it into a synonym for progressive or liberal-radical.

10. Reverend Moon's "Americanism" clearly has a tactical dimension; he is more concerned with South Korea than with America. However seeking to influence anticommunist power centers is an essential characteristic of his ministry; hence his ties to the Park regime in South Korea, his support of Nixon, and his current attempts to influence congressmen (*New York Times*, December 21, 1975). Despite the tactical nature of Reverend Moon's ministry to America, the dynamic growth of his movement in the United States represents a totalistic response to the problem of mass society, as well as a militant sectarianization of American civil religion.

11. This research was supported by Public Health Service grant 5-R01-DA00407-04.

References

Anthony, Dick, and Thomas Robbins, 1974. "The Meher Baba Movement: Its Effect on Post-Adolescent Social Alienation." In Irving Zaretsky and Mark Leone, eds., *Religious Movements in Contemporary America.* Princeton, Princeton University Press. Pp. 479–511.

Anthony, Dick, and Thomas Robbins, 1975. "Young Culture Religious Ferment and the Confusion of Moral Meanings." Paper read at the annual meeting of the Society for the Scientific Study of Religion, Milwaukee, Wis.

Bell, Daniel, 1960. *The End of Ideology.* New York, Free Press.

Bellah, Robert N., 1970. "Civil Religion in America." In Robert Bellah, ed., *Beyond Belief.* New York, Harper and Row. Pp. 168–192.

———, 1974. "New Religious Consciousness." *The New Republic* 1971, 21:33–41.

———, 1975. *The Broken Covenant.* New York, Seabury.

Bronfenbrenner, Urie, 1974. "The Origins of Alienation." *Scientific American* 4, 2:53–61.

Coleman, John, 1970. "Civil Religion." *Sociological Analysis* 31, 2:67–77.

Coleman, James S., 1970. "Social Inventions." *Social Forces* 49: 163–173.

Divine Principle, 1974. Washington, D.C., Holy Spirit Association for the Unification of World Christianity.

Douglas, Jack D., 1974. "Watergate: Harbinger of the New American Prince." *Theory and Society* 1:89–97.

Fenn, Richard, 1972. "Towards a New Sociology of Religion." *Journal for the Scientific Study of Religion* 11:16–32.

Gezurian, Dorothy, 1974. "The Cult of the Guru Maharaj-ji." Honors paper, Queens College.

Kornhauser, William, 1959. *The Politics of Mass Society.* New York, Free Press.

Lofland, John, 1966. *Doomsday Cult.* Englewood Cliffs, N.J., Prentice-Hall.

Lofland, John, and Rodney Stark, 1965. "Becoming a World-Saver: A Theory of Conversion to a Deviant Perspective." *American Sociological Review* 30:862–875.

Luckmann, Thomas, 1967. *The Invisible Religion.* New York, Macmillan.

Marx, John H., and David L. Ellison, 1975. "Sensitivity Training and Communes: Contemporary Quests for Community." *Pacific Sociological Review* 18, 4:442–462.

Mauss, Armand L., and Donald W. Petersen, 1974. "Prodigals as Preachers: The 'Jesus Freaks' and the Return to Respectability." *Social Compass* 21:2–18.

Messer, Jean, 1976. "Who Is Guru Maharaj-ji?" In Robert Bellah and Charles Glock, eds., *Consciousness and Youth.* Berkeley, University of California Press.

Moon, Reverend, 1973a. New Hope, Pa. Holy Spirit Association for the Unification of World Christianity.

———, 1973b. "Answer to Watergate." Washington, D.C., National Prayer and Fast for the Watergate Crisis.

———, 1974a. New Hope, Holy Spirit Association for the Unification of World Christianity.

———, 1974b. "The Hope of Youth." *The Way of the World* 7:3–18.

Nolan, James, 1971. "Jesus Now: Hogwash and Holy Water." *Ramparts* 10:20–26.

Petersen, W., and Armand L. Mauss, 1973. "The Cross and the Commune: An Interpretation of the Jesus People." In Charles Y. Glock, ed., *Religion in Sociological Perspective.* Belmont, Cal., Wadsworth. Pp. 261–280.

Rice, Berkeley, 1976. "Messiah from Korea: Honor They Father Moon. *Psychology Today* 9, 8:36–47.

Richardson, James T., 1973. "Causes and Consequences of the Jesus Movement." *Social Studies: Irish Journal of Sociology* 2, 5:457–474.

Robbins, Thomas, 1974. "Field Notes on the Unification Church." Unpublished manuscript. October.

———, 1975. Interviews with Members of the Unification Church. Unpublished manuscript. Spring.

Robbins, Thomas, and Dick Anthony, 1972. "Getting Straight with Meher Baba: A Study of Drug-Rehabilitation, Mysticism and Post Adolescent Role Conflict." *Journal for the Scientific Study of Religion* 11, 2:122–140.

Stauffer, Robert E., 1974. "Radical Symbols and Conservative Functions: The Politics of Political Myths." Paper read at the annual meeting of the Society for the Scientific Study of Religion, Washington, D.C.

Szymanski, Albert, 1974. "The Decline and Fall of the U.S. Eagle." *Social Policy* 4, 5:5–15.

Vidich, Arthur J., 1975. "Social Conflict in an Era of Détente." *Social Research* 42, 1:64–87.

Walzer, Michael, 1975. "Civility and Civic Virtue in Contemporary America." *Social Research* 41, 4:593–611.

Wilson, Bryan, 1966. *Religion in Secular Society.* Baltimore, Penguin.

5

Jews and Judaism in Reverend Moon's *Divine Principle*

A. James Rudin

There are several levels of significance implied for the American people, and especially for the Jewish community, in this study of the basic text of the Reverend Sun Myung Moon's movement— the first systematic study, to my knowledge, that has been published of the scriptures of Moonism. The first is that Reverend Moon is contributing to a theologically reactionary mentality whose traditional fixations on anti-Semitism have been repudiated in recent decades by virtually every major Catholic, Protestant, Greek Orthodox, and evangelical group and leader— from Vatican Council II, the World and National Council of Churches, to Dr. Billy Graham and the Southern Baptist Convention. At a time when the majority of enlightened Christian leadership throughout the world is laboring to uproot the sources of the pathology of anti-Jewish hatred that culminated in the Nazi holocaust, Reverend Moon appears to be embarked on a contrary course of seeking to reinfect the spiritual bloodstream of mankind with his cancerous version of contempt for Jews and Judaism. On this level, therefore, this study is a clinical diagnosis intended to expose the Moon infection in order that both Christian and Jewish leadership will be vigilant to the need for combatting any effort of Reverend Moon and his followers to enter the mainstream of American religion and culture with his horrendous baggage of bigotry.

A second consideration is that we are now dealing not only

with an ersatz spiritual phenomenon but one that has potentially serious political implications as well. The recent revelations that Reverend Moon and his Unification church are allegedly involved as a front group for the South Korean intelligence forces in the United States, who are charged with illegal lobbying and bribery, raise the serious issue of whether Moon's anti-Semitism is intended to be used for the ideological objectives of his political backers. If that is the case, then the American people must be alert to the emergence in the Moon phenomenon of an ideological campaign whose antecedents trace back to the Nazis and to Stalinist communism. Those totalitarian movements consciously and cynically employed anti-Jewish hatred as a major vehicle for realizing their apocalyptic goal of undermining the biblical and democratic values of Western civilization. The troubling question cannot be evaded: Why are Reverend Moon and his political backers resorting to the Nazi model of exploiting anti-Semitism for ideological purposes? Every American congressman, senator, and public official who is approached by the Moon movement ought to be alert to this ideological landmine of fanatic hatred when courted for support by Reverend Moon and his backers.

Finally this essay is directed to the consciences of Jewish young people who, most incredibly, have been enticed or seduced to become Moonies. It has been estimated that nearly 30 percent of the Moonies today are Jewish young men and women who have been subjected to this latest form of totalitarian brainwashing. During the Korean War the communists captured 3,778 American soldiers and subjected them to psychological coercion, which involved, first, a mind-conditioning phase in which the American prisoners were intensively persuaded to hate their own country, and, second, a so-called suction phase in which they were taught that life was superior under communism and they should spread the gospel of communism. Whatever the psychological or sociological reasons for their attraction to Reverend Moon's movement, at some time in their search for personal meaning Jewish youth must confront the realization that they are being asked to find salvation in a "third messiah" whose gospel is the hatred for and destruction of their own people, their religion and culture, their very families. In the face of this understanding of what Reverend Moon is really teaching about Jews, a continued involvement in his movement can be nothing other than an exercise in self-hatred and self-debasement. Surely young Jews and Christians have other, more humane alternatives for finding meaning for their existence and self-fulfillment.

The Reverend Sun Myung Moon is a Korean-born (1920) religious leader who moved to the United States in 1973. Since then his teachings and beliefs have received extraordinary attention in the Western world as he embarked upon a widespread and highly visible campaign to gain new members for his Unification church. It has been a campaign filled with bitter controversy, including a congressional investigation of his tax-exempt status and an acrimonious court case that was instituted by the parents of a new convert to his church. Since 1973 nearly 30,000 Americans, most of them under thirty years of age, have flocked to Reverend Moon's banner and have become active and committed members of the Unification church. Reverend Moon claims a worldwide membership of over 60,000.

While public attention has been focused on many aspects of his movement, very little has been said about his—and the Unification church's—attitudes and beliefs regarding Judaism and the Jewish people as reflected in *Divine Principle*, the basic text of Reverend Moon's movement. The work has gone through several revisions and enlargements since it was first published in Korean nearly twenty years ago. This study is based on the 1974 English edition, published by the Holy Spirit Association for the Unification of World Christianity. A systematic analysis of this 536-page document reveals an orientation of almost unrelieved hostility toward the Jewish people, exemplified in pejorative language, stereotyped imagery, and sweeping accusations of collective sin and guilt.

Whether he is discussing the "Israelites" of the Hebrew Bible or the "Jews" as referred to in writings of the New Testament period, Reverend Moon portrays their behavior as reprobate, their intentions as evil (often diabolical), and their religious mission as eclipsed. There are over thirty-six specific references in *Divine Principle* to the Israelites of the Hebrew Bible (Old Testament), every one of them pejorative. The "faithlessness" of the Israelites is mentioned four times on a single page. Moreover the accusation is leveled collectively: "The Israelites all fell into faithlessness" (p. 315); "All the Israelites centering on Moses fell into faithlessness" (p. 320); "The Israelites repeatedly fell into faithlessness" (p. 343).

In similar fashion *Divine Principle* records some sixty-five specific references to the attitudes and behavior of the Jewish people towards Jesus and their role in his crucifixion, again, every one hostile and anti-Jewish. Thus not only were the Jewish people of Jesus's day "filled with ignorance" (p. 162), "rebellion" (against God) (p. 359), and "disbelief" (p. 146), but they "betrayed" (p. 453), "persecuted" (p. 155), and "derided" Jesus (p. 135), finally "delivering him to be crucified" (p. 200). Reverend Moon goes even beyond the infamous deicide "Christ killer" charge against the Jewish people. In two separate instances in *Divine Principle* (pp. 357, 510), he specifically links the Jews with Satan in bringing about the death of Jesus:

As a matter of fact, Satan confronted Jesus, working through the Jewish people, centering on the chief priests and scribes who had fallen faithless, and especially through Judas Iscariot, the disciple who had betrayed Jesus.

Nevertheless, due to the Jewish people's rebellion against him, the physical body of Jesus was delivered into the hands of Satan as the condition of ransom for the restoration of the Jews and the whole of mankind back to God's bosom. His body was invaded by Satan.

The anti-Jewish thrust of Reverend Moon's writings about the ancient Israelites and the Jews of Jesus's time carries forward into his interpretation of Jewish history and of the current status of Jews and Judaism.

There are some twenty-six pertinent references in *Divine Principle*. In tone and in substance they are viciously anti-Jewish, reflecting the worst aspects of traditional Christian displacement theology and viewing the persecution of Jews across the ages as punishment for their sins: "the Jewish nation was destroyed" (p. 431); because of "the Israelites' faithlessness, God's heritage [has been] taken away from the Jewish people" (p. 519); "the chosen nation of Israel has been punished for the sin of rejecting Jesus and crucifying Him" (p. 226). Reverend Moon also brings his teachings up to modern times: "Jesus came as the Messiah; but due to the disbelief of and persecution by the people he was crucified. Since then the Jews have lost their qualification as the chosen people and have been scattered, suffering persecution through the present day." (p. 147). About the Nazi holocaust the *Divine Principle* says: "Hitler imposed the strict primitive Germanic religious ideology by concluding a pact with the Pope of Rome, thus founding a national religion, and then tried to control all Protestantism under the supervision of bishops throughout the country. Therefore, the Catholics as well as the Protestants were strongly opposed to Hitler. Furthermore, Hitler massacred six million Jews" (p. 485).

It is true that many of Reverend Moon's most virulent teachings about Jews and Judaism have their parallels (if not their sources) in a tradition of Christian anti-Jewish polemic that stretches from the early church fathers to the Oberammergau Passion Play. Saint John Chrysostom (d. 407 C.E.) wrote of the Jewish people: "Of their rapine, their cupidity, their deception of the poor . . . they are inveterate murderers, destroyers, men possessed by the devil . . . they are impure and impious." Tertullian (d. 222), another church father, attempted to refute Judaism, especially the permanent validity of the Mosaic covenant. Saint Justin (d. 165), one of the first Christian leaders to link the Jewish people with the crucifixion of Jesus, wrote, "The tribulations were justly imposed upon you, for you have murdered the Just One." Saint Hippolytus (d. 235 or 236) taught that Jews will always be slaves because "they killed the Son of their Benefactor." Origen (d. 254), echoed the deicide and punishment theme: "We say with confidence that they will never be restored to their former condition. For they committed a crime of the most unhallowed kind, in conspiring against the Saviour of the human race." Chrysostom believed that the rejections and dispersion of the Jews was the work of God, not history: "It was done by the wrath of God and His absolute abandon of you." A fourth-century Christian historian, Sulpicius Severus, wrote, "Jews are beheld scattered through the whole world that they have been punished on no other account than for the impious hands which they laid on Christ."

All of these themes—the faithlessness of Israel, the abrogation of the covenant, collective guilt and punishment—come together in the Oberammergau Passion Play, which is presented every ten years in Germany. In it Jesus renounces Judaism: "The Old Covenant which my Father made with Abraham, Isaac, and Jacob has reached its end" (1970 ed., pp. 41ff.) The Jewish crowd cries, "Drive him with violence that we get on to Calvary. . . . On, drive him with blows . . . He deserves crucifixion" (1970 ed., pp. 106, 109.) The so-called blood curse is clearly directed at the entire Jewish people:

Chorus: Jerusalem! Jerusalem!
        The blood of His Son will yet avenge on you the Lord.

People: His blood be on us, and our children!

Chorus: Be it upon you, and your children. (1970 ed., p. 99)

These and many other examples attest to the anti-Jewish sources in Christian tradition from which Reverend Moon has obviously drawn. But in recent years Christian church leaders have made vast efforts to repudiate the most negative and hostile elements of this anti-Jewish legacy and to affirm the ongoing validity of God's covenant with the Jewish people. The Roman Catholic church in its "Declaration on Non-Christian Religions" (1965) affirmed that responsibility for Jesus's death could not be laid to the Jews and asserted: "The Jews should not be presented as rejected or accursed by God, as if this followed from Holy Scriptures." The Lutheran Council in the United States, representing three Lutheran bodies, advised in 1971: "Christians should make it clear that there is no Biblical or theological basis for anti-Semitism. Supposed theological or Biblical bases for anti-Semitism are to be examined and repudiated." The twelve-million member Southern Baptist Convention resolved in 1972 "to work positively to replace all anti-Semitic bias with the Christian attitude and practice of love for Jews, who along with all other men, are equally beloved of God." The newly revised Book of Confession of the Presbyterian church in the United States affirms: "We can never lay exclusive claim to being God's people as though we have replaced those to whom the covenant, the law and the promises belong. We affirm that God has not rejected His people, the Jews. The Lord does not take back His promises." The archdiocese of Cincinnati, in 1971 guidelines, declared: "The Jewish people is not collectively guilty of the passion and death of Jesus Christ, nor of the rejection of Jesus as Messiah. The Jewish people is not damned, nor bereft of its election. Their suffering, dispersion, and persecution are not punishments for the crucifixion or the rejection of Jesus."

These are among the many indications of a growing sense of responsibility among Christian leaders to teach positively and fairly about Jews and Judaism. It is profoundly unfortunate that these developments find no echo and no acknowledgment in Reverend Moon's teachings. Having drawn upon the most anti-Jewish elements in Christian tradition, Reverend Moon has totally ignored the conscientious efforts of Christians to correct them. Moreover the holocaust, when one-third of the Jewish people were murdered by the Nazis, is gratuitously mentioned by Reverend Moon, and nowhere in *Divine Principle* are there any calls for repentance or for self-examination. The United Methodist church in 1972 expressed "clear repentance and a resolve to repudiate past injustice and to seek its elimination in the present." But not Reverend Moon.

Two leading Christian bodies, the National Council of Churches and the Roman Catholic archdiocese of New York, are sharply critical of Reverend Moon's teachings. A working paper prepared by the Faith and Order Commission of the NCC asserts that many principles of the Unification church differ substantially from accepted Christian theology and that it finds serious fault with Reverend Moon's major beliefs:

Divine Principle contains a legalistic theology of indemnity in which grace and forgiveness play little part. The central figures of providence fail even when they are not believed—a vicarious failure is certainly not central to Christian affirmation. That is, Christ failed because the Jews did not believe in Him and put Him to death. That is double indemnity indeed, and its penalties are continuing anti-Semitism and the requirement that another savior come to complete the salvation of Jesus Christ.

Dr. Jorge Lara-Braud, a member of the Presbyterian church in the United States, and Dr. William L. Hendricks of the Southwestern Baptist Theological Seminary were the principal authors of the working paper. The Roman Catholic archdiocese of New York has warned its priests about the "acute dangers" that the Unification church presents for believing Christians. "It is important to bear in mind that several points of Rev. Moon's teaching are in direct conflict with Catholic theology, and therefore render his movement suspect for Catholic participation," Father James L. LeBar, an official of the archdiocesan communications office, said in a letter to pastors.

There are over 125 examples of an unremitting litany of anti-Jewish teachings in *Divine Principle*. But nowhere does Reverend Moon acknowledge the authenticity and integrity of Jews or Judaism, either ancient or modern. From Abraham until the present day, Jews are seen only as a people devoid and emptied of any genuine faith and spiritual qualities: "The inner contents are corrupt" (p. 532). The Jewish people, allies of Satan, are depicted as collectively responsible for the crucifixion of Jesus. They have been replaced by a "second Israel" (who interestingly enough, must soon be replaced by the "third Israel": the followers of Reverend Moon). Further the Jews have lost God's "heritage" and are still being "punished" for their many, many sins.

Reverend Moon's *Divine Principle* is a feculent breeding ground for fostering anti-Semitism. Because of his unrelieved hostility toward Jews and Judaism, a demonic picture emerges from the pages of his major work. One can only speculate on what negative and anti-Jewish impact *Divine Principle* may have upon Reverend Moon's followers.

In apparent response to the American Jewish Committee's recent study of his basic teachings, the Reverend Moon has categorically condemned anti-Semitism and has declared his support of Israel's right to secure existence (*New York Times*, December 19, 1976).

We trust that the Reverend Moon's declaration that the Unification movement "categorically condemns anti-Semitism, the most hideous, abject and cruel form of hatred" will now result in concrete actions demonstrating that he means what he professes. A comprehensive and systematic removal of negative and hostile references to Jews and Judaism that abound in his *Divine Principle*, the basic teachings of the Unification movement, would be one such demonstration that his statements are made in good faith and are not simply public relations pieties.

Reverend Moon attributes the murder of six million Jews during the European holocaust to "political short-sightedness and lack of moral responsibility on the part of Germany's political and religious leaders, and statesmen from among other nations, in the period between the Two World Wars." While these realities cannot be denied, the actual foundation blocks for the holocaust were laid centuries before that, and the destruction of European Jewry cannot be viewed apart from a tradition of theological and cultural anti-Semitism that dehumanized Jews, heaped contempt upon them, and justified their persecution on religious grounds.

The numerous references to Jews and Judaism documented in

the American Jewish Committee study of the *Divine Principle*—especially the teachings that the entire Jewish people betrayed, rejected, and crucified Jesus, that Jewish suffering and persecution "through the present day" are punishment for the collective sin of the "Christ-killers," that God's heritage has been taken away from the Jewish people—all conform to that invidious tradition and, in fact, reinforce it.

In light of the fact that all major Christian bodies and religious authorities have unambiguously repudiated these anti-Jewish canards, we call upon Reverend Moon not to be guilty of replanting these poisonous weeds, which so many faithful people have labored over decades to uproot.

Since the American Jewish Committee study was confined to a content analysis of the *Divine Principle*, I have restricted this response mainly to the issues of anti-Semitism. That concentrated focus should not be taken to mean that the American Jewish Committee is not equally concerned about the proselytizing activities and the reputed mind-conditioning methods of indoctrination practiced by Reverend Moon and his followers, as well as their ideological stance, which appears to be a religious justification of regimes that practice oppression and denial of human rights.

6

**Some Thoughts about the
Unification Movement
and the Churches**

Barbara W. Hargrove

Certainly one of the most controversial Eastern religious groups now in the United States is that headed by the Reverend Sun Myung Moon and known as the Unification church. It has fallen heir to charges of recruitment by brainwashing, which we first heard leveled at such groups as the Children of God. Suspicion has been raised by the group's support of the Park government of South Korea, linking the activities of the Moonies to the scandals of Korean influence peddling in Washington, D.C. Sinister motives have been ascribed to the group's economic activities, which include not only Moon's extensive business holdings in Korea but also his purchase of valuable property in New York and elsewhere (including the former New Yorker Hotel, the Columbia University Club, a large estate in Tarrytown, New York, and a former Christian Brothers monastery in Barrytown, which now serves as their seminary). People in Boston and Norfolk, Virginia, have begun legal battles to stop the competition engendered as they have invested in fisheries and staffed them with unpaid church members. Charges of sexual irregularity in the group have arisen, along with contrasting ones claiming the movement over-controls members' sex lives. Protestant, Catholic, and Jewish leaders have recently condemned the group as anti-Semitic, anti-Christian, and antidemocratic. And even the normally unconcerned public has tended to have a negative impression of the eager young Moonies who buttonhole people in terminals and parking lots and try to sell products or solicit contributions.

Yet the movement grows. What is its appeal? Why have

the arguments against it carried so little weight? After some admittedly sketchy study of the group, I have come to a few tentative conclusions.

Current Criticisms

It is counterproductive to concentrate criticism of the group on their recruitment methods as brainwashing. There are at least three reasons to take this stand.

First, discussions of brainwashing, at least those emanating from the religious community, beg the question of the nature of religious conversion. A common assumption about religion is that it provides the basis for a person's world view. It is from religion that one finds a sense of meaning in life by which priorities are ordered, authorities accepted, and values chosen. This is a personalized rather than an institutional definition, but it is one commonly accepted among students of religion, who see religious institutions as the continuing repositories and purveyors of those world views, so that they are expressed both socially and in personal life. In such a frame of reference religious conversion may be seen as stepping from one world view into another, where not only institutional membership is changed but the priorities and authorities upon which reasoning is built and one's life is ordered. Such a change is seldom made in any lasting sense without social support; one needs other people to share a world view or face doubts about one's sanity. Obviously this has happened with recruits to the Unification church—as it has happened to sincere converts to any new religious perspective through the ages. It is also clear that when such a conversion occurs, it becomes harder to share important concerns with those who still live within the old frame of reference, so a rift may develop between converts and their families and former friends, reinforced by the fact that they seem impossible to reason with because of the change in basic assumptions upon which the reasoning takes place. Thus while it is clear that Moonies may be alienated from their families, it does not necessarily follow that this alienation is deliberately fostered. And if it is brainwashing to persuade a person to accept a world view one has found valuable, then the Christian church stands guilty of having practiced it for generations in its programs of evangelism and missions.

A second weakness of the brainwashing accusation lies in the ease with which it can be refuted. Many persons who have had contact with the Unification church report that they have not felt pressured or manipulated by indoctrination sessions, and many have indeed left those sessions unconvinced. True brainwashing involves a degree of coercion, which is hard to prove in this case. Such coercion is clearly more evident in the deprogramming undertaken by those who would "save" people from the movement.

The third weakness is that it tends to lead to refutation through ad hominem argument. When families or churches level such accusations at any other group, they lay themselves open to charges that they are reacting out of envy toward a group that has succeeded in attracting the devotion of young people they themselves have failed to inspire and attract. Charges of breaking up families are hard to take seriously in a society where most families expect and often assist young people to leave home for schooling or employment in distant places. In fact psychologists state that many young people are attracted to such movements when they are cut off from family life by these sorts of circumstances. They enjoy the richness of a large family-like group, which provides the kind of variety and sociability that has been lost as industrialization has broken extended families into small nuclear units. It is not the fault of the modern family that it is caught in this situation, but it does not require some sinister methodology for the Unification church to meet such needs. Similarly churches in their own self-studies recognize difficulties in meeting the needs and stimulating the enthusiasm of young people. Consequently when churches or families accuse the Unification church of brainwashing, it becomes believable that the difference between what they call brainwashing and their definition of true religion or filial piety is simply its success: "That which succeeds where I have failed must be supported by sinister means."

For all these reasons I find the brainwashing argument some-what of a red herring in the consideration of the Unification church.

There are serious problems with many of the theological objections raised against the Unification church. In an age when the desire for ecu-menical cooperation has made charges of heresy inappropriate, those who accuse the movement of deviation from normative Christianity expose themselves to rebuttals that question the exis-tence of such a norm. While the total theological argument of the Unification church is indeed unique—as is that of each major church—it contains elements congenial to a wide range of Christian traditions, even when they are not accepted by all.

Their unification theme, for example, is a logical extension of the ecumenical movement in that they would unite all religions under the banner of a monotheistic God. The movement gives evidence of its belief in worldwide brotherhood both in its full fel-lowship of Caucasians and Orientals (few American blacks have been attracted) and in the international character of a member-ship, which is shifted around enough so that direct personal contact with persons of other cultures is frequent. It is as easy to accuse the American churches of a racist reaction to the idea of a Korean messiah as it is to define the Unification church as narrow sectarianism.

At the same time much of Unification theology is based on the kind of conservative Christianity that found root in Korea through the efforts of American missionaries. Thus there are themes with appeal for conservatives, who might not be attracted by the movement's ecumenism. There is a tendency toward bib-lical literalism, though interpretations are sometimes unique. Much of their understanding of history is consistent with the kind of "dispensationalism" popularized by the old Scofield Reference Bible and still current in some conservative circles. At the same time their strict code of personal morals—no liquor, no tobacco, no drugs, no extramarital sex—and their strong work ethic are consistent with the stance of conservative Christians on such matters.

Another element of the Unification faith picks up themes from the social gospel movement. While the Moonies may put it in more eschatalogical terms, their efforts at building the kingdom of God on earth through action in political and social institutions are certainly reminiscent of that movement in the churches. It strikes me as strange when I hear people at places like Yale Divinity School expressing concern about the movement because it is "so political," because it engages in informal lobbying. One may indeed question the group's political orientation, but it is another thing to question its desire to engage in political action. The assumptions of the 1970s that religion is a private affair are open to question.

The Unification church cannot be dismissed as simply another version of youth-based "new religions" of the 1970s. Most of the so-called new religions, whether specifically religious or a secular search for salvation, have properly been accused of contributing to the trend toward the privatization of religion; that is, they reinforce a definition of religion as a matter of personal opinion and voluntary association, with no import for the public sector of the society. In this way no matter how personally satisfying or stimulating the religious practice, it provides little basis for responsible action in the public sector of the society. Its only relevance to the centers of power and decision will be that which Marx saw, an opiate for the masses by which they may endure a life made otherwise unendurable by the greed of the powerful. Certainly there is little in the current scene to refute such criticism or to indicate that any basic social change is resulting from the new religious consciousness.

But the Unification church does have a public dimension. For good or ill, its adherents are concerned with political policy and in touch with those who create it. They are involved in economic structures on a worldwide basis. The Unification church is a form of civil religion.[1] Its ideology revives the messianic notion of America as a light to the nations, and it is in this way that it has attracted many bright, idealistic converts who have been disappointed both by the shoddiness of American politics and by the inaction of the churches, yet who desire a more meaningful life than the pursuit of financial success or personal religious assurance.

The Unification church also cannot be classified with other new religions in their trend toward an early demise. In 1966 John Lofland published a study of the Unification movement, *Doomsday Cult,* in which he carefully protected its identity so that informants would not be embarrassed when the movement failed—an event he assumed was near at hand. Instead the movement has grown and solidified, and it has an economic base that makes its imminent disappearance improbable.

Sources of Concern

I am not, however, prepared to argue for the acceptance of the Unification church as a legitimate religious movement that deserves the cooperation, if not the support, of other major faiths, for it has other elements that tend to be less consistent with the values of American religion. Most of these revolve around the nature of the messianism, which is central to Unification theology.

One way to approach messianism is to look at the full-page advertisement Moon took out in the *New York Times,* on December 19, 1976, attempting to refute charges of anti-Semitism that had been raised. Point 6 of that statement reads, "The Unification Movement is grateful to God, to His true and righteous prophets and saints of our common spiritual tradition who prepared the foundations on which we stand and organize our struggle. We consider ourselves to be the younger brother of our Jewish and Christian brethren, all of whom are children of our Heavenly Father."

The Unification theology is closely related to the Christian interpretation of Jewish messianism, which claims that Jesus went first to the "lost sheep of the house of Israel," and only after they failed to recognize him as their messiah was the Christian church founded as spiritual heir to the promise given to Abraham, to become God's chosen people. This, of course, is not the only interpretation of the relationship of Judaism to Christianity, or even the most widely accepted in the churches today. But it is still present, and such studies as Charles Glock and Rodney Stark's *Christian Beliefs and Anti-Semitism* have linked it to secular anti-Semitism when certain other conditions are present. To that extent Unification teaching may be considered anti-Semitic, though no clear indication has been given yet that the other necessary conditions for anti-Semitism are present in the organization.

At the same time, there is an equal amount of anti-Christian potential. Unification theology teaches that because the Jews failed to accept Jesus as their messiah, the full messianic function has not yet been fulfilled, a statement that can find support, though for very different reasons, from both Jews and Christians who take seriously and literally the Second Coming of Christ as that fulfillment. The point of potential conflict, however, is in the assumption that Christians of the present age may fall into a similar error and refuse to recognize the messianic claims of the Lord of the Second Advent, who may be Moon himself. Should this happen, today's Christians could find themselves in the dubious spiritual state of having prevented once again the fulfillment of God's redemptive plan for humankind. Thus the basis is laid for the same attitude toward Christians as that which has led to the persecution of Jews in the Christian world.

The messianic fulfillment is expected to involve the purification of both the physical and the social orders. Perhaps the most difficult of Moon's ideas to deal with is his definition of original sin as coming from immature and wrongfully motivated sexual intercourse between Adam and Eve, and its cure being the establishment of a perfect family where children are the product of mature spiritual love cleansed by the blessing of the leader. It is these cleansed people and their innately pure offspring who may be trusted to create a just society, based on true love and the unification of all peoples.

There are teeth in this idealistic picture, for the proof that anyone really is the Lord of the Second Advent lies in his (or her) ability to bring this state of affairs into being. Thus so far Moon is only potentially the messiah, his confirmation in that position depending upon the behavior of those who have thrown their lot in with him. This explains the great effort being made to legitimate the movement in the eyes of established religious leaders, as well as the scientific, academic community, shown in the well-run and well-financed international conferences on the unity of the sciences, as well as their attempts to attract established religious scholars to teach in their seminary and to have it accredited. It will be much harder to bring in the kingdom of the messiah if the messiah is once again rejected by the establishment.

This idealistic picture also explains much of the determined cheerfulness and friendliness of the Moonies. If they have truly been cleansed by the new messiah, they have no reason not to be happy. Their behavior becomes the kind of works-righteousness attributed to Calvinists who knew that God has preordained each to be elect or damned but continued to work to show signs of their election. In this case, though, there is even more at stake: a failure to live up to the standards not only endangers the standing of the individual but also threatens the whole movement, giving evidence that their leader does not have the necessary salvational power to be the messiah. One can imagine the pressures on parents and children alike as these young people enter into sanctioned marriage and produce children who are expected to be perfect. Only the truly committed could view such an expectation as psychologically healthy.

Consequently one negative evaluation of the group embraces the psychological dimension. While evidence of brainwashing is unclear and immediate psychological consequences of joining may be quite positive as the convert finds meaning in life and a strong supportive community, the long-range psychological pressures appear to be extreme (unless, of course, their ideology is literally true).

Other portions of their theology are potentially dangerous to values claimed, if not always lived up to, by most other churches.

One concern arises from the strong dualistic tendency in their teaching. Though it maintains the supremacy of a transcendent God, it grants significant power to Satan. It divides humanity into two opposing camps. On the one hand are the Abel types, who have the potential for good even though they are marred by original sin. In contrast Cain-types are the children of Satan, inherently opposed to the plan of God. The Cain influence is directly equated with modern communism, and an apocalyptic battle between these evil forces and the legions of good is taken for granted. The nature of human life in the present age is characterized by this struggle between the forces of good and those of evil. And only the Lord of the Second Advent has the power to lead a successful fight against the satanic forces of communism.

These echoes of cold war–Far Right rhetoric tend to raise fears of an authoritarianism of the Right, which are not laid to rest by pronouncements of Unification leaders, although some apologists cite Moon's personal experience as a prisoner of the communists as a reasonable excuse for such rhetoric and others lay it to the Korean penchant for overstatement. This, however, is not the only instance of a tendency toward what may be described as a nascent fascism. Their version of American civil religion may be so interpreted. One example of their approach may be found in the bicentennial issue of their periodical, *News World* (July 4, 1976), which provides not only a sketch of the questionable numerology on which they base their belief in the nearness of the Apocalypse but also gives their version of the highlights of American history. Several themes emerge: the traditional civil religion theme of America as the promised land, the chosen people, a light to the nation; typical American rejoicing in technological development and progress, a tendency to see periods of centralization of government power as high points, decentralization as negative; strong support for political leaders as exercising God-given power; and a celebration of international economic structures as sources of worldwide organization and distribution.

Unification, they say, will come about through the centralization of economic and political power in the right hands. Thus their worldwide investments in basic commodities and industry are consistent with the placement of Moonies in the offices of influential congressional and other government leaders where they can gently persuade and influence decisions. Both are efforts to consolidate power—power that can be used to battle the forces of godless communism, power that does not ward off but ensures victory in the inevitable Armageddon of World War III.

Aside from an aversion to such warlike expectations, there are at least two other reasons to question such a view of the world, one theological and one pragmatic. Theologically unless one is willing to accept the movement's assumptions about being involved in a Second Advent in which the messiah returns with power, this orientation seems dangerously close to what traditional Christianity has described as a temptation of Satan, which Jesus resisted at the beginning of his ministry: having all the kingdoms of the world delivered into his hand. Faithfulness to his leadership would appear to require the church to renounce such earthly power.

Pragmatically whenever that lesson has been forgotten and the church has achieved political and economic dominance, its secular power has overwhelmed its religious message, and corruption and disintegration have ensued. There is no reason, outside accepting their ideology literally and completely, why the Moon movement should be exempt from that process.

An ideology that justifies the seeking of power in order to do battle with forces of evil, on the assumption that one's own movement is pure and totally right, also justifies repressive methods in the attainment and exercise of that power. Regardless of whether they are currently using them, the Unification church has the potential for exercising highly authoritarian, repressive methods, as well as sanctioning their use by others considered to be on the side of the right. While Moon's followers may regret the public relations of the Park regime of South Korea, there is no reason in their ideology for them to denounce it. Similarly while brainwashing and manipulation of members may not be as prevalent as their critics claim, there are fewer correctives in their teachings against such manipulative practices than are found in most Christian and Jewish groups at the present time. The perfect society they hope to establish has even more potential for repression than utopias of the past.

Implications for the Churches

If the movement, then, is contrary to some important values of American churches, there is reason for concern about its attractiveness and its growing power. This implies that attention be directed in several areas, some of which follow.

Other churches need to reconsider the ways in which they are attached to economic and political power centers in ways that limit their freedom to be faithful to their own values. If indeed they criticize the relationship of the Unification church to such power centers, they must examine such things as the privileged tax status of the churches, their investment practices, and other ways in which they may have compromised their ability to speak their own message and support their own values in the political and economic worlds.

Churches must also direct their attention to the trend toward privatization of religion. It is not just the new religious groups that have emphasized a definition of religion as purely personal and subjective. Christian churches, both liberal and conservative, have contributed to this trend.

Liberals, concerned with affirming cultural pluralism in the modern world, have been loath to advance particularistic claims as having universal application. As a consequence they tend to play down specific faith claims and spend much of their public rhetoric on questions of organization and policy rather than on the sources of the values assumed in their discussions. Young people trained in such a religious climate are unlikely to ask hard questions of any new group they encounter, which would uncover the ideological sources of their action. Rather they treat such issues as matters of personal opinion and base their evaluation of the group heavily upon surface phenomena such as their friendliness and sense of mission. On the other hand conservatives have maintained a high level of commitment and participation by focusing their interests on individual salvation and personal piety. Thus where specific faith stands are spelled out more clearly, they tend to be focused on the individual and private behavior. Until liberals are willing to articulate religious reasons for their public pronouncements, or conservatives admit to a public relevance to their religiosity, idealistic and genuinely religious young people are likely to be attracted to a group that seems to do both.

The idealism of young people needs to be taken seriously. Our society in the past several decades has consistently increased the period between physical maturity, which is significantly earlier now, and social responsibility. In spite of lower voting ages, young people are denied full adult status while they pursue longer and longer courses of study. Little that they do is taken seriously, except as preparation for some receding future. They know that one reason they stay in school is that there is no place for them in the job market, and those who drop out receive painful confirmation of that fact. It is not surprising if they begin to have doubts about ever having significance in the society. The churches do not help matters when they segregate young people into youth groups that discuss problems of adolescence or engage only in recreational activities. What young people need, in the churches and out of them, is a sense of significance. Movements such as Moon's provide it. Privatized churches may have little significance to grant, but often they do not offer young people that which they could provide—a responsible place in their own structure.

Churches need to provide young people with genuine community. Catering to individual needs has led churches to act as spiritual service stations, to which people come for a regular fill-up or an occasional tuneup before they go out to involve themselves in the "real world." The problem with that is that every other involvement is equally partial and periodic, so that there is no center around which to organize life. We depend on the nuclear family for this, but it is both too small and too fragmented to serve that function alone.

Parents have been faulted for not having a sufficiently rich family life to protect their children from the appeal of Moon's or other religious communities. But they can hardly be expected to provide the kind of group support available in extended families of the past. In the church, however, there is the possibility of finding people who care, who share values, and who represent peers and parents—and grandparents and aunts and uncles as well—in the nearest approximation of the extended family available in urban, industiralized, Western society. If that kind of care were fostered and these shared values acted out in the church in continuing and deep ways, young people would not be so surprised and attracted by the atmosphere of love and caring exhibited in Moonie centers but would actually have more than that already available.

Finally the churches are challenged by such movements to become more theologically responsible. The Unification church appeals to people who are seriously religious and who want to put that religion into practice. There must be reasons why they choose it instead of traditional churches, which are tied to the way in which those churches interpret their message. Or maybe, more rightly, one may question the way in which such interpretations are made real in the lives of the faithful.

Most of the weaknesses in the ability of the churches to provide a responsible critique of this movement have been centered not around high-level, systematic theology but around the kind of popular religion that is assimilated by average Americans, including faithful church members. The question may be why there should be such a gap between these two expressions of Christianity in our society today. We need to take seriously Jurgen Moltmann's words on this subject: "Faith, the church and theology must demonstrate what they really believe and hope about the man from Nazareth who was crucified under Pontius Pilate, and what practical consequences they wish to draw from this."[2]

Perhaps enough has been said already in the discussion of privatization concerning being serious about what we believe and hope. But a discussion of the practical consequences of this involves other factors as well. The churches, like the rest of modern society, have fallen victim to the overspecialization of the age. Theology all too often speaks only to its own internal structure and seldom to the problems encountered by ordinary Christians in the world of everyday existence. Churches too often concern themselves only with life within the institution and not their relation to the other involvements of members. In a world where literary and artistic emphases are on the meaninglessness of existence, religious institutions whose symbolic and organizational focuses are removed from the common life leave an opening to any group that will present an ideology that invests the daily life of its members with ultimate meaning.

It does not help that many young people in the churches are allowed to grow up as biblical illiterates. They cannot deal responsibly with ideologies based on new interpretations of texts said to be sacred to their tradition but that are unfamiliar to them, both in content and in context. Young people are apparently attracted to groups where they see people dealing seriously with what they believe and what that means in a societal context. They find the church to be serious about such things very infrequently. Movements such as Moon's challenge the churches to articulate their distinctive values and put them into practice, or else not to complain if the next generation looks elsewhere for religious meaning and involvement.[3]

Notes

1. Thomas Robbins; Dick Anthony; Madeline Doucas; and Thomas Curtis, *Sociological Analysis* "The Last Civil Religion: Reverend Moon and the Unification Church," 37:2 (Summer 1976): 111–125.
2. Jurgen Moltmann, *The Crucified God* (New York: Harper and Row, 1974), p. 3.
3. My sources of information concerning the beliefs and practices of the Unification church include, in addition to personal discussions with members and panelists in the series "Faith and Fractionalism" at Yale Divinity School, the following Unification publications: Young Oon Kim, *Unification Theology and Christian Thought*; Sun Myung Moon, *Christianity in Crisis: New Hope, God's Hope for America, New Hope, The New Future of Christianity*, and *The Divine Principle*; and Herbert Richardson, ed., *Documents Concerning the Theology of the Unification Church.*

7

**Critique of the Theology
of the Unification Church
as Set Forth
in *Divine Principle***

Agnes Cunningham
J. Robert Nelson
William L. Hendricks
Jorge Lara-Braud

For several months the National Council of the Churches of Christ's Commission on Faith and Order has been frequently requested to clarify the claim to Christian identity made by the Unification church, whose official name contains that claim: the Holy Spirit Association for the Unification of World Christianity. In pursuit of its membership application to the Council of Churches of the City of New York, the Unification church filed in the supreme court of the state of New York on September 4, 1975, a notice of petition identifying itself as "a Christian Church committed to the ministry of spreading by word and deed, the gospel of the Divine Lord and Saviour, Jesus Christ." We have since received solicited and unsolicited authoritative statements of self-clarification from the Unification church and some of its sympathizers. For the sake of keeping discourse entirely within the realm of what is authoritative and in the public domain, the commission has chosen to confine itself to the official doctrinal text of the Unification church: *Divine Principle* (the version used is the second edition, published in 1974).

This process, engaging the entire commission, has resulted in this critique. Although it is primarily a response to those who have requested our theological assessment, it is also made available to anyone else upon request. Nothing would be more

This is an official study document of the Commission on Faith and Order of the National Council of the Churches of Christ in the U.S.A. As with other study documents, this does not become official policy of the whole council unless, through an appropriate process, its governing board approves it.

contrary to the spirit of this critique than for it to be used for arbitrary or punitive purposes. The commission is wholeheartedly committed to the inalienable rights of civil and religious liberties enjoyed in the United States by all religious groups, whether they are the critics or the criticized.

Divine Principle: Review and Critique
Its Purpose

The purpose of this book, according to the anonymous introduction, is to set forth the "new, ultimate, final truth" (p. 15), which "has already appeared" (p. 16). The God-sent messenger of this truth is Sun Myung Moon, who will "resolve the fundamental questions of life and the universe" (p. 16). Victorious over the bitterest of trials and over Satanic forces, he has come "in contact with many saints in Paradise and with Jesus," thus bringing "into light all the heavenly secrets through his communion with God" (p. 16). The "Divine Principle" is part of "the new truth." What is recorded here is "what Sun Myung Moon's disciples have hitherto heard and witnessed" (p. 16). The new truth "should be able to resolve completely the problems of religion and science" (p. 121).

The vast program undertaken in *Divine Principle* is reflected in topics discussed in the contents of the volume: part I chapters are "Principle of Creation," "Fall of Man" (male language designating both sexes is used in *Divine Principle*; we have retained it for the sake of consistency), "Consummation of Human History," "Advent of the Messiah," "Resurrection," "Predestination," and "Christology." Part II chapters are "Providential Age for the Foundation of Restoration," "Providence of Restoration Centering on Moses and Jesus," "Formation and Length of Each Age in the History of Providence," "Providential Age of Restoration and Age of the Prolongation of Restoration from the Standpoint of Providential Time-Identity," and "Preparation Period for the Second Advent of the Messiah," and "Second Advent."

Definition of the Principle

The divine principle is the principle of creation, which is the reality of existence and its movement toward perfection. All reality, including God, has the dual nature of internal-external characteristics composed of the essentialities of positive-negative poles, which interact in reciprocal relationships.

Existence passes through the threefold movement of origin-division-union. It must also pass through the stages of formation-growth-perfection (p. 53). God's purpose of creation is realized in the establishment of a "fourfold position foundation" based upon himself. Adam and Eve were to have propagated children of goodness, forming a trinity based on God. "However, due to the fall, Adam and Eve established the four position foundation centered on Satan" (p. 217). Their descendants also "formed trinities centered on Satan, and have brought about a human society of corruption" (p. 217).

This condition requires new parents for the race who will effect a trinity centered on God. Jesus (the masculine principle) and the Holy Spirit (the feminine principle) were to have formed such a trinity based on God, "but because of the undue death of Jesus, he and the Holy Spirit have fulfilled only the mission of spiritual True Parents" (p. 217). A further trinity must be effected by the "Christ" who comes again and who will become "the True Parent both spiritually and physically" (p. 218), by forming the substantial trinity centered on God.

Presuppositions

Duality and Esoteric Knowledge   There are several presuppositions underlying the doctrines in *Divine Principle*. From the beginning, duality is firmly established as essentially and existentially real at every level of being (pp. 2, 4, 20–64). The concept of duality—whether in God, creation, human life, or the individual—is necessary for an understanding of the teachings set forth in the volume. *Divine Principle* emphasizes the duality of all things and claims an esoteric knowledge of a truth and an understanding of this truth never before available in the history of the world (pp. 19, 66, 88, 119, 130, 131, 136, 170, 176, 205, 509, 535).

Stress on Materiality   Another presupposition is a stress on
materiality, which is strikingly evident in the concepts of salvation presented in *Divine Principle*. "God's purpose of creation is to
establish the Kingdom of Heaven on earth" (p. 102). This implies
domination "of all things," subduing "the natural world through
highly developed science," and bringing about an "extremely
pleasant social environment on earth" (p. 87). "Social revolution" is "unavoidable when the circumstances of the age cannot
satisfy the desires of the men belonging to the age" (p. 95).

Jesus was not able to provide physical salvation. He was not
supposed to die. In dying "his body was invaded by Satan"
(p. 148). His death accomplished only spiritual salvation. It
remains for the Lord of the Second Advent, "by engrafting the
whole of mankind spiritually and physically" on the foundation
he establishes, "to restore them to be children of God's direct
image, having removed the original sin" (p. 369).

Adultery as the Root of All Sin   A further presupposition is
that "the root of man's sin stems from adultery" (p. 75). Eve's
blood relationship with the angel Lucifer caused the spiritual fall,
and her blood relationship with Adam caused the physical fall
(p. 77). Since then mankind has multiplied in sin, "thus perpetu-
ating the lineage of Satan" (p. 80). No matter how devout Christians may be, they, like the Old Testament saints, have not been
able "to liquidate original sin coming down through the flesh" or
"to remove themselves from the lineage of Satan" (p. 368).
"Therefore, the Lord of the Second Advent must come to restore
the whole of mankind to be children of God's direct lineage"
(p. 369).

**Responsibility of Jews and Christians for the Restoration of
Fallen Humanity**   Still another presupposition is the peculiar
responsibility of Judaism and Christianity for the restoration of
fallen humanity. The Jews failed, and Christians are in danger
of doing the same. It is clearly stated that "the history of the
Israelite nation is the central focus of the providential history of
restoration" (p. 283). This is so because of the failure of the

Israelites on every occasion to show fidelity and cooperation with all that God gave to them to realize salvation.

Repeatedly the Israelites failed to multiply goodness (p. 298). They "all fell into faithlessness" (pp. 315, 316, 319, 323), which became the reason for the failure both of Moses (p. 316) and of Jesus (p. 145). Because of the "ignorance and disbelief of the Jewish people," Jesus was crucified (p. 145), and the Lord of the Second Advent will not come from this people (pp. 430, 431, 518). Christians who fail or refuse to acknowledge the Lord of the Second Advent will be like the Jews who failed to acknowledge or recognize Jesus as Messiah (p. 535).

Doctrines Emerging from Presuppositions

These presuppositions underlie the doctrinal affirmations of *Divine Principle*. Several doctrines are significant.

Scripture and Authority   The Bible, "not the truth itself, but a textbook teaching the truth," is to be supplemented by a new expression of truth, which has already appeared (p. 9). Just as Jesus appeared at the close of the Old Testament age, "Christ" will come at the close of the New Testament age "and will give us new words for the building of a new age" (p. 35). God will reveal "all the secrets of the Second Advent of the Lord before actualizing it" (p. 497). These secrets include the coming of Christ a second time, outside of the descendants of Abraham (p. 520); his birth in an Eastern nation, which will be "none other than Korea" (p. 520); and an inevitable third world war, when the world of democracy (the heavenly side) will vanquish the world of communism (the Satanic side), either "by force of arms or an ideological battle" (p. 493).

The Nature of God as Triune   The God portrayed in *Divine Principle* is monotheistic. His deity is dualistic in nature (p. 20), consisting of "essential positivity" ("essential character") and "essential negativity" ("essential form") (p. 29). In the words of *Divine Principle*, "God is the subject who consists of the dual characteristics of essential character and essential form. . . . He is a subject consisting of the dual characteristics of masculinity and femininity. . . . In relationship to the whole creation, God is the masculine subject representing its internal character" (p. 25).

God "is the reality of the number 'three' . . . , the absolute reality, the existing neutral center of the two essentialities" (p. 53). For this reason "God has worked to restore the number 'three' " (p. 53). If Adam and Eve "had perfected themselves without the fall," they would have formed "a trinity as the True Parents centered on God" (p. 217). However Jesus too failed in his mission. He and "the Holy Spirit have fulfilled only the mission of spiritual True Parents, by forming the spiritual Trinity centered on God." The "substantial Trinity centered on God" will be formed only when "Christ" comes again "in flesh" (p. 218). Who is this "Christ," and what is this "Second Advent"?

Christology Several major sections of *Divine Principle* are devoted expressly to what is included in the Christian understanding of Christology: part I, section 4, "Advent of the Messiah"; part I, section 7, "Christology"; part II, section 2, "Providence of Restoration Centering on Moses and Jesus"; and part II, section 6, "Second Advent." In addition other references to Jesus, his life, and mission appear in the book.

The first reference to Jesus lists the ways in which "God has worked to restore the number 'three' " (p. 53), since God "is the reality of the number 'three' " (p. 53). Jesus had "thirty years of private life and three years of public ministry," "three major disciples," "three temptations," "three prayers at Gethsemane"; Peter denied Jesus three times; there were "three hours of darkness during the crucifixion and Jesus' resurrection after three days." However such a catalog does not contribute to our understanding of who Jesus is thought to be or how his mission is comprehended.

"Jesus came," we are told, "as a perfected man in flesh and spirit. . . . Jesus is our savior. He came to the world in order to perfect fallen men by striving to have them unite with him" (p. 63). He came "as the Tree of Life to fulfill the hope of the Old Testament saints, who had waited for his advent" (p. 68). "Jesus came to restore the ideal world in the form intended at the creation" (p. 113). Jesus came "as the incarnation of the Word (John 1:14), proclaiming the Word of Life" (p. 116). With the Holy Spirit Jesus forms "the spiritual Trinity" centered on God (p. 217). What is the meaning of these statements?

"Jesus Christ came as the Messiah," but only in the sense of the "Messianic expectations of the Israelites" (p. 139). Although "Jesus was a man who had attained the purpose of creation" (p. 210), he is one of a series of "central figures," each of whom appeared in a respective new age: Noah, Abraham, Moses, Jesus (p. 134). The mission of Jesus surpassed that of Abraham and Moses because it was "worldwide" (p. 187).

While the "Principle does not deny the attitude of faith held by many Christians that Jesus is God, . . . the principle of creation sees the original value of perfected man as being equal to that of Jesus" (p. 209). Since "a perfected man is one body with God" (p. 209), "Jesus, as a man having fulfilled the purpose of creation, is one body with God" (p. 210). However Jesus "can by no means be God Himself" (p. 211). He is "a second God (image of God)" (p. 211). Because he "has been interceding for us before God, . . . just as he did on earth; because Jesus was tempted by Satan, and finally crucified by the evil force, . . . it becomes clear that Jesus is not God Himself" (p. 213).

Jesus came as the Messiah, that is, as "Christ"; the "Lord," as Jesus promised, will come on the day of the Second Advent (p. 498). Jesus was born as the Messiah "after the 2000 years of the 'providential age of restoration by indemnity' " (p. 499); the "Christ" of the Second Advent will be born not from "among the lineal descendants of Abraham, but to the nation that would take their heritage and produce the fruits of it . . . Korea" (p. 520). Jesus has achieved his mission: limited and "spiritual." The Lord of the Second Advent will achieve his: complete and universal restoration.

"Jesus did not come to die on the cross" (p. 143). The "crucifixion was the result of the ignorance and disbelief of the Jewish people" (p. 145). Jesus "should have fulfilled the salvation of both spirit and body" (p. 147). However the work of Jesus was a failure (p. 196). Thus the "physical salvation of mankind was left unfulfilled, and Jesus died, promising it would be realized when the Lord would come again" (p. 511).

The "Lord, who is to come," like Jesus, "must come as a man perfected both spiritually and physically" (p. 511). The "Lord" of the "Second Advent" must realize the kingdom of God as really as intended at Jesus's coming" (p. 511). Accordingly "the Lord must be born in the flesh on the earth, as in the First Advent" (p. 511).

Redemption by Indemnity   Adam and Eve fell "in the perfection level of the growth stage and [man] has remained ever since under the dominion of Satan" (p. 221). However man "must first restore himself to the perfection level of the growth stage" before he can receive the Messiah (p. 222). Once he has received the Messiah, man, through rebirth, will "be restored to the position before the fall of Adam and Eve" (p. 222).

The process by which man is restored so that he can fulfill the purpose of creation is called *indemnity*. Indemnity proceeds through three stages: paying the exact amount of the loss incurred; paying a lesser amount than the loss incurred; paying a larger amount than the loss incurred. This third stage occurs because of the insufficiency of the second (pp. 224–225) and is required because "when a certain figure in the providence is to set the condition of indemnity again, he must include what was left undone due to the failure of previous persons, in addition to what he himself had to set originally" (p. 225).

Central figures who have paid the indemnity for mankind are Adam's family, Noah's family, Abraham's family, Moses's family, and Jesus. John the Baptist was supposed to prepare the way for Jesus's mission, but he "failed to accomplish his mission" (p. 348). Jesus himself "had to suffer the tribulations which John the Baptist" (p. 348) was supposed to have suffered. Hence Jesus died and accomplished only a portion of his mission. Thus a new messiah is required who will accomplish the full payment of indemnity and restore creation to its intended position.

In the process of indemnity God "does not interfere with man's own portion of responsibility" (p. 371). The principle of creation moves by the process described to the inexorable eschatological state of perfection.

Church and the Means of Grace   The first reference to "church" in *Divine Principle* says, "Christ is the head of the church (Eph. 1:22), and we are his body and members (1 Cor. 12:27)" (p. 213). Our relationship to Jesus is then spelled out in the light of several scriptural texts (John 15:5, Rom. 11:12, John 15:14, 1 John 3:2, 1 Cor. 15:23).

No fuller explanation of "church" is given, but Christianity, according to *Divine Principle*, is "different from other religions" because "its purpose is to restore the one great world family which God had intended at the creation" (p. 123). The "Kingdom of God in heaven can be realized only after the realization of the Kingdom of God on earth" (p. 62). Since it is only in "a home formed around the parents" that "true brotherly love" can occur (p.129), it is "upon the Second Advent of the Lord as the True Parent of mankind" that all will come "to live harmoniously in the garden as one family" (p. 129).

As for the means of grace, belief in "the redemption through the cross," baptism, and the sacrament of holy communion are examples of "lesser indemnity" (p. 225). The Lord of the Second Advent alone "is to come in the completion of the providence of restoration" (p. 238). Then "all the missions of all the ages which the prophets and saints . . . have left unaccomplished" (p. 238) will be realized.

Creation and Eschatology   The origins of human life and of the entire created universe are discussed at noticeable length in *Divine Principle* (pp. 19–64). Here the principle is operative in the explanation of God's work of creation. Duality is present here, along with interpretation of the scriptural account of Genesis. There is also an effort in this section to combine Oriental philosophic thought with Christian teachings and categories of scientific analogy.

More significant, perhaps, is the teaching on eschatology, including a vision of the course and goal of human history. There are political implications in the teachings of the Unification church, as, for example, in the distinctions between the "good" nations and the "bad," which will meet in a final war between God and Satan following allegedly revealed predictions. In the reading of human history, individuals and peoples are either "satanic" or "heavenly" insofar as they threaten or foster the "foundation stage" of restoring "the Heavenly sovereignty by forming a wide and firm basis of politics and economy" (p. 482; cf. also pp. 449–496).

The role of the nation of Korea is foretold for this time of the "Last Days." According to Revelation 7:2–4 and a pre-Christian Korean prophecy revealed in *Chung Gam Nok* (p. 528), the Lord of the Second Advent will be born in Korea (pp. 519–532) and the millennium will be established (p. 527). Then it will be possible for the new heaven and the new earth to be brought about, on the condition that the moment and the central figure are recognized and accepted. All religions will be finally "united into one religion; namely, Christianity" (p. 528).

Theological Critique of *Divine Principle*
Introductory Comments

Any criticism of a religious doctrine that claims to be launched from "*the* Christian position" must be qualified because there is much diversity in Christian belief and theology and thus internal disagreement. Moreover criticisms leveled against other religions by Christians may often be directed against fellow Christians. Orthodox doctrine in its pure state is difficult to define.

As we examine the teachings of *Divine Principle*, therefore, we are mindful of the diversities within Christianity. Nevertheless we believe that the contemporary ecumenical convergence is making certain dimensions of Christian doctrine stand out in sharp detail as essential and indispensable to whatever may be called Christian faith.

The recent rise of the Unification church has confused many Christians and others by advancing teachings that are either at variance with generally recognized Christian doctrines or are subtle modifications of them. This critique of *Divine Principle* does not in any way call into question the freedom of the Unification church to exist and propagate its beliefs under the protections of the First Amendment of the U.S. Constitution. Such analysis is required to see whether *Divine Principle* is in accord with the revelations of God and the saving work of Jesus Christ.

In commenting upon the major presuppositions and doctrines of *Divine Principle*, we offer three kinds of criticism: a questioning of meaning and intelligibility, a direct challenge to veracity or credibility, and an indication of either insufficiency or total lack of Christian expression of belief.

Particular Teachings of Presuppositions

Dualism Duality, a prevalent characteristic of *Divine Principle*, is in fact an inherent teaching of cosmic dualism, which conflicts with Christian biblically-based teaching. First, the eternal unity of the one God is jeopardized by the assertion that upon such dual essentialities as positive and negative, masculine and feminine depends the very being of God (pp. 24, 26). Second, although Christian faith emphasizes the active relation of the Creator God to the created world and human creatures, the dualism of *Divine Principle* posits a gulf between the Creator and creation that prevents God from crossing for the purpose of historical intervention (pp. 105, 148). Whatever the divine will may be, God has only "indirect dominion" over creation (pp. 55–57). Third, reflections upon the mystery of good and evil always raises the thought of dual powers at work. Granted the difficulties in dealing with this mystery, authentic Christian teaching has never allowed an absolute dualism of God and Satan. *Divine Principle* so elevates the power of Satan as to teach what inevitably appears to be a second, rival god. Fourth, *Divine Principle* posits a dualism in human nature as "spirit man" and "physical man" (p. 61). Christian theology has not always fully appreciated the biblical view of the human being as an essential unity of body-spirit (soul), but it has not allowed a dualism that minimizes the goodness of the body and militates against the Christian doctrine of resurrection. Finally, the fall of man is explained in a way incompatible with the Bible and Christian theology. The mythical figure of Lucifer, the fallen angel of light, is presented as the external source of evil and sin, which he transmits by sexual union to Eve, who passes it on to Adam by the same mode. Such unwarranted mythology seeks a facile answer to a most profound and inscrutable mystery, which becomes a basis for questionable teachings and practices of sex and marriage.

Secret Revelations   Without reiterating the antimaterial heresies of ancient gnosticism, *Divine Principle* repeats the claim for secret, esoteric truth. Knowledge of the principle is the key to acquiring "new truth," which illuminates all problems of "life and the universe" (pp. 14–16, 88, 100). Such claims, similar to occult schemes of various character, cannot be admitted into Christian thought without distorting it.

Materialism   In one sense Christianity is "materialistic"; it takes creation, man and incarnation, most seriously as God's work. This is contrary to "spiritualizing" all life and experience at the expense of creation. However *Divine Principle* elevates what is material at the expense of the spiritual. Its very concept of salvation is materialistic. *Divine Principle* reduces the saving work of Jesus Christ as having only or merely spiritual consequences. Jesus could not achieve the "material" salvation, which *Divine Principle* promises. This is an earthly kingdom of comforts and satisfactions, apparently achieved as much by the uses of scientific technology and a democratic political order as by divine intervention (p. 102). Granted that all people, including Christians, desire a "pleasant social environment" in a good society, the projected vision of *Divine Principle* appears to be more a utopia achieved through human means, rather than through a divine reign of righteousness (Matthew 6:33).

Anti-Semitism   There is a recurrent emphasis in *Divine Principle* on the responsibility of the Jewish nation for the failure of the mission of Jesus (pp. 113, 118, 143, 144, 147, 152, 153, 154, 156, 157, 196, 232, 343, 347, 357, 359, 369–370, 418, 479–480, 516–519). The "ignorance," "disbelief," and "stubbornness" of the

Jewish people placed them "on the side of Satan" (p. 480). The attitude expressed toward the Jewish people throughout *Divine Principle* is consistently and unrelievedly negative. It amounts to a prevailing condemnation of an entire people and results in an inevitable anti-Semitism.

It cannot be denied that Christians in the past have written and spoken in a manner that was anti-Semitic. That day is not completely gone, but it is openly regretted by the followers of Jesus. Jesus Christ is not served by any type of discrimination, whether of race, color, creed, sex, or economic status. The anti-Semitism of *Divine Principle* is incompatible with authentic Christian teaching and practice.

Revitalizing Scripture   The Bible is frequently cited in *Divine Principle,* giving the initial impression to some readers that this work is in accord with the Scriptures. The use of biblical texts is arbitrary, however. They are more often cited to provide the names of actors in the drama of restoration than to serve as primal instances of revelation or else, in the manner of many Christian literalists, the texts are adduced to prove the truth of teachings drawn from nonbiblical sources. Yet of Christians who depend literalistically upon Scripture, *Divine Principle* says they are "captives to scriptural words" (p. 533). *Divine Principle* appeals to other revelations, which contradict basic elements of the Christian faith.

Within the diverse communions and traditions of Christianity, there are many ways of understanding scriptural authority and interpretation. Nevertheless for Christians, the biblical witness remains the normative authority. This is not the case in *Divine Principle,* which acknowledges the higher authority of Sun Myung Moon.

The Triune God   The doctrine of the triune God, as set forth in *Divine Principle,* is incompatible with Christian teaching. The concept of a "trinity" formed with Adam and Eve as "true parents centered on God" (p. 218) is inconsistent with Christian understanding of this doctrine. The explanation of a "spiritual trinity" consisting of Jesus and the Holy Spirit "as spiritual True Parents . . . centered on God" (p. 218) is not in harmony with Christian teaching.

This "trinity" is to be replaced when "Christ" comes as the Lord of the Second Advent, to "become the True Parent both spiritually and physically by forming the substantial Trinity centered on God" (p. 218). This "True Parent" will give spiritual and physical rebirth to "all fallen men" and have them also "form [by couples] substantial trinities centered on God" (p. 218). The doctrine of the triune nature of God cannot be acknowledged as Christian.

Salvation, Restoration, and Eschatology   The doctrine of salvation, according to *Divine Principle,* consists in "restoration through indemnity," which within Christian teaching is based further on the absence, in *Divine Principle,* of any clear indication of the existence of the Christian community as church and the role of grace and divine intervention by God in human history.

It is "man, who lost the original position or status endowed at the creation" who "must set up certain necessary conditions to restore himself" (p. 224). The Lord of the Second Advent will "restore through indemnity the providential course of restoration left unachieved at the time of the first coming" (p. 364). Since salvation ("restoration") in *Divine Principle* is explained in terms of the failure of Jesus to fulfill "the salvation of both spirit and body" (p. 147), this doctrine cannot be affirmed as Christian. Similarly, since the fullness of restoration is to be achieved by another than Jesus—by the "Lord of the Second Advent" (p. 369)—this doctrine must be rejected as unchristian.

The political implications of the teachings of the Unification church on eschatology are such as to cause serious concern for members of Christian churches. Facile and categorical distinctions between the "good" nations and the "bad" (pp. 483–490, 491–493) are included in allegedly revealed predictions of a final warfare between God and Satan (pp. 490–496).

Christian eschatology cannot accept an interpretation of human history whereby individuals, as well as peoples, are arbitrarily identified as "satanic" or "heavenly" in terms of a "foundation stage" of restoring "the Heavenly sovereignty by forming a wide and firm basis of politics and economy" (p. 482; also pp. 449–496). It is not faithful Christian teaching to elevate any nation to a messianic role. Hence Christians cannot accept the role assigned to the nation of Korea by *Divine Principle* for the "last days" (pp. 520–532). *Divine Principle* claims that the Lord of the Second Advent is to be born in "none other than Korea" (p. 520). It also holds that "the Korean People . . . will become the Third Israel" (p. 521) and that "many spiritual signs regarding the Lord coming again in Korea are appearing" (p. 529). This eschatology is incompatible in critical and essential ways with that acknowledged, recognized, and taught in Christian churches throughout the world.

Conclusions

The Commission on Faith and Order of the National Council of Churches has defined "continuity with the Christian faith" in the following affirmations: (1) Essential to Christian identity is the biblical affirmation that Jesus of Nazareth is the Christ, the eternal Word of God made flesh. (2) The life, death, and resurrection of Jesus are the ground and means of the salvation of persons and of the whole creation. (3) The triune God—Father, Son, and Holy Spirit—has acted as Creator, Redeemer, and Sanctifier identifying with the suffering and need of the world and is effectively saving it from sin, death, and the powers of evil. (4) There is an essential relationship between faith in the saving work of the triune God and obedient response of the believing community. In the light of this definition of continuity with the Christian faith, we conclude that the Unification Church is not a Christian church because its doctrine of the nature of the triune God is erroneous; its Christology is incompatible with Christian teaching and belief; and its teaching on salvation and the means of grace is inadequate and faulty. We further conclude that the claims of the Unification church to Christian identity cannot be recognized because the role and authority of Scripture are compromised in the teachings of the Unification church; revelations invoked as divine and normative in *Divine Principle* contradict basic elements of Christian faith; and a "new, ultimate, final truth" is presented to complete and supplant all previously recognized religious teachings, including those of Christianity.

III

The Politics of Moon

8

**The Activities of
the Korean Central
Intelligence Agency
in the United States**

Jai Hyon Lee

I appreciate the opportunity to appear before the Subcommittee on International Organizations of the Committee on International Relations of the House of Representatives to testify on activities of the Korean Central Intelligence Agency, KCIA, in the United States in the context of U.S. policy toward Korea and developments affecting the human rights in that country [September 1976].

Last summer when I testified before this committee with regard to the repression of human rights in South Korea and its implications for U.S. policy, I pointed out the existence at the Korean embassy in Washington of KCIA plans for clandestine operations in the United States. I testified that, in the spring of 1973, the ambassador called frequent staff meetings at which I had been also present as chief cultural and information attaché and, concurrently, director of the Korean Information Office in the United States. In these meetings, the KCIA station chief and his senior aides oriented the key embassy staff to the clandestine operational schemes. After a few sessions I realized that the meeting were in fact an initiation of converting all the diplomatic and consular officers into KCIA auxiliaries.

Plans for Clandestine Operation in the United States

From my own personal knowledge, I testified to you last June that Park's plans for clandestine operations in this country included (1) to seduce and, if possible, buy off American leaders—particularly in Congress; (2) to apply covert pressure on the important American businessmen who have vested interests in Korea to exercise their influence in the Congress and the administration to support Park's repressive policies; (3) to organize American and Korean business groups that would voice support for Park; (4) to organize professional associations and societies of Korean scholars and scientists in the United States with a reward of embassy entertainment and possibly all-expense-free VIP trips to Korea; (5) to organize indirectly, or to finance covertly, scholastic meetings, seminars, and symposia of Korean and American professors to rationalize Park's dictatorship or, or least, to curb their criticism; (6) to publish through its collaborators and front men pro-Park Korean community newspapers in the United States; (7) to operate and finance Park's propaganda broadcasting; (8) to regiment Korean communities in the United States by infiltrating Korean resident associations; (9) to intimidate "uncooperative" Koreans and Korean-Americans through their families, relatives, and close friends in Korea to silence their criticism, and to make already silent ones more "cooperative."

In that testimony I made a number of serious charges regarding the KCIA's illicit activities within the United States, citing specific incidents that fell in with the pattern of that master plan. Since then those charges have been further reinforced by new facts and more evidences provided in the March 17, 1976, testimonies before this committee by Mr. Donald L. Ranard, former director of Korean Affairs Office at the Department of State from early 1970 to the end of 1974; Professor Gregory Henderson, an expert of Korean affairs who had twice served as a diplomat with the American embassy in Korea; and Mr. Woon-ha Kim, publisher of a Los Angeles Korean community weekly, who is one of the victims of such KCIA operations. Therefore I need not take up the time of this committee by restating what is already on the record. In my testimony today I will simply elaborate some of those evidences where I deem it necessary and add my new observations.

Now that the KCIA has become the complete control mechanism of Park's dictatorship, which monitors, controls, and manipulates virtually all aspects of Korean life—political, economic, cultural, and academic—and which attempts to do the same in the United States, ambassadors and diplomatic and consular officers are in actuality nothing other than a slightly more respectable facade of the KCIA. Some are willing collaborators and others are marionettes at best of dictator Park's control apparatus.

KCIA and Consulate in San Francisco

For example, not only KCIA but also Korea consulate staff have unlawfully interfered with the U.S. Constitution-guaranteed rights of Korean-Americans and Korean residents during the recent elections for president and vice-president of the Korean Resident Association of San Francisco. It is alleged that the KCIA and Korean consulate at San Francisco were bitterly opposed to one slate, which ran against the KCIA and Korean consulate-supported candidates. Many evidences indicate that the KCIA and Korean consulate were engaged in questionable practices to defeat presidential candidate Young-baik Kim. Several of Young-baik Kim's campaign workers were allegedly warned by KCIA agent Sun Man Lim not to support Young-baik Kim. At least one businessman was also told this. Another supporter of Young-baik Kim was reported to have received a telephone call from his family in Korea urging him not to work for Young-baik Kim.

The running mate of Young-baik Kim was also called by his family in Korea and was told that "the other side is supported by the (South Korean) government, so it is best not to run." It is important to note in these two cases that neither of them had previously let their families in Korea know anything about their activities on behalf of Young-baik Kim.

Buddhist priest Han Sang Lee, who presides over the Monterey Korean community's Sambo-sa temple, was reported to be pressured by the KCIA and Korean consulate to bring his congregation up to San Francisco to vote. When such illegal activities were exposed in the *Korea Journal*, published fortnightly in the

Korean community in the Bay Area, Korean Consul General
Dong Won Shin issued an arrogant and threatening public state-
ment against this paper. That official statement was quoted in
The Dong-A Ilbo's Los Angeles edition, known as *Mijoo Dong-A*, of
March 11, 1976. As I translate the direct quote from the consul
general's statement in Korean, it reads, "Hoping that *The Korea
Journal* will repent of its conduct and will place itself on the right
track of journalism, I issue a stern warning to this newspaper."
This is an open intimidation and improper challenge by an
accredited foreign government representative to the American
constitutional guarantee of free press. Apparently misusing the
privileges of diplomatic and consular immunities, Park's consul
general Shin is openly and unlawfully meddling in the internal
affairs of the lawful residents and citizens of the United States.

Since I testified last year, there have been other cases in Los
Angeles, Chicago, and New York where the KCIA and Korean
consulates have attempted to influence the selection of officers for
the various Korean resident associations and have tried to
influence their policies, particularly with respect to support of the
Park regime.

Ambassador Threatened the *Christian Science Monitor* Editor

Threats and intimidation are common practices of dictator Park
Chung Hee's representatives even within the United States.
Another instance is the implied threat made against Elizabeth
Pond, a *Christian Science Monitor* correspondent, by Park's ambassador to this country, Pyong Choon Hahm. According to the
Christian Science Monitor article, Hahm told the *Monitor*'s editor
John Hughes in early June 1974 that she might be "received dis-
courteously" if she visited South Korea again. Asked whether the
statement implied physical violence, Hahm suggested that his
government might not be able to control an "incident manufactured by North Korean subversives posing as South Korean
thugs."

KCIA Continues Harassment Tactics in the United States

Last year I enumerated such examples as the disruption by KCIA agents and karate strongmen of a meeting of Korean-Americans and residents Kim Dae Jung was to address in San Francisco before he was kidnapped by the KCIA from a Tokyo hotel; a telephone call from the KCIA headquarters in Seoul—obviously coordinated by its agents in this country—to the master of ceremonies at an assembly of Korean Christian scholars in St. Louis warning him against delivering an anti-Park statement; taking pictures of demonstrators protesting against Park's dictatorship to identify them, to create fears among them, and to intimidate them through their families or relatives in Korea (by the way such a photographer in action was recently filmed by NBC and aired in its "Weekend Report" of May 1); death threat by telephone calls; threat of violence by kicking the door well after midnight and then running away; attempts to break up meetings against Park's repression; organizing deceitful rallies in support of the Park regime; extorting money from Korean businessmen (NBC also interviewed a victim recently and filmed him in shadow). South Korean diplomatic and consular missions in this country still continue to carry out these tactics to harass and intimidate people within the United States.

Attempts to Manipulate Academics

Although less visible, the KCIA also has been active among the academics. Professor Sugwon Kang of Hartwick College at Oneonta, New York, did research and wrote a scholastic paper on this subject, which was published in the October–December edition of the *Bulletin of Concerned Scholars* and in the January–February issue of *Worldview*. This paper contains an extensive collection of facts to which any attempt of summary would do only injustice. Therefore I would like to submit for inclusion in the record a copy of Professor Kang's paper, "President Park and His Learned Friends: Some Observations on Contemporary Korean Statecraft."

Last March there was a conference on Asian Studies in

Toronto, Canada, which was attended by many American and Korean scholars from the United States. Attendants later reported that a KCIA front offered the conference $3,000 to pay the expenses of pro-Park scholars coming from the United States. The conference refused the offer, and the refusal became a point of heated debate between some of the participating members. With regard to this conference, the aforementioned NBC television program reported: "Two months later, Professor T. C. Rhee was advised by the (Korean) Embassy to either dilute his paper or not present it. The paper was anti-Park. Rhee, who is an American citizen, tells how part of the telephone conversation went." Then the report was followed by a filmed interview of Professor Rhee.

"Weekend Report" on KCIA and NBC's Corrections

At this point, Mr. Chairman, I would like to submit for inclusion in the record this transcript, which I made from the actual broadcast of the NBC television's "Weekend Report" of May 1, 1976: "KCIA in the United States," by James Gannon. Considering the difficulty of televising such a subject matter, it was an excellent in-depth report on the KCIA's activities in the United States. The substance was thoroughly comprehensive and accurate in every aspect, and the presentation was factual, fair, and well balanced. But a month later, on June 5, 1976, during the "Week-end Report," the NBC made some strange corrections. It said:

In last month's report on the Korean CIA, we made two errors. We said KCIA censors are in Korean newspaper offices. We should have said they used to be. They were withdrawn about a year ago following a protest strike. We also said these eight men were hanged before they could appeal their death sentences. They did appeal to the Korean Supreme Court but still had two other appeals open when they were executed, despite a Korean government prosecutor's assurance that they would not be. Neither error alters the report's basic point; the Korean CIA operates illegally in this country, and our government appears to be doing nothing to stop it.

The second point is only a further elaboration of the fact

originally stated; so there is no problem. But the first one is different because the original report of May 1 was entirely correct, and NBC nevertheless took the pain of correcting it to become wrong. This is extraordinary!

There have been reports from Seoul by American correspondents that indicate otherwise. Datelined Seoul, May 19, 1975, Don Oberdorfer of the *Washington Post* reported: "Within hours of Park's new decree last Tuesday (Presidential Emergency Measure No. 9 of May 13, 1975), agents of the Korean CIA moved back into newspaper offices on a full-time basis to monitor and virtually edit the news." On September 19, 1975, Richard Halloran of the *New York Times* reported from Seoul that "the press, according to all sources here, is under complete censorship." I have other impeccable sources who confirm to this effect.

Professionally speaking I am curious about this most unusual practice of NBC. Knowing the KCIA as I do, knowing the KCIA's master plan, which includes among other things, the use of influential American businessmen, knowing the pressure the Park regime brought to bear upon the *Christian Science Monitor*, and knowing the vested interest in South Korea of NBC's sister company, RCA, I would like to find out if there was the invisible hand of the Park regime behind NBC's making this reverse correction. As a professor of journalism, I also have an academic interest in such problems of the press. So the next day I sent a mailgram to the president of NBC requesting equal time for rebuttal or answers to my questions; therefore I expect to hear from NBC.

The Case of SP5 Michael E. Kerr

Such seemingly improbable things are highly probable with the KCIA as I have known it. In this regard there is another case, which may seem hardly probable to most people—the ambiguous circumstances in which U.S. Army Specialist Five Michael E. Kerr was ejected from Korea by the U.S. Army unit while he was serving in Korea. Since Professor Henderson has already taken up this incident in his testimony before this committee, I will only add that I am of the same conclusion after my own independent assessment of Michael Kerr's documentation of the case, which warrants a thorough investigation for possible KCIA influence on the U.S. Army field commanders in Korea and their superiors in Washington.

Broadcasting by Front Men

With regard to the broadcast media, I pointed out before this committee last year the KCIA's plan to operate, finance, or subsidize pro-Park propaganda Korean language broadcasting in the United States. After my testimony I received a telephone call followed by a letter signed by a high-ranking official of a South Korean government mission in the United States. His letter tells me how it is done, at least in this particular case of which he has personal knowledge. Other than the brief community news that the broadcasting organization produces only in voice, all other programs are produced in film or tape by the government-owned and -operated Korean Broadcasting System in Seoul, specifically for such overseas use and sent over here by diplomatic pouch. With this subsidy in kind, his production cost is almost nil and his advertising revenue is all his. Other inside sources tell me that at least some of them also receive money from the Korean government sources.

Political Activities of Sun Myung Moon

Nowadays virtually every business in Korea—including the media business—must have close connections with the regime and the KCIA in particular. A business that requires foreign loans or foreign exchange absolutely must have KCIA approval at every turn. In this respect what draws my particular attention, because of its financial scope, is the vigorous and strange political activities in the United States of South Korean industrialist-evangelist Sun Myung Moon since Park turned South Korea into a police state.

For instance, in 1973, Moon came to the United States and mounted a dynamic coast-to-coast campaign of the "Day of

Hope," with full-page advertisements in the *New York Times*, the *Washington Post*, and other major dailies, proclaiming, "At this moment in history God has chosen Richard Nixon to be President of the United States." Apparently bidding for favor Moon proclaimed Watergate-besieged President Nixon as a leader by divine right, and later Moon was invited to the White House, where he embraced Mr. Nixon. Toward the end of 1973, and in the beginning of 1974, Moon crusaded in behalf of President Nixon with two "evangelical" themes of "Forgive, Unite," and "God Loves Nixon," through full-page newspaper ads, mass rallies, and street demonstrations in the United States, Europe, and the Far East. Of course the scene was repeated in South Korea. The point is that Moon staged massive demonstrations in Seoul where such rallies have been strictly banned by the "emergency decrees" of dictator Park.

The KCIA is involved in virtually every aspect of Korean life; therefore it is entirely unthinkable that the omnipresent KCIA simply overlooked Moon's movement. On the contrary the KCIA would be most interested in putting some Korean like Moon, who supports all of its goals, in a position to work and lobby for the Park regime's position on the American political scene. Indeed as most Koreans know, Moon's huge constellation of business enterprises in Korea and his cult have risen to a flourishing empire under the Park government despite his early days of arrest on morals charges, controversy, and scandalous reports in the leading Korean dailies.

Among many things, it is strange to note that Moon operates, through his Unification church–controlled Federation for Victory over Communism, an anticommunist indoctrination center for Korean government employees and military officers. By the KCIA's unpublicized charter, however, this area of "anti-Communist indoctrination and internal propaganda" is explicitly under the control of the KCIA's Second Bureau, which also controls the press with censors and supervising agents in each newspaper and broadcasting station.

"Little Angels" and Korean Cultural and Freedom Foundation

For another thing, only in 1973, I learned from a calling card that Moon is the founder and chairman of the board of the "Little Angels" Korean children's dance troupe, which has performed throughout the world as the officially endorsed emissary of the Park government. But the Little Angels has always been a show-case exhibit of another organization in Washington, D.C.—the Korean Cultural and Freedom Foundation of which the founder and president is now a retired lieutenant colonel of the Korean army who was initially sent to South Korea's Washington embassy as assistant military attaché in 1961 by Park Chung Hee's military junta. Recently it became known that he is also an important member of Moon's Unification church and his translator and constant traveling companion during his tours of the United States.

Park's Government and Korean Cultural and Freedom Foundation

Another of the Korean Cultural and Freedom Foundation's few programs was "Radio of Free Asia," which had no transmitters of its own but used the government-owned and -operated Korean Broadcasting System's transmission facility and its broadcasting time for free of charge to beam its programs to Vietnam. I also remember that in 1970 or 1971, Park Chung Hee sent out a personal letter, signed on the government stationery as president of the republic of Korea, to at least 60,000 prominent Americans, including many senators, congressmen, bankers, and business-men, and so forth, soliciting contributions for the Korean Cultural and Freedom Foundation, Inc. It was also in this period that, by sheer accident, I came to know that the Korean Cultural and Freedom Foundation had access to the South Korean embassy's cable channel to Seoul, which goes only to the foreign minister, director of the KCIA, prime minister, and the president.

In Washington, D.C., there is another organization of which Moon is also the founder and chairman of the board, namely, the

Freedom Leadership Foundation with which KCIA agents in the Korean embassy maintained contact while I was still with the embassy. I remember that at least three American secretaries in South Korea's Washington embassy had been hired upon recommendations of the Freedom Leadership Foundation, which furnished candidates at the request of the embassy's KCIA agents. When these not-too-visible links are viewed along with the strange political activities of Sun Myung Moon in the United States following Park's "Yushin" coup in office, there appears to be a curious working relationship between Park's dictatorial regime, Korean Cultural and Freedom Foundation, "Little Angels," Moon's Unification church–affiliated organizations, and the KCIA—let alone dictator Park's patronage for Moon's multimillion dollar ventures in South Korea.

KCIA and Consulate-Organized Fund Raising for Senator Tunney

Since Park Chung Hee's power is essentially dependent on his control mechanism, KCIA, and American aid, Park apparently intends to do everything from shameless to lawless for continued American support. For that purpose Park wants to use every corrupt and even repressive method in this country as he does in Korea. In September 1975 the KCIA and Korean consulate at Los Angeles covertly organized a group called the "Friends of U.S. Senator Tunney" and stage-managed a $100-a-plate fundraising dinner for Senator John V. Tunney, who had not been sympathetic to Korean aid bills in the past. Fortunately the Los Angeles Korean weekly *New Korea* learned of this conspiracy and informed the innocent victim, whereupon the senator canceled the event.

Recently there were news reports on the FBI's investigation of allegations that two congressmen accepted bribes from Park's government last year. Maxine Chesire reported in the *Washington Post* of February 19, 1976, that a member of the House Speaker's staff gave many parties for congressmen and their wives, at which a frequent guest was the Korean embassy's KCIA station chief,

Yung Hwan Kim. The two congressmen met KCIA station chief Kim through this member of the House Speaker's staff. Judging from the detailed reports in the *Washington Post* and the *New York Times*, the KCIA appears to have well-established contacts in the office of the House Speaker and the House Appropriations and Armed Services Committee—to say the least. As I testified last summer, I knew Park's ambassador was trying to bribe American lawmakers. It was part of the KCIA's master plan. But there seem to be some other ways to tempt U.S. Congress.

Morton Kondracke reported in the *Chicago Sun-Times*, June 6, 1976, that dictator Park's officials extended to Congressman Don L. Bonker offers of a $200 digital watch and "an attractive woman who would be pleased to meet with the congressman on matters of mutual interest." Of course Congressman Bonker rejected the offers as the *Sun-Times* reported. He never saw the woman and sent back the watch left on his desk by the Korean embassy's KCIA agent, Colonel Yae-heun Choi, and National Assemblyman Young-dal Ohm. By the way this news article explains how the Park regime attempts to corrupt American lawmakers with wine, woman, song, and gift.

Park's incredible attempts to buy off American leaders do not stop there. The Park regime even attempted to purchase the Nixon White House in 1974. According to the *Washington Post* of February 29, 1976, dictator Park's appointed National Assemblyman Chin Hwan Row made a "blanket" offer to a White House aide, sometime before the August 9, 1974, resignation of President Nixon, "to contribute to anyone in Congress recommended by the Nixon administration." This report was confirmed by Mr. Ranard in his testimony last March; therefore I will not make any further comment on it.

Attitude and Policy of the Administration

If I sum up what I have observed, Park's KCIA agents and other officials are actively engaged in a vast clandestine operation of seduction, intimidation, threats, coercion, extortion, and bribery within the United States for the purpose of manipulating U.S.

policy and legislation by purchasing American leaders in the government, business, and academia and by suppressing the press and individuals who speak out. What puzzles me most is the attitude of the United States government—the administration in particular. There are strong indications that President Richard M. Nixon and Secretary of State Henry A. Kissinger tacitly consented to dictator Park's destruction of democratic institutions and human rights in South Korea, as Don Oberforfer reported in the *Washington Post* of May 17, 1976.

In another article by John Saar, John Goshko, and Bill Richards, the *Washington Post*, May 23, 1976, also reported in this regard as follows:

Many present and former State Department officials say privately that the tendency within the Department, particularly during the presidency of Richard M. Nixon, was "not to make too much noise" about the KCIA. One put it this way: "You couldn't call it a coverup or anything like that; I never heard anyone say specifically that this is an area to stay away from. It was more that you sensed a lack of enthusiasm about pursuing complaints. The feeling seemed to be that we were dealing not with the Soviets and the KGB but with an important ally, and that, like it or not, we had to avert our gaze a little bit."

With his firsthand knowledge Don Ranard made a similar reference to this attitude of the last two administrations in his testimony of March 17, 1976, before this committee.

The Ford administration seemed to carry on the same old Korea policy the Nixon administration had laid as the deeds indicate. For example, President Gerald Ford went to see Park in Seoul despite the strong protest from the democratic forces and foreign observers in South Korea. Moreover he did not sneeze a word about human rights or democratic institutions while he was visiting Korea.

In early April 1976, when 119 members of Congress wrote a letter to President Ford advising him that "since military power is directly associated with governmental control over the population, many Americans and Koreans suspect that United States military support somehow condones or even contributes to the long wave of repression, in the absence of strong public signals to the contrary from our government."

KCIA Operation Is a Consequence of U.S. Policy

Indeed such attitude and policy of the United States government has emboldened the Park regime to an incredible extent of even exporting his corrupt and repressive methods into the United States. Hence I cannot help but view these illegal activities of the KCIA agents and Park's other officials within the United States as a consequence of the current U.S. policy in regard to Park's dictatorial government. In this same context I have profound admiration and deepest respect for your courage, Mr. Chairman. For three consecutive years, against all these odds within your own government, you have been almost singlehandedly carrying out your congressional responsibilities regarding this matter for what is right for the United States as well as for other countries like Korea.

I know the current administration has two prominent excuses for its inaction, repeated time and again in various public statements: first, South Korea's defense against the communist North is important to the United States; second, U.S. policy is not to interfere with domestic affairs of other governments. I deplore this bureaucratic "nonspeaking" of government spokesmen, which is even dishonest. Heaven knows these two statements are contradicting each other.

U.S. aid to Korea and the presence of 42,000 American troops in South Korea are already a massive intervention in Korean affairs. Destruction of democratic institutions and human rights in South Korea behind the American shield deprives South Koreans of their value and life-style for which they would defend themselves against any communist attack or subversion. Therefore the current U.S. policy is neither in the interest of U.S. security nor in the benefit of South Korean defense. Certainly under any circumstances it cannot be an excuse for not protecting U.S. citizens and residents from the harassment and other illegal activities of foreign agents within the United States. Speaking out against repression of human rights is surely not the kind of action the sensible "doctrine of noninterference" was intended to avoid. The administration is simply using it as an excuse to circumvent American responsibility to the United States' own principles. Hence the current administration's policy regarding South Korea is not only dishonorable and inconsistent with American ideals but also self-defeating.

The Administration's Policy Is Discriminatory

Now I find it even discriminatory. Betraying his own words the same U.S. policy maker loudly spoke out in Santiago de Chile two weeks ago, calling for human rights in Latin America. Challenging violations of human rights in his host country, Chile, he declared that "the condition of human rights . . . has impaired our relationship with Chile and will continue to do so" and called for the removal of the "obstacles raised by the conditions." In order to help make his strong words more than lip-service, the Ford administration is not seeking military aid for the anticommunist Chilean junta this year. I wholeheartedly support this policy. But what has he done to South Korea in the last three years while so many Americans and Koreans called for a strong U.S. stand in support of human rights in South Korea?

Recommendations

Mr. Chairman, since the illegal activities of dictator Park's KCIA and other officials within this country are in part consequences of the attitude and policy of the U.S. government in regard to the Park regime as I have elaborated, I will begin my recommendations with regard to U.S. policy in South Korea.

The United States should adopt a no-nonsense approach to the violation of human rights with the Park regime.

Both publicly and privately the United States should inform Park Chung Hee that it believes in protecting democracies and respecting human rights and that if he does not do so, the United

States will bow out of any commitment of U.S. troops, arms, grains, sales credits, or loans now being provided.

Just as Secretary Kissinger did in Chile, the United States should publicly spell out this stand while withholding U.S. aid until the Park regime cleans up its mess. Such a policy, in both words and deeds, will also restore this country's credibility not only as a guardian of its own rights but also a supporter of the human rights of others. This is not only ethically correct but also pragmatically important for the United States to align itself with the legitimate aspirations of people everywhere.

Only so determined, the administration can seriously investigate and stamp out illegal activities of Park's KCIA agents, other officials, and their companion collaborators in this country. As for specific action to accompany the above policy, I also submit the following recommendations:

The secretary of state in the strongest possible diplomatic means of formal communication inform the Korean government that it will not permit the present role and conduct of the Korean Central Intelligence Agency in the United States.

In so doing the secretary of state should make emphatically clear to the Korean government that the only acceptable function of the KCIA in the United States is intelligence liaison with its U.S. counterparts and that intelligence liaison representatives may be assigned only to the Korean embassy in Washington, D.C.

The Department of State should set a limit on the number of such intelligence representatives it is prepared to accredit, prohibiting the assignment of intelligence personnel to any of the Korean consulates in the United States.

The substance of such expression and communication to the Korean government should be made public.

The Federal Bureau of Investigation should make a serious and thorough investigation into the alleged clandestine operations and intelligence activities of the Korean government, as well as the activities of Koreans suspected of having repressive aims in the United States.

The Department of Justice should make sure that all organizations and individuals in the United States that receive support directly or indirectly from the Korean government sources be registered under the Foreign Agents Registration Act.

The Internal Revenue Service should make certain that the total revenue of such organizations and individuals is properly reported.

References

Anderson, Jack. "CIA Condones Foreign Secret Cops in U.S." *Chicago Daily News*, October 27, 1976.

————. "Koreans Woo Hill on Two Levels." *Washington Post*, November 5, 1976.

————, and Les Whitten. "U.S. Might Have Curbed Oil Prices." *Washington Post*, December 15, 1976.

Anonymous. "A Side of the Moon Hidden from Seoul." *Far Eastern Economic Review*, June 25, 1976.

————. "Albert Blocks Move Faulting South Korea." *Washington Post*, September 23, 1976.

————. "Banker Hits U.S. Aides." *Washington Post*, June 21, 1976.

————. "Koreagate on Capitol Hill?" *Time*, November 29, 1976.

————. "Moon Produces Weapons Parts." *Washington Post*, June 7, 1976.

————. "Ousted Korean CIA Aide Linked to Kidnapping of Foes of Regime." *New York Times*, November 15, 1976.

————. "Pleas by 'Threatened' Korean Publisher Spark Two Probes." *San Francisco Examiner*, December 16, 1976.

————. "S. Korean Agents in U.S. Are Called Goons, Sent Home." *Washington Post*, October 17, 1976.

————. "Seoul Assembly Weighs Protest on Its Foes in U.S." *New York Times*, July 3, 1977.

————. "Seoul's Man in the U.S. Is Mr. Lee and Mr. Yang." *New York Times*, August 17, 1973.

————. "South Korea Lifts Visa of *Monitor* Reporter." *Christian Science Monitor*, June 6, 1974.

————. "South Korea's Sordid Spooks." *Newsweek*, October 8, 1973.

————. "Spooking Capitol Hill." *Time*, November 15, 1976.

————. "The Spooks of Namsan." *Newsweek*, October 22, 1973.

————. "2 California Representatives Admit Gifts of Money from South Korea." *New York Times*, November 5, 1976.

————. "U.S.—No Trespassing." *New York Times*, November 5, 1976.

————. "Washington's Korea Lobby." *Newsweek*, November 22, 1976.

————. "Western Teacher Urges KCIA Probe." *Macomb* (Illinois) *Daily Journal*, December 2, 1976.

Armstrong, Scott. "Columnist to Quit Role with Bank: Jack Anderson to Avoid Interest Conflict." *Washington Post*, November 22, 1976.

————. "Diplomat National Bank Head Quits, Cites Probe." *Washington Post*, April 26, 1977.

————. "13 Congressmen Aided Tongsun Park." *Washington Post*, April 27, 1977.

Armstrong, Scott, and Maxine Cheshire. "Bank Stock Owned by Park, Pak." *Washington Post*, November 14, 1976.

————. "Korean CIA Tied to Moon Rallies Supporting Nixon." *Washington Post*, November 7, 1976.

————. "Korean Ties to Congress Are Probed: Tongsun Park Among Those Under Scrutiny." *Washington Post*, October 15, 1976.

————. "McFall Admits He Got Cash from Park." *Washington Post*, November 5, 1976.

————. "McFall Says He Got $4,000 from Park." *Washington Post*, November 27, 1976.

————. "U.S. Probes S. Korean's Banking Data." *Washington Post*, October 26, 1976.

Associated Press. "Korea Scandal Seen Involving 50 on Hill." *Washington Post*, January 24, 1977.

————. "Korean Tactics Probed." *Washington Star*, June 8, 1973.

————. "Lawmakers Tied to Korea's Park." *Chicago Tribune*, April 27, 1977.

————. "Louisiana Chief Admits Wife Took Korean Cash." *Chicago Sun-Times*, October 26, 1976.

————. "Panel to Seek Probe of Moon's Interest in Washington Bank." *Baltimore Sun*, June 20, 1976.

————. "Report S. Korea Lobbyists Coached by Nixon Officials." *Chicago Sun-Times*, November 22, 1976.

————. "Rev. Moon Aides Term Criticism Distorted, Unfair." *Los Angeles Times*, December 30, 1976.

————. "Seoul Denies Links with Businessmen Involved in Probe of Capitol Hill Bribery. *Baltimore Evening Sun*, October 27, 1976.

————. "3 Religious Groups Join in Attack on Moon's Church." *Los Angeles Times*, December 29, 1976.

_____. "Verify Rep. Brademas Got $4,650 Cash from Korea." *Chicago Sun-Times*, October 27, 1976.

Babcock, Charles R. "Dispute Keeps Little Angels at Home in Seoul." *Washington Post*, February 16, 1977.

_____. "Hill GOP Aide Pushed Asian Lobbies." *Washington Post*, December 14, 1976.

_____. "Hill Trips to Taiwan, Korea Are Paid by National Groups: 2 Groups Paid for Hill Trips." *Washington Post*, November 13, 1976.

_____. "Justice Probing Ex-Rep. Minshall–Tongsun Park Relationship." *Washington Post*, December 20, 1976.

_____. "Korean Charity Fund Abuse Cited: 2 U.S. Officials Seek Court Trustee." *Washington Post*, February 16, 1977.

_____. Korean Foundation under Two Probes." *Washington Post*, October 31, 1976.

_____. "McFall Not a Target of Korea Probe." *Washington Post*, March 23, 1977.

_____. "McFall's Ties to S. Korean Test Ethics Committee." *Washington Post*, June 1, 1977.

_____. "Moon Disciples Own 44% of Bank Here." *Washington Post*, June 19, 1976.

_____. "Tongsun Park's Paper Jigsaw Puzzle Solved." *Washington Post*, May 13, 1977.

Babcock, Charles R., and Maxine Cheshire. "House Members Listed in Tongsun Park's Little Black Books: Korean Lobby, U.S. Rice Aid Seem Linked." *Washington Post*, July 17, 1977.

Babcock, Charles R., and Bill McAllister. "Legislators Recall Korean Offers of Cash, Favors." *Washington Post*, November 28, 1976.

Baldwin, Frank. "The Korean Lobby." *Christianity and Crisis Vol.* 36 no. 12 (July 19, 1976).

Binder, David. "Threat to Koreans in U.S. by Seoul Stirs Concern." *New York Times*, August 17, 1973.

Blau, Eleanor. "Korean Solicitors Curbed by Albany." *New York Times*, January 26, 1977.

Bradsher, Henry S. "Korean CIA Flap Has Some of Its Roots in Langley: Our CIA Taught Orientals Many Tricks of Trade." *Washington Star*, November 27, 1976.

Brancatelli, Joe. "Fast-growing Moon Cult Collides with Suburbia." *Village Voice*, April 19, 1976.

Butterfield, Fox. "Seoul Seeks to Link Dissidents with Regime in North." *New York Times*, November 26, 1974.

Cheshire, Maxine. "Bribe Taking Alleged: Two House Members Probed." *Washington Post*, February 19, 1976.

————. "Gallagher Says Park Cashed Bonds." *Washington Post*, February 13, 1976.

————. "Korean's 1974 Gift Offers Here Bared." *Washington Post*, February 29, 1976.

————. "The Korean Connection." *Washington Post*, April 22, 1976.

————. "Two House Members Probed." *Washington Post*, February 19, 1976.

————. "Watchword for an Untimely Gift." *Washington Post*, March 25, 1976.

————, and Scott Armstrong. "Data Links Korea Chief to Charges: Sources Report Tapes May Tie Park to Bribes." *Washington Post*, October 27, 1976.

————. "Korean-American Named as Conduit for KCIA Funds." *Washington Post*, March 1, 1977.

————. "Nixon Aides Turned Down Korean Gifts." *Washington Post*, October 20, 1976.

————. "Rep. Robert Leggett: Life of Immense Complications." *Washington Post*, July 18, 1976.

————. "Seoul Gave Millions to U.S. Officials." *Washington Post*, October 24, 1976.

Cheshire, Maxine, and Charles R. Babcock. "Letters Reveal Legislators' Ties to Korean." *Washington Post*, April 17, 1977.

————. "Probe of S. Koreans' Activities Widens: U.S. to Question 2 Here in Korean Influence-peddling Probe." *Washington Post*, November 2, 1976.

Claiborne, William. "New York Accuses Korean Foundation of Charity Fraud." *Washington Post*, February 21, 1977.

————. "News World's Low Ad Rates." *Washington Post*, January 21, 1977.

————. "3 Major Faiths Mount Harsh Attack on Moon." *Washington Post*, December 29, 1976.

Coates, James. "S. Korea Nabs Moonies to Placate U.S." *Washington Post*, March 30, 1977.

————, and John Maclean. "Congressmen Offered Seoul Junket." *Chicago Tribune*, December 9, 1976.

————. "Korea Agent's Profits on U.S. Food Aid Told: Secret Nixon Pact with Seoul Bared." *Chicago Tribune*, November 1, 1976.

————. "Korean Embassy's Cash Handouts on Capitol Hill Bared." *Chicago Tribune*, November 25, 1976.

————. "U.S. Probes S. Korean CIA Funding of Rev. Sun Moon." *Chicago Tribune*, October 28, 1976.

Colgan, Paul. "WIU Professor Tells How Cash Sent to U.S." *Quincy* (Illinois) *Herald-Whig*, December 1, 1976.

Crittenden, Ann. "Moon's Sect Pushes pro-Seoul Activities." *New York Times*, May 25, 1976.

Elkin, Neal. "US Corruption Supports Park Dictatorship." *Michigan Free Press* (Detroit), February 7–13, 1977.

Fraker, Susan, and Anthony Marro. "Washington's Korea Lobby." *Newsweek*, November 22, 1976.

Gannon, James. "Weekend," May 1, 1976.

Glaser, Vera. "Aide Urged Korea Bribe Probe in '71." *Chicago Tribune*, November 7, 1976.

Halloran, Richard. "A New Korean Agent Reported in Capital: Sources Say Operative to Replace Park Tong Sun Was Given $600,000 for Lobbying." *New York Times*, February 27, 1977.

―――. "Counsel for Koreans Quit Over Bribe Case: Seoul Envoy Rejected Advice by Ex-Congressman to Cooperate with Justice Department." *New York Times*, May 1, 1977.

―――. "Ex-Korea Aide Says Park Envoy Told Him He Should Be Silent." *New York Times*, July 3, 1977.

―――. "Former K.C.I.A. Head Says Park Tong Sun Was Korean Agent: Lobbyist Linked to Congress; The Assertion Contradicts Denials by Seoul That Park Acted for the Government." *New York Times*, June 5, 1977.

―――. "Governor of Louisiana Defends Gift of $10,000 to His Wife by Korean." *New York Times*, June 15, 1977.

―――. "Inaction on Lobbying by Korea Is Linked to Its Vietnam Role." *New York Times*, November 14, 1976.

―――. "Inquiries May Force Koreans to Quit U.S." *New York Times*, October 25, 1976.

―――. "Inquiry Raises Possibility That U.S. Citizens Work Illegally for Seoul." *New York Times*, October 30, 1976.

―――. "Inquiry Suggests Agents of Korea Tried to Take Over Bank in U.S." *New York Times*, May 31, 1977.

―――. "Korean Bribe Figure Tied to Bank Inquiry: Park Tong Sun Called Organizer of $2 Million Capital Venture under Federal Investigation." *New York Times*, February 10, 1977.

―――. "Korean Chief Linked to Illegal Lobbying: Intelligence Sources Tell of Effort to Sway Congress." *New York Times*, November 9, 1976.

―――. "Korean Dissidents in Washington Report Threats by Seoul's Agents." *New York Times*, May 22, 1977.

―――. "Koreans Linked to Bid 'Use' U.S. Educators." *New York Times*, December 16, 1976.

―――. "Laird Says He Warned State Dept. about South Korean Lobby in 1970: He Recalls Asking for Inquiry." *New York Times*, November 10, 1976.

―――. "Lobbying by Korean Apparently Paid Off: 60 Congressmen Voting against Legislation Opposed by Seoul Got Some Form of Favor." *New York Times*, December 6, 1976.

————. "New Korean Inquiry by U.S. Is Disclosed: Charge That Seoul Agents Harass Residents Here Investigated." *New York Times*, October 29, 1976.

————. "Offer to American U. by Korean Reported: Rejected Fund Said to Have Been for Lobbying Post in Capital." *New York Times*, March 2, 1977.

————. "Seoul Bids Lobbyist Stay away From U.S." *New York Times*, November 15, 1976.

————. "Seoul's Vast Intelligence Agency Stirs Wide Fear." *New York Times*, August 20, 1973.

————. "South Korean C.I.A. Extends U.S. Activities, Seeking to Influence American Policies." *New York Times*, October 2, 1976.

————. "U.S. Envoy Said to Have Protested to Seoul on Lobby in Washington." *New York Times*, February 3, 1977.

————, Marjorie Hunter, and Jo Thomas. "Ethics Panel Finds More Congressmen Took Korean Favors: 115 Apparently Are Involved." *New York Times*, July 11, 1977.

Hopkins, Elaine. "Ex-S. Korean Official in Macomb Tells Story of Corruption, Bribery." *Journal-Star* (Peoria, Illinois), November 28, 1976.

Horrock, Nicholas M. "Aide to Moon Denies Press Charges." *New York Times*, November 2, 1976.

————. "Gallagher Is Reported Subpoenaed in Inquiry on South Korea Bribery." *New York Times*, December 5, 1976.

————. "Inquiry on Korean Influence in U.S. Focuses on a List of 90 in Congress." *New York Times*, October 28, 1976.

————. "Korean Lobbyist's Absence May Affect U.S. Inquiry." *New York Times*, November 16, 1976.

————. "State Department Said to Have Urged Korea Inquiry in '75: Investigation of Park Tong Sun Followed Testimony in Senate on Payments by Gulf Oil." *New York Times*, October 31, 1976.

Hyer, Marjorie. "Rev. Moon Tied to Korean CIA." *Washington Post*, June 23, 1976.

————. "Rev. Moon's Church Held Not Christian." *Washington Post*, June 21, 1977.

————, and William R. MacKaye. "Controversy Ruffles Prayer Breakfast." *Washington Post*, January 31, 1974.

Jackson, Robert L. "Ethics Panel Member Took Free Trip to Korea." *Los Angeles Times*, May 25, 1977.

————. "Moon Not Korean Agent, Aide Says: Bribe Furore Criticized as 'Out of Proportion.'" *Los Angeles Times*, June 13, 1977.

Jameson, Sam. "Seoul Agents Watching L.A. Koreans, Official Says: Foreign Minister Calls Such Surveillance in U.S. Legitimate Diplomatic Information-Gathering." *Los Angeles Times*, April 15, 1977.

Jhabvala, Darius S. "State Dept. Tells Koreans: In US Do as Constitution Says." *Boston Globe*, June 10, 1973.

Johnson, Thomas A. "Moon's Sect Denies Link with South Korean Regime." *New York Times*, May 20, 1976.

Kang, K. Connie. "A Hard Look: Why Koreans Here Fear Seoul's CIA." *San Francisco Examiner*, December 10, 1976.

Kang, Sugwon. "President Park and His Learned Friends: Some Observations on Contemporary Korean Statecraft." *Bulletin of Concerned Asian Scholars* (October–December 1975): 28–32.

Keller, Bill. "NW Congressman Says Korea Offered Sex, Gift." *Portland Oregonian*, June 9, 1976.

Kirk, Donald. "Dirty Trick Korean Style." *Saturday Review*, January 8, 1977.

Knight News Service. "Probers Say CIA Winked at Korean Bribery." *Chicago Tribune*, November 18, 1976.

Kondracke, Morton. "Korea Tempts Congress with Women, Watches: But Freshman Bonker Is One Who Says 'No.' " *Sunday Sun-Times* (Chicago, Illinois), June 6, 1976.

Kook, Yung-Gill. "KCIA Gets on Tunney's Campaign Trail." *New Korea* (Los Angeles, California), September 11, 1975.

LaPierre, Frank. "Publisher Charges 'Korean CIA Terror Extends to Bay Area.' " *San Mateo* (California) *Times*, November 19, 1976.

Lee, Jai Hyon. "Statement of Jai Hyon Lee, Associate Professor of Journalism, Western Illinois University." *Human Rights in South Korea and the Philippines: Implications for U.S. Policy*. Hearings before the Subcommittee on International Organizations of the Committee on International Relations, House of Representatives, 94th Cong., 1st sess., May 20, 22, June 3, 5, 10, 12, 17, 24, 1975, Washington, pp. 177–185, 198–224.

Lindsey, Robert. "Seoul's Intelligence Agents Harass Korean Community in Los Angeles." *New York Times*, October 30, 1976.

Lynch, William. "Gov. Edwards Denies Gift from Park." *Washington Post*, January 26, 1977.

———. "Park's Customs Run-in Is Topic of Memo." *Washington Post*, February 5, 1977.

Lynton, Stephen. "Dead Husband of Mrs. Ford's Aide Called Alcoholic under Psychiatric Care." *Los Angeles Times*, April 12, 1975.

Lyons, Richard D. "Arkansas Governor Says He Got Fund Offers from South Koreans." *New York Times*, November 11, 1976.

———. "Legality of Junkets Is Questioned Anew: Inquiry into Capitol Hill

Lobby of South Koreans Draws Attention to Congressman's Far East Trips." *New York Times*, November 28, 1976.

————. "McFall, Victim of Korean Scandal, Will Also Lose Job as House Whip." *New York Times*, December 7, 1976.

McAllister, Bill. "Korean Probe Deals Blow to Karate School Owner." *Washington Post*, December 30, 1976.

————. "Koreans Offer Degrees, Trips to Congressmen." *Washington Post*, August 23, 1976.

McAllister, Bill, and Scott Armstrong. "Campaign Funds Converted to Personal Use." *Washington Post*, December 5, 1976.

————. "Park, Korea Balk on Aide in U.S. Probe: Embassy Aide, Lawyer Agree." *Washington Post*, November 13, 1976.

Maclean, John, and James Coates. "Korea President Sent Bribes to U.S., Aide Says." *Chicago Tribune*, December 2, 1976.

Marks, John D. "From Korea with Love." *Washington Monthly* (February 1974).

Mathews, Jay. "Harassment by Korean CIA Alleged." *Washington Post*, March 18, 1976.

Meyer, Eugene L. "Moon Church Campaigning Is Charged by Ex-member." *Washington Post*, September 26, 1976.

————. "Moon Defection: P.C. Candleakers Felt Ignored." *Washington Post*, September 15, 1976.

Morgan, Donald, and Scott Armstrong. "Ex-Aide Testifies Edwards Given Cash by Park." *Washington Post*, January 25, 1977.

Nussbaum, Bruce. "Diplomat NB Control by Moon Scrutinized." *American Banker*, June 14, 1976.

————. "Probing the Dark Side of the Moon." *Far Eastern Economic Review*, June 18, 1976.

Oberdorfer, Don. "Mystery Surrounds Death of Korean Law Professor." *Washington Post*, November 9, 1973.

————. "Probe of S. Korea Payments Puts New Strain on U.S. Ties." *Washington Post*, October 31, 1976.

————. "S. Korean Abuses Tolerated: U.S. Reportedly Tolerated S. Korean Rights Abuses." *Washington Post*, May 17, 1976.

————. "U.S. Envoy to Korea Protested Strongly Gift to Nixon Aide." *Washington Post*, October 30, 1976.

Oppenheimer, Jerry. "Ex-Rep. Waldie Admits Korea Aid, Gifts." *Washington Star*, November 4, 1976.

————. "Korean's $1,000 Went to Office Account: McFall Reports '72 Gift from Park." *Washington Star*, November 27, 1976.

————. "Mystery Cloaks KCIA Connection to Research Unit." *Washington Star*, November 14, 1976.

Polk, James, and Paul Soroka. "NBC Evening News," October 16, 1976.

Powers, Charles T. "Immigration Service Fails to Press Inquiries on Alien 'Moonies.' " *Los Angeles Times,* April 12, 1977.

Riley, John. "The Korean CIA's Reign of Terror in Southern California." *New West,* November 22, 1976.

Robbins, William. "Agriculture Aides' Queries in Inquiry Linked to Korea." *New York Times,* November 1, 1976.

Ross, Andrew. "KCIA's Illegal U.S. Activities Exposed." *Berkley Barb,* March 19–25, 1976.

————. "Korean CIA Wages Illegal U.S. Campaign." *McDonough Times* (Macomb, Illinois), December 2, 1976.

————. "Moonies Move into Banking." *Berkley Barb,* February 6–12, 1976.

————. "Moon's Friends in S. Korea, the Japanese Right and the CIA." *Berkley Barb,* January 23–29, 1976.

————. "Today the Bay Area, Tomorrow the World: We Wish You a Merry Moonmas??" *Berkley Barb,* December 26, 1975–January 1, 1976.

Ross, Barbara. "Rev. Moon's Korean Ties Face U.S. Investigation." *Reiorter Dispatch* (White Plains, N.YQ.(— Hay 28, 19$)9

Rothman, Steve. "$330 Million Worth of Rice U.S. Sent to wsouth UQTREANS Is Resold to Enrich gdictator's Corrupt RVEGIME." *N/tion/l Enquirer' April 26, 1977.*

————, and John I. Jones. "You the Taxpayer Supply the Cash for South Koreans to Bribe U.S. Congressmen." *National Enquirer,* April 19, 1977.

Saar, John. "Probe of S. Koreans' Activities Widens: Seoul Was Warned." *Washington Post,* November 2, 1976.

————. "S. Korea Accuses Post of 'Malicious, Sensational Reporting.' " *Washington Post,* October 29, 1976.

————. "S. Korean Aide Defects Here: S. Korea Diplomat Here Defects to U.S., Fears Reprisal." *Washington Post,* June 7, 1973.

————. "S. Korean CIA: Power Grows, Fear Spreads." *Washington Post,* May 23, 1976.

————. "South Korea Censors Keep Gift Scandal Quiet." *Washington Post,* October 28, 1976.

————. "This Thriller 'Third Rate' to Park Aide." *Washington Post,* October 30, 1976.

Safire, William. "If You Know Suzy." *New York Times,* May 12, 1977.

————. "The Back Channel." *New York Times,* March 10, 1977.

Seib, Charles B. "Journalistic Conflicts." *Washington Post,* November 26, 1976.

Sharkey, Joe, Joe Davidson, Bruce Boyle, and Alfonso D. Brown, Jr. "Phila. Koreans Tell of Intimidation." *Philadelphia Evening Bulletin,* December 20, 1976.

Shaw, Gaylord. "S. Korea President Denies Role in Gifts." *Los Angeles Times,* December 30, 1976.

————. "Stakes Are Global in Korea Lobby Probe." *Los Angeles Times,* November 21, 1976.

————, and Robert L. Jackson. "Koreans in U.S. Tell of Seoul Intimidation: Minister Says There Are Spies in His Congregation, Others Cite Harassment." *Los Angeles Times,* December 12, 1976.

Siddon, Arthur, and James Coates. "Congressional 'Junket' May Top $2 Million." *Chicago Tribune,* April 17, 1977.

Snow, Jr., Crocker. "A Korean Crunch at Harvard." *Boston Globe,* September 12, 1975.

Southerland, Daniel. "Harassment in U.S. Continues, Korean Editor Charges." *Christian Science Monitor,* November 19, 1976.

————. "Korean Lobbying Traced: Writer Tells of Threat by Seoul Agents." *Christian Science Monitor,* November 1, 1976.

Srodes, James. "Testing Time for the Asian Lobby." *Far Eastern Economic Review,* April 16, 1976.

Stecklow, Steve. "A Moonie Nightmare: How I Fled—Singing, Lectures, Love and Fear." *Philadelphia Sunday Bulletin,* March 27, 1977.

Stein, Jerry, and Ed Murray. "The Moon Connection: Korean Lobby's Twenty Year Ties to Top U.S. Officials." *Washington Newswork,* September 9–15, 1976.

Stentzel, James. "Rev. Moon and His Bicentennial Blitz." *Christianity and Crisis,* July 19, 1976.

Sterba, James P. "Koreans and Americans in Seoul Doubt Park Didn't Know of Gifts." *New York Times,* November 8, 1976.

————. "Nixon officials said to have given guidance to South Korea lobbyists." *New York Times,* November 21, 1976.

————. "President Park Ousts South Korean CIA Official Reportedly in Charge of Operations in Washington." *New York Times,* November 14, 1976.

————. "Seoul Says Americans Misunderstood Hospitality." *New York Times,* November 7, 1976.

————. "U.S. Ties with Seoul under Acute Strain." *New York Times,* November 5, 1976.

Stern, Laurence, and William R. MacKaye. "Rev. Moon: Nixon Backer." *Washington Post,* February 15, 1974.

Stuart, Peter C. "South Korean Lobby Mounts Attack: Pressure from Seoul to Maintain U.S. Forces." *Christian Science Monitor,* August 4, 1976.

Szulc, Tad. "Inside South Korea's C.I.A." *New York Times Magazine,* March 6, 1977.

————. "Too Much Rice, the Original Sin." *New Republic,* January 29, 1977.

Tolchin, Martin. "Members of Congress from New York City Got Favors from Koreans." *New York Times*, December 12, 1976.

U.S. House of Representatives. *Activities of the Korean Central Intelligence Agency in the United States*. Hearings before the Subcommittee on International Organizations of the Committee on International Relations, House of Representatives, 94th Cong., 2d sess., March 17, 25, 1976, part I.

————. *Activities of the Korean Central Intelligence Agency in the United States*. Hearings before the Subcommittee on International Organizations of the Committee on International Relations, House of Representatives, 94th Cong., 2d sess., June 22, September 27, 30, 1976, part II.

U.S. Senate. *United States Security Agreements and Commitments Abroad, Part 6—Republic of Korea*. Hearings before the Subcommittee on United States Security Agreements and Commitments Abroad of the Committee on Foreign Relations, United States Senate, 91st Cong., 2d sess., February 24, 25, 26, 1970.

United Press International. "Edwards Believes Bribes Overseas Should Be OK." *Chicago Daily News*, October 28, 1976.

————. "Korea CIA Arranged Nixon Rally." *Chicago Tribune*, November 8, 1976.

————. "Moon-Sponsored N.Y. Daily Paper Starts Publishing." *Washington Post*, January 1, 1977.

————. "Papers Found near Park Office Mention Nearly 100 Congressmen." *Christian Science Monitor*, May 27, 1977.

————. "Seoul's Agents Are Accused of Harassing Koreans in U.S." *New York Times*, June 9, 1973.

Wallace, Mike, and Barry Lando. "60 Minutes," December 19, 1976.

Weaver, Jr., Warren. "Rep. McFall's Tie to Seoul Lobby Draws Attention to 'Slush Funds.' " *New York Times*, December 3, 1976.

Whymant, Robert. "S. Korea: It Pays for Its Way." *Chicago Daily News*, November 4, 1976.

Williams, Lena. "Immigration Service Begins Deportation Proceedings against 178 Members of the Moon Church." *New York Times*, April 24, 1977.

Wilson, George C. "Army Says Seoul Rigs Contract Bids." *Washington Post*, October 29, 1976.

Wong, Ken. "Foe of President Park: Death Threat to Korean Here." *San Francisco Examiner*, August 24, 1974.

Wood, Connie. "Moonies in Disneyland: Weekend with the Brainwashed." *Berkley Barb*, December 26, 1975–January 1, 1976.

Woodward, Kenneth L., Henry McGee, William J. Book, and Sylvester Monroe. "Life with Father Moon." *Newsweek*, June 14, 1976.

9

**Profits, Politics, Power:
The Heart of the
Controversy**

Marianne Lester

To some, he is the new messiah. To others he is a power-hungry maniac, a cruel genius who destroys families. He is the Reverend Sun Myung Moon, and since 1972 his rise to fame in the United States has been phenomenal. Moon's Unification church claims to have 30,000 members in the country, most of them young people in their twenties. His philosophy, the divine principle, is a bizarre blend of Christianity, Eastern mysticism, and almost paranoid anticommunism. But it is not simply his philosophy that has made Moon one of the most controversial figures of our time. Moon and his movement have brought a nightmare of division to thousands of families, many of them military families. Though Unification church officials deny they encourage Moon's followers to sever relations with their families, it is a common result when young people join the church.

Retired Air Force Lieutenant Colonel Marvin Jensen and his wife, Penny, are one couple whose lives have been affected by the Moon cult. Their twenty-three-year-old son Dave joined the church in 1973 when he ws a freshman in college. Since then, he has dropped out of school and left his home in Arizona to travel across the country as he devotes his life to Moon's organization. Today he is the Washington bureau chief of a church-funded newspaper, *The News World*. His parents are also devoting much of their life to Reverend Moon—"to exposing him for what he is," Penny Jensen says bitterly. Like many other critics of Moon's movement, the Jensens believe the Unification church recruits and holds onto its members through a form of brainwashing. Unlike some other desperate parents, they have promised their son they will never kidnap and deprogram him from the church's teachings. "It is no longer a fight between us and our son," Penny Jensen says. "We want to enlighten other parents about Moon. People must realize that this is not just another silly cult. It's dangerous. And it's not a religion!"

Moon's religious teachings aside, there are other aspects of his movement that disturb the Jensens and other critics of the church. Many of them believe the religious aspects of his cult are simply a cloak for more sinister goals: that Moon is using the church just to amass personal wealth or that Moon is part of a larger South Korean effort to build American support for the government of President Park Chung Hee. In "The Moon Movement Part I" (July 11, 1976) *The Times Magazine* told the personal story of the Jensens and Dave, describing Moon's background and philosophy and the kind of young people he attracts. In this article *The Times Magazine* examines additional allegations against Moon and the Unification church and how they affect church members and their families. What is it about Reverend Moon and his church that makes a normally moderate woman like Penny Jensen cry out emotionally, "It's like waking up to find your son has joined the Hitler Youth!"?

Moon: Prophet for Profit?

"I wonder if Dave and these other kids realize just how wealthy Moon is," Penny Jensen says. Like many other critics of the Unification church, the Jensens struggle constantly to fathom Moon's motives. Sometimes they think the whole movement is just a way for Moon to accumulate incredible wealth. And the Unification church has made money. "Christians think the Messiah must be poor and miserable," says a "classified" Unification church training manual *The Times Magazine* has obtained. "He did not come for this. Messiah must be the richest. Only he is qualified to have dominion over things, and unless the Messiah can have dominion over things, and unless the Messiah can have dominion over things neither God nor the Messiah can be happy."

This "messiah" must certainly be happy. Because it is a tax-exempt, nonprofit religious organization, the Holy Spirit Association for the Unification of World Christianity is not required to report its income, even to the Internal Revenue Service. Church spokesmen say the American church has an income of about $12 million yearly and holds $20 million in properties. Moon has in fact become a profitable prophet. Among the church holdings in New York alone are the multimillion-dollar New Yorker Hotel in Manhattan, a mansion on a 350-acre estate in Tarrytown worth several million dollars, and a former Catholic monastery in Barrytown, which cost more than a million dollars and is used now as a training center for Moon's followers. Church spokesmen hasten to point out that they have mortgages like everybody else.

The church also has made investments in retail businesses— service stations, fish markets, commercial fishing. Moon and some of his associates have acquired a controlling interest in stock in the Diplomat National Bank in Washington, D.C. In 1976 the church began financing its full-color morning Daily in New York City, *The News World.* Moon himself enjoys a lavish life-style, suitable to a potentate if not a messiah. Church members told *The Times Magazine* that his Tudor mansion in New York is filled with antiques, he travels in limousines, sends his children to private schools, occasionally goes nightclubbing in Las Vegas. A few of his followers said they were troubled by reports of Moon's personal wealth, though they insist part of it is necessary for security precautions.

Others remain confident in the "master's" judgment. Dave Jensen, for example, says he doesn't object to the apparent "Life of Riley" Moon enjoys: "His life has been hell, and now we can afford to house him in the dignity which he deserves." But another young church member was so disturbed by what she saw of Moon's wealth that she left the church in disgust. Nancy, an army colonel's daughter, joined the church while in college. Later she worked for the church near Moon's home in New York State and had a chance to observe the way he and his family lived. "His kids are chauffeured to private schools in limousines with bodyguards," she said. "He's got two lovely yachts and he spends a lot of spare time tuna fishing. His family, and all the top leaders and public relations people, were given expensive wardrobes. It was such a contrast to what I'd seen in the field—kids living a subsistence life-style and sending in all the money they made fundraising to support Moon. There were special fund-raising drives all over the country to raise money for expensive presents for the Moon family on holidays.

"I began to see that the church was just a self-perpetuating thing. What were we really doing for others? What had happened to the goals and ideals I joined for? Who were we helping besides Moon himself?"

Moon has taken a personal interest in organizing the church to produce more profits, stressing the importance of constant fund-raising by young church members. *The Times Magazine* has seen internal church transcripts of Moon's speeches in which he exhorts his followers to raise $80 to $100 each a day. A Unification church training manual puts it graphically: "Do you like to make green bills happy? When green bills are in the hands of a fallen man, can they be happy? Why don't you make them happy? So many green bills are crying. . . . They are all destined to go to Father [Moon]." The manual continues: "Money should be reported to Father. . . . We must offer it to Heavenly Father through Father to use for a heavenly purpose."

The purpose may or may not be heavenly, but Moon's disciples certainly have made a lot of green bills happy. Some of Moon's followers told *The Times Magazine* that as many as a thousand church members are currently in mobile fundraising teams, the church's primary source of known income. MFT's consist of groups of five to ten young people who travel in vans and raise money selling flowers, candy, or ginseng tea on the streets. Moon's critics charge that his church is less a religion than an enormously profitable panhandling operation. Items are "sold for donations" for as much as a 400 percent markup. Working as long as twelve hours a day at shopping centers, airports, and busy intersections, each MFT member can produce as much as $100 a day after expenses. And occasionally there are special drives to make money for specific purposes. On Christmas Eve 1975 in Phoenix, Arizona, for example, in a twenty-four-hour sales effort, twenty young church members netted $20,000 selling carnations.

Although church officials deny that they encourage deception in fund raising, many former MFT members say it is a common practice. "I soon found out that if I mentioned Reverend Moon or the church, people were hesitant to give money," one for Moonie, the son of an army sergeant, told *The Times Magazine.* "So I started using false pretenses—saying I was with a drug abuse program, or raising money for underprivileged children or for a Christian youth center. Almost everybody would buy something then."

I watched Unification church members selling carnations at two airports—Washington's National Airport and Miami International Airport. Airport spokesmen were using loudspeakers to warn passengers that they were not obligated to buy the flowers, though the broadcasts made no mention of the Unification church or Reverend Moon. Neither did the sellers. Dozens of pretty young women were marching confidently up to arriving or departing businessmen, pinning carnations on their lapels before they had a chance to protest. As soon as the startled men accepted the flowers, the women made their pitch for money. Few turned them down. Those who questioned what group was selling the flowers were told a variety of stories, but even persistent questions never revealed that the sellers were in fact Unification church members. "I though they were here for a drug clinic," one man said later.

Young Moonies Live the Church
What is life like for the young church members, many of whom leave home and school to live in church centers and become full-time fundraisers? *The Times Magazine* talked to half a dozen

military dependents who had worked for the church. They painted a bleak picture of the street-selling life. Even still-active church members admit the work is grueling, though they believe it is an important part of training. But the Jensens are torn by worry when they hear about the way some young church members are living. "I've even heard reports that some young people were driven to suicide by this life-style," Penny Jensen says. "It tears a mother apart ot wonder how her child is, whether he's eating well, getting medical attention."

Living expenses for the MFT members are kept to a minimum. "There was a lot of competition to see which team could send in the most profit," one former fundraiser remembers. "So we ate a lot of beans and rice. We were never starving, but of course the nutrition was lousy." The regimen is strict: drugs and alcohol are forbidden; Unification church teachings stress an unyielding segregation of the sexes; even for married members (called "blessed couples" because Moon himself often selects the mates and performs the wedding ceremony) sex is forbidden until Moon grants a sort of dispensation allowing the marriage to be consummated. Some married couples have waited as long as three years for that permission. For unmarried members sex is even more severely discouraged. Male and female members often eat at separate tables, work in separate groups. "They were very careful to see that none of us formed an attachment with a member of the opposite sex," says Nancy, the army colonel's daughter. "They taught us that we could conquer our natural desires by taking a lot of cold showers—'Satan hates cold showers!' they would say.

"We were all very worried about Satan. The church teaches that anything or anyone still outside the church is under the influence of Satan, so we had almost no contact with anyone not a church member." Other former disciples confirm Nancy's story. The church, they say, became their lives. After long hours of street selling or domestic work in the communal houses, members spend hours in prayer and study. "There was almost no privacy," recalls another former Moonie, the son of a navy officer. "I could stand the hard work because I really believed in what we were doing. But I missed the chance to get off by myself and think. They don't leave you any time to reconsider what you're doing."

Soldiers in the Army of Moon

From the beginning Moon's movement has had decidedly political overtones. Its staunch anticommunism and emphasis on U.S. support for the South Korean government of President Park Chung Hee have caused some Moon critics to charge that the Unification church is nothing more than a political arm of the South Korean government. Dave Jensen's father is deeply concerned about Moon's political activities. "I'm as firmly anticommunist as anybody else," he says. "But a lot of people are taken in by all this anticommunism. I believe we should support the South Korean government—hell, I fought there myself. But if we should ever go to war for South Korea, it should be a careful decision of our government. Why should our military die to protect a place just because it's Moon's birthplace? I get angry when I read about the South Korean lobbying in Congress—and I think Moon's just part of all that."

Moon has enjoyed at least tacit approval from the Park regime, and the church may have received more tangible support as well. For example, a performing arts center in Korea for the Moon-sponsored Little Angels singing group has been built on land "donated by the government," according to a church publication. Moon's support for the Park government has been unflagging. He and other church officials often give rousing anticommunist speeches to church members, deploring what they call the "questionable" American commitment to South Korea, and urging a new determination to fight communism, especially in Korea. In fact many Moon disciples told *The Times Magazine* they had taken a vow to fight for South Korea in the event of a North Korean invasion. "To us, it's like the Holy Land," says one current church member. "Of course we would go to war for the Father's [Moon's] birthplace."

The Unification church maintains a coterie of twenty to

twenty-five members on Capitol Hill. The "Capitol Hill ministry" as the church calls it, is not a registered lobby, and church spokesmen deny that they try to influence specific legislation. "They attend prayer meetings, talk with congressmen and their aides, drop off gifts and copies of the *Divine Principle*," says a church official. "They're trying to bring a spirit of God back into the government." The impact of their efforts is hard to measure. Ann Gordon, a former air force dependent, was a church member for a year and a half until her parents had her deprogrammed. She was a member of Moon's Capitol Hill ministry in 1975. At a meeting of concerned citizens chaired by Senator Robert Dole in 1976, she described her job: "We . . . were told to be somewhat 'vague' when dealing with Capitol Hill contacts in order to protect our presence there, but we were to try to influence our contacts to support Moon and South Korea." U.S. support for South Korea is essential to that country, which relies heavily on American financial and military aid. South Korea has received billions of dollars in economic and military assistance, and today the United States has more than 40,000 troops there. In 1976 and 1977 there were numerous revelations of a widespread South Korean lobbying effort to maintain and increase that assistance. The Justice Department has been investigating massive influence-buying in Congress, and some reports say the Koreans poured as much as $1 million a year into their Capitol Hill effort. More than a dozen present and former congressmen have been accused of receiving cash and gifts from the South Koreans in exchange for legislative support.

In the course of these investigations a number of Moon's associates and Moon-sponsored organizations have cropped up. While the Justice Department is not investigating the church as such, it is investigating any connections that might exist between the church and the Korean bribery scheme. Prominent in the federal investigation has been the name of Pak Bo Hi, Moon's translator, constant companion, and chief aide. Pak, a former Korean army colonel, was a military attaché at the South Korean embassy in Washington, D.C., until 1964. That year he left the

service of his government to found the Korean Cultural and Freedom Foundation, a tax-exempt foundation whose stated purpose
was "containing communism on the Asiatic continent."

But although Pak vehemently denies the charge, there have
been persistent accusations by other South Koreans that he was,
and is, an agent of the Korean Central Intelligence Agency,
whose activities have been investigated in connection with bribery
on Capitol Hill. Justice Department spokesmen told *The Times
Magazine* they could not comment on any individuals while the
case was still under investigation, but sources close to the
investigation have told reporters from *The Washington Post* that
Pak attended a meeting with Korean President Park at the South
Korean presidential mansion, where the original plan to funnel
cash and gifts to U.S. officials was discussed. Pak has denied
attending such a meeting.

In summer 1976 the House Subcommittee on International
Organizations, headed by Congressman Donald Fraser, held
hearings on the activities of the KCIA in the United States.
Several witnesses testified that Colonel Pak and other Moon
associates and foundations had direct links to the KCIA and
President Park. Dr. Jai Hyon Lee, a former cultural and information officer at the Korean embassy, testified that long after Pak
officially left the embassy and joined Moon's movement, he was
allowed to use the embassy's cable channel to Seoul, "which goes
only to the foreign minister, director of the KCIA, prime minister,
and the President." Lee also testified that the embassy maintained a close relationship with the Moon-sponsored Freedom
Leadership Foundation, another nonprofit organization whose
purpose is to educate young Americans about the dangers of communism. That group's founder was Neil A. Salonen, who is also
president of the Unification Church of America.

The church has denied that the Freedom Leadership Foundation has any more than a coincidental relationship with the
church. But Allen Tate Wood, a former church member who was
president of the foundation, told Fraser's subcommittee that it
was funded by the church and received its orders directly from

Moon. Tate testified that he met Moon at a conference in Korea, where "he outlined to us his plans for America. The gist of it was that through the Unification Church and its numerous front orgainzations Moon wanted to acquire enough influence in America so that he would be able to dictate policy on major issues. Of paramount importance was the issue of guaranteeing unlimited American military assistance to South Korea in the event of the breakout of hostilities between North and South Korea."

There was further testimony from Robert W. Roland, an airline pilot and former marine whose wife and daughter had joined the Unification church. Roland testified that he had been a personal friend of Colonel Pak during the 1960's when Pak was still at the South Korean embassy. He said Pak told him part of his duties involved serving as a liaison between Korean and U.S. intelligence agencies. Pak, Roland testified, said he knew Moon had met with Korean President Park on "a number of occasions." Pak also spoke to Roland about the Korean Cultural and Freedom Foundation. "He stated that the purpose of KCFF would be to gain influence and raise money for Moon's cause."

In fall 1976 the Justice Department began investigating the foundation to determine if money raised for it had been channeled into the elaborate Korean lobbying effort on the Hill. And in January 1977 the New York State Board of Social Welfare revoked the foundation's right to solicit funds in the state. The board accused the group of using less than 7 percent of the $1.5 million it raised in one year for children's relief and other purposes for which its appeals were made. The evidence of Moon's connection with the Korean government and its political efforts in the United States is still mostly circumstantial, and church officials deny any tie at all. In a press conference in summer 1976, church president Neil Salonen said, "There is not now and never has been any connection whatsoever between the Unification Church of America or the Freedom Leadership Foundation and the government of South Korea or its Central Intelligence Agency."

Church members like Dave Jensen remain convinced that Moon's movement is essentially a religious one. "It's not political except as it hopes to bring God back to the country," he says. "We need to remember our nation's motto, 'In God We Trust.' " Dave says he is unconcerned about reports of church ties to the Korean government. "I'm convinced Reverend Moon is a true prophet. I have no questions at all about his sincerity."

Is Moon's Eclipse Coming?

In the end Sun Myung Moon's motives remain a mystery. Moon himself grants no interviews to the outside press, and *The Times Magazine*'s request for an interview was routinely denied. Even a reading of Moon's own rambling, sometimes unintelligible speeches offers little clue to his real purpose. At times in the speeches he sounds as if he truly believes he is the new messiah. At the other times he seems more like an ardent Korean patriot. Occasionally he sounds like nothing more than a shrewd businessman, advising his followers on the techniques of establishing of credit and reaping huge profits. Yet for all the fervent loyalty he inspires in some of his disciples, a number of them have become disillusioned with Moon and his cause. *The Times Magazine* talked to several young people who had left the church on their own, disturbed by reports of shady dealings, tired of hard work, no pay, and few vestiges of the idealistic goals that brought them into the Unification church in the first place. A few church members said privately they were afraid that Moon himself may have been duped by those around him and been used as a propaganda tool in a larger scheme of Korean dealings.

Moon's rallies in 1976 had disappointing turnouts. Although the church claims 30,000 members in the United States, church officials admit that only 7,000 of them are "core members," full-time disciples—hardly enough to support Moon's avowed goal that he and his church will "conquer and subjugate the world." Reverend Moon's eclipse, if it comes, may result more from disillusionment within his band of followers than from their parents' concern or government investigations.

10

The Korea Lobby   Frank Baldwin

The House of Representatives on June 3, 1976, voted 241 to 159 against an attempt by Congressmen Donald M. Fraser and others to reduce military aid to the Republic of Korea (ROK) because of human rights violations by the Park Chung Hee dictatorship. According to one Congressional aide the Park government now "has a green light to continue its repressive measures without fear of a reduction in military assistance."

The vote was a bitter defeat for religious and human rights groups that had urged concrete actions to pressure the Park regime on basic democratic rights. But it was a sweet victory for the Korea lobby, perhaps the longest running open raid on the U.S. treasury since the cold war started. (The ROK has received $12 billion in economic and military assistance since World War II, and it will get another $754 million in fiscal years 1976 and 1977 as a result of the House action. The cost of U.S. troops stationed there is approximately an additional $600 million per year.)

The Korea lobby is a loose coalition of individuals, groups, and institutions that promote the Park government's interests. It presently centers on Ambassador Hahm Pyung Choon and Yung Hwan Kim, the Korean Central Intelligence Agency (KCIA) station chief in the ROK embassy, and includes key individuals in the U.S. national security bureaucracy, the Congress, the Council

Reprinted from the July 19, 1976, issue of *Christianity and Crisis,* copyright ©1976 by Christianity and Crisis, Inc.
The author wishes to thank Bruce Cumings for his assistance in the preparation of this article.

on Foreign Relations, a few universities, and the media. Members' motives are as mixed as the membership itself: anti-communism, balance-of-power geopolitics vis-à-vis the Soviet Union, financial stakes in profits from cheap South Korean labor and grain sales and credits, psychological gratification, acceptance of bribes and gratuities, and the joys of all-expense-paid junkets to Seoul filled with sexual fun and games.

The major overt forces opposed to limitations on military aid to Seoul in the June vote were the Defense and State departments, the farm bloc, a clique of pro-Park Congresspersons and academics, and a larger congressional circle that votes conservatively on national security issues. Putative elements include the banks, which have loaned the ROK about $2.3 billion, and the oil companies that have an interest in oil explorations off the Korean coast—notably Gulf, which secretly contributed $4 million to Park Chung Hee in 1967 and 1971.

The Korea lobby as a power in American politics is a post–World War II phenomenon. It began with the U.S. military occupation and government of southern Korea in 1945 to 1948, was spurred by the formation of the ROK in 1948, and became a fixture in Washington after the Korean War in 1950. For more than a quarter of a century South Korea has watched and wooed Congress with a persuasive brand of mendicant mendacity. Senior congressional leaders have been voting funds for Seoul their entire political lives.

The Cultivation of Congress
Donald L. Ranard, State Department country director for Korea from 1970 to 1974, testified before the House Subcommittee on International Organizations and Movements on March 17, 1976, that

the KCIA has made it its business to follow Congressional actions on a day-to-day basis to know the status of military and economic assistance legislation; the views of individual Congressmen and influential chairmen regarding stationing of forces, human rights and other issues affecting Korea; their overseas travel; and their election campaigns. Indeed, Korean ambassadors as well as [KCIA] station chiefs are only so popular in the Blue House as they are able to demonstrate an influence with our Congress.

The ROK embassy assiduously cultivates Congress by wining and dining influential congressional leaders. In the process South Korean ambassadors have earned reputations as tireless and imaginative hosts. Former Ambassador Kim Dong Jo (later foreign minister) joined all the important clubs in Washington, slapped backs with a flair, and gave extraordinary parties attended by the patron saints of the China lobby like Anna Chan Chennault, doyens of the House and Senate, and young swingers from Capitol Hill. (Ambassador Kim was also ready to help with the mundane side of lobbying. A former embassy official testified that in the spring of 1973 the ambassador packed $100 bills into envelopes as rewards for unidentified congressional supporters.) A younger generation of U.S.-educated South Koreans form an auxiliary of hosts and hostesses.

Hundreds of congresspersons have been invited to Seoul where they received heroes' welcomes, were feted like princes of the blood, and loaded down with honorary degrees and presents. They were taken on tours to the demilitarized zone between South and North Korea, to Panmunjom, to the battlefields of the Korean War. Government hosts repeated the same themes: eternal gratitude for U.S. assistance during the Korean War, a plea for continued aid for a "few more years because of the threat from the North," and an earnest appeal for understanding that democratic rights are an impermissible luxury.

ROK dignitaries from Seoul visiting Washington have never failed to pay their respects to senior congresspersons. "We are your only true friends in Asia," they usually say. During the Vietnam War when President Lyndon Johnson was unwelcome across the United States, the Park Administration turned out vast crowds to greet him. In recent years American officials and academics (particularly the latter) discredited by the Vietnam disaster have found a friendly port in South Korea where their messages of military intervention are still received as revealed truth.

While ROK ambassadors have worked the public social circuit, embassy KCIA operatives have utilized other routes to power. For example, Korea-born Suzi Park Thompson, since 1971 a $15,000-a-year aide to former House Speaker Carl Albert, has a reputation as a "junior grade Perle Mesta." Her forte is intimate dinner parties where eight guests are served Oriental delicacies, and she specializes in annual birthday parties for congresspersons and their spouses. Her birthday parties for New York Congressman Joseph Addabbo have been major social events. Thompson has also given large parties costing up to $1,000, according to her former husband.

An article in the *Washington Post* (February 19, 1976) by Maxine Cheshire provides details of Thompson's travels and companions. In 1971 she accompanied a congressional delegation to South Korea headed by Speaker Albert. The trip stirred up dust back in Albert's Oklahoma when Thompson told reporters that she was going with him "to visit her homeland." In August 1975 Thompson was part of a delegation to Seoul led by Congressman Lester Wolff, for whom she had worked as a secretary before moving to Albert's office. She returned to the ROK two months later with another congressional delegation, invited by the Park regime to commemorate the twenty-fifth anniversary of the Korean War. On both of the latter trips she was listed as an "interpreter," even though the U.S. embassy normally provides interpreters for congressional visitors. (Thompson also accompanied Congressman Robert L. Leggett on a visit to the Far East in 1973.)

Just another Washington hustle? Not at all. KCIA man Yung Hwan Kim frequently attended Suzi Thompson's parties, and both Leggett and Addabbo have acknowledged that they met Kim through Thompson.

The Federal Bureau of Investigation is now looking into this chain of associations as a result of allegations that Leggett and Addabbo accepted bribes from the Park government in late 1975.

This highly sensitive investigation was personally authorized by Attorney General Edward H. Levi. Both congressmen have denied any wrongdoing. Whether Tongsun Park, a young businessman who parlayed suaveness and political influence into quick financial success in Washington, was working primarily for his own interests or the ROK's, or both, is still unclear. But he entertained lavishly at fashionable dinner parties attended by Washington's political elite, including Vice-President and Mrs. Ford, Speaker Albert, and Majority Leader Thomas O'Neill, Jr.

Park reportedly made a fortune in grain sales and was well placed to make another from business interests in Washington when his star fell with a whoosh of scandal. Colonel James W. Howe, husband of Betty Ford's press secretary, Nancy Howe, committed suicide after the couple's acceptance of Park's hospitality on a vacation trip to the Dominican Republic was revealed. It was Park's second fall from grace; he had been implicated earlier in the conviction of former Congressman Cornelius Gallagher. The KCIA also went straight to the Nixon White House. According to the *Washington Post,* Chin Hwan Row, a pro-Park national assemblyman and former head of the Korean Residents Association in Washington, in 1974 made a "blanket offer . . . to contribute to anyone in Congress recommended by the Nixon administration" (February 29, 1976). John E. Nidecker, former special assistant to Nixon, reported the offer to his White House superiors and to the State Department's Korea desk. At about the same time Row also offered money to Congressman Charles E. Wiggins. He told Wiggins, who declined the offer, that a group in South Korea "wanted to assist friendly American Congressmen."

South Korea's New Packaging
In the 1950s and early 1960s South Korea had few problems with Congress or the American public. McCarthyism and the China lobby rode high. Any discussion of withdrawal from or accommodation to communism in Asia was taboo. This situation changed abruptly in the late 1960s as the Vietnam War turned

irretrievably sour after the Tet offensive. Hearings in 1970 by the Senate Foreign Relations Committee's Subcommittee on U.S. Security Agreements Abroad revealed that ROK forces in Vietnam were paid secret bonuses (concealed from Congress by State Department, Pentagon, and Park regime collusion). Senator William Fulbright denounced the South Koreans as mercenaries, and administration officials admitted that Seoul's "support" had a multibillion dollar price tag, which is still being paid. Revelations that ROK forces had systematically committed some of the most heinous atrocities of that bloody war distressed many Americans.

Financial pressures from the war forced cutbacks in marginal areas. One U.S. infantry division was withdrawn from South Korea in 1970–1971, and a reassessment of the commitment to Seoul began. The Nixon visit to China in 1971 and the promise of détente all but erased the strategic value of the ROK as a forward defense area. The times were changing for South Korea. Park Chung Hee compounded these negative (from his point of view) trends in October 1972 by declaring martial law, suspending the constitution, and dissolving the National Assembly. A new constitution made him president for life. Electoral politics were at an end, a rubber-stamp assembly was subservient to Park, and the modest civil liberties tolerated before were curtailed. KCIA surveillance spread to the media, the churches, and the universities. Peaceful dissent was equated with treason. The Park regime's dizzying descent into rule by draconian emergency decrees and an utterly depraved KCIA was underway.

The present activities and style of South Korea and its lobby reflect the difficult task of convincing post-Vietnam America to continue support for Park Chung Hee—or any other regime in Seoul. To create a pro-Seoul bloc, since there is no large ethnic constituency for South Korea in America, the ROK and its lobby have turned to bribery, prostitutes, corrupt academics, and an expensive public relations firm. These traditional methods of influence have been complemented by intelligence operatives with a penchant for secret manipulation and bare-knuckle tactics.

(Korean Christian scholars meeting in St. Louis three years ago were warned against making an anti-Park statement; a rally for opposition leader Kim Dae Jung in San Francisco was physically disrupted by KCIA agents; recent testimony before the Fraser subcommittee indicates that the harassment of dissidents continues.)

Sun Myung Moon and his Unification church are yet another facet of South Korea's new packaging. The weaker the product, the harder the sell. The function that Moon and the Unification church perform in the Korea lobby is to blend religion and anti-communism into support for Park Chung Hee. As a "religion" the Unification church is tax exempt and protected from investigation under the First Amendment. Moon has a freedom of action and security not available even to the ROK embassy or KCIA fronts. He is able to engage in political activities through satellite organizations linked to the Unification church by interlocking boards of directors, personnel, and secret funding.

The Freedom Leadership Foundation (FLF) was established in 1969 by Neil A. Salonen, who is its president; he is also president of the Unification church in America. Former members have stated that the FLF was formed upon Moon's orders, is entirely financed by the Unification church, and consists almost entirely of church members. The foundation carried out an intensive propaganda campaign between 1969 and 1970 in support of the Vietnam War and the invasion of Cambodia. And it stuck with Richard Nixon to the day of his resignation. Through its biweekly, the *Rising Tide,* and other publications the FLF churns out an ultraconservative alarm. At more than a hundred college and university chapters, it spreads a gospel of anticommunism, often sponsoring conservative members of Congress as speakers.

The Unification church itself has an active lobbying effort on Capitol Hill. Activities have included prayer breakfasts, direct appeals to individual members, and offers of financial and other support. The church has even placed one young woman member in Speaker Albert's office. Further, as reported by Ann Crittenden in the *New York Times* (May 25, 1976), the Unification church has access to the ROK embassy's communications system and diplomatic pouch. It can thus transmit funds for political activities and other purposes unhampered by the currency controls required for other mortals. Moon will be even more efficient when the Diplomats National Bank begins operations in Washington. A list of persons associated with this new bank reads like a who's who of the Korea lobby and the Unification church; it includes columnist Jack Anderson, the Park regime's long-time favorite media person.

Wooing Academia

Every lobby needs a few savants to provide a semblance of truth and intellectual respectability. The current KCIA blitz to enlist academia began in the spring of 1973. According to Professor Jai Hyon Lee, who served for three years as the cultural and information attaché of the ROK Embassy until he defected in June 1973, the KCIA initiated a plan of "clandestine operations to mute criticism of Park's totalitarianism." The academic component called for the KCIA "to organize indirectly, or to finance covertly, scholastic meetings, seminars and symposia for Korean and American professors to rationalize Park's dictatorship, or, at least, to curb their criticism." The latter bears special emphasis: to silence the academics was sufficient for KCIA purposes. Alarmed at the intellectual and campus opposition in America to the Vietnam War, the Park administration desperately sought to create support for the ROK.

An early example of this plan was the symposium, "Korea and the Powers in the 1970's," jointly sponsored by the Institute for Asian Studies in Washington and South Korea's Kyung Nam University. The institute, part of the Pan-Asian Foundation which is funded by the South Korean government, is a paper organization. The head of the foundation is Kwang Neun Hahn, who has been identified in congressional testimony as publisher of a KCIA-funded newspaper in Washington. Kyung Nam University's chief claim to excellence is that its president's brother is the notorious Park Chong Gyu, former chief bodyguard of President Park. Kyung Nam University sponsored another meeting in Seoul in January 1974, "An International Symposium on Peace and Security in East Asia." The meeting was organized by Professor Sungjoo Han of Brooklyn College. Not the slightest pretense of scholarly purpose graced the gathering. Professor Sugwon Kang of Hartwick College observed that "none of the 11 American scholars had anything directly to do with Korean studies and [that] they had been picked merely by virtue of their being either a former professor, present colleague or an associate of one of the organizers."

These counterfeit institutes and conferences often attract well-known scholars. The Korean Institute of International Studies (KIIS) held a conference in June 1974 on the lofty theme, "Search for Peace: Alternatives to Confrontation in East Asia." Fifteen academics (including six from the United States), thirty-four participants from South Korea, and an array of dignitaries and foreign ambassadors were so uncritical in their remarks that even the controlled ROK press was moved to comment, "the contents of their papers are either obsolete, i.e., stuff which they may have used in some journals many years ago, or collections of platitudes. One wonders if this is attributable to their hectic schedules." The KIIS journal *Tonga Ilbo* dismissed the conference papers as "stale stories" and deplored the waste of "precious foreign exchange and research funds."

The purpose of these conferences was, of course, political influence, not scholarly exchange. Thus the KIIS journal lists an International Advisory Board that includes Roger Hilsman, Herman Kahn, Robert Scalapino, Zbigniew Brzezinski, A. Doak Barnett, and George Beckmann. This learned journal regularly prints President Park Chung Hee's speeches, including a New Year's press conference. The Council on Foreign Relations (CFR) is hardly an instrument of the KCIA, yet "friends of South Korea" are well placed to defend Seoul's interests. In December 1974 the council formed a "discussion group on the role of the two Koreas in East Asian affairs." A concern that the ROK might not "be able to cope with the changes occurring on the international economic scene" was given as one reason for the discussions. The groups included representatives from the Department of Defense, the CIA, the Agency for International Development, the State Department, investment firms, and eastern universities, as well as critics of the Park regime.

Three of the five discussions were led by pro-Seoul individuals, including Chong-sik Lee, University of Pennsylvania, and Robert Scalapino, University of California, anticommunist scholars who championed the Vietnam War and the ROK expeditionary force's role in it. James Morley of Columbia University, also a Vietnam hawk and a participant in several of the recent conferences, was a chairman of the meetings. No academics sympathetic to North Korea were included. Can the mistaken men and ideas of Vietnam be recycled for Korea? Not very likely. Certainly not as long as they are the men who have supped at Park Chung Hee's table for more than a decade. But they can contribute to a climate of opinion among international affairs specialists and the Congress that opposes restrictions on military aid to Seoul. The CFR would never share the platform with Sun Myung Moon at Yankee Staduim, but both have a common interest in Yankee establishment imperialism.

Seoul was fun city for co-opted academics in the summer of 1975. The Park regime had just summarily executed nine dissidents in April on trumped-up charges, but the scholars blithely tripped over each other at the freebies. Most of the early so-called conferences gathered scholars in the social sciences, the policy-making disciplines. The humanities made a strong comeback when the Korean National Academy of Sciences held the International Symposium to Commemorate the Thirtieth Anniversary of Korea's Liberation in Seoul from August 11 to 14. The approximately fifty participants, including outstanding academicians from Harvard, Yale, Indiana University, and other similar institutions, had all their expenses paid to read papers on . . . anything. Again it was the presence of the scholars, not their papers, that was important. One participant sheepishly called the gathering a "buddy, buddy thing" and laughed at its supposed scholarly purposes.

Respectability and Repression

To create an image and "mute the critics" requires a multi-dimensional approach. The Korean Traders Association (KTA), a 2,000-member business federation with headquarters in Seoul and a New York City office, has tried two joint political ventures with the eastern establishment. In April 1975 it retained the public relations firm of Hill and Knowlton to polish the Park regime's tarnished image. The KTA apparently expected that the $300,000 fee would change the news accounts of events in South Korea. When asked why the contract was not renewed this spring, Ock Kim, director of the KTA in New York, said that "unfavorable stories are still appearing in the *New York Times*."

The KTA probed again for the soft underbelly of American scruples. According to the official version of events, this initiative began with J. T. Coolidge, a businessman in the ROK who is a Harvard alumnus and fund raiser for the university's East Asian studies program. Against the background of the Park regime's crackdown on dissent and the Christian churches in 1973 and 1974, Coolidge approached the KTA to donate a chair in Korean studies to Harvard. The timing hardly seemed auspicious. South Korea was hard hit by the 1973 oil crisis, exports had slumped because of the international recession, and the ROK was forced to borrow extensively abroad (almost $4 billion in 1974–1975). Foreign indebtedness climbed from $3.3 billion in 1973 to $5.9 billion by late 1975. Nevertheless the KTA was responsive to the request and agreed in December 1974 to a $1 million contribution. Was all that money actually to come from the KTA, or was part of it from the government? An independent audit or investigation is impossible, so there is no way to know. Yet the KTA acknowledges its close relationship with the government, and the KCIA has long manipulated business organizations for its own purposes.

Another fundamental question is why an impoverished nation should be donating $1 million to one of the world's richest universities. KTA members' profits are a result of the low wages paid to South Korean workers. According to recent ROK official statistics, 81.9 percent of wage earners are below the government-designated poverty line. The ethics of squeezing the poor of South Korea to enhance the image of Park Chung Hee apparently presented no problem at Harvard. (Columbia University's East Asian scholars are facing the same issue. They have requested several million dollars from Seoul for a Korean studies program.) In the spring of 1975 the KTA raised questions about the political views of persons to be appointed to the Harvard position. They were concerned that "adverse criticism of South Korea not result from the gift." John K. Fairbank, director of Harvard's East Asian Research Center, reassured the KTA while maintaining the liberal rhetoric of "no strings attached," a posture struck partly to rebut critical articles like this one.

Harvard sources insist that the KTA did not improperly influence faculty decisions on use of the funds. The facts, however, suggest otherwise. The ROK approved the donation, and the first appointments have gone to an unabashed defender of the Park government and to a graduate student who, despite years of experience in South Korea and being privately critical of the Park regime, has yet to take a public position on the dictatorship. To appoint scholars critical of the Park government would have betrayed the spirit of the gift and its acceptance—and future donations. Who needs strings when the Harvard administration puppets and the KTA/KCIA puppeteers both dance to the same tune?

On the most charitable reading the timing of the final negotiations and the presentation of the KTA grant showed an extreme insensitivity on the part of the American scholars. It was on April 9, 1975, that the nine alleged members of the so-called People's Revolutionary party (PRP), a government fabrication, were summarily executed. (The PRP men had been arrested in 1974 as a warning to dissidents that anyone might be charged as a communist agent.) Two foreign missionaries were forced out of South Korea because of their inquiries into the case. The Reverend George Ogle, a United Methodist, was deported in December 1974 when his personal research, undertaken at the request of the prisoners' wives, indicated that the charges were false. In April 1975 Father James Sinott, a Maryknoll priest stationed in South Korea since 1960, was forced out for protesting the killings.

Other missionaries in Seoul led a protest at the U.S. embassy. Church groups in Japan and America protested. Many journalists—American, Korean, Japanese, and British—took real risks to cover the PRP case, the executions, and other gross violations of human rights. But through it all Professor John Fairbank and his colleagues assured the KTA that they would not regret their gift to Harvard. According to one faculty member no one in Asian studies at the university publicly protested the executions. On June 16, 1975, Harvard announced the KTA grant with a press release stating that the money would go toward "enhancing the base for the objective study of Korea."

The Korea lobby has a mischief-making record worthy of its erstwhile colleagues, the China and Vietnam lobbies. A minor involvement in 1945 has been sanctified into a sacred cow of commitment. Support for the ROK is equated with national security and firmness toward the Soviet Union, powerful cant in an election year when the Congress has unconditionally surrendered on the Pentagon budget. In a mutation of the domino theory South Korea is now described as important to Japan's defense. The Japanese government (but not the Japanese people) cynically agrees, as it did on Vietnam, but it wisely refrains from sharing the costs or the risks.

Attempts in Congress to support human rights in the ROK are voted down because of an exaggerated, nearly imaginary "threat from the North." The basic facts are obfuscated: South Korea has almost two and a half times the population of the North, and the presence of U.S. atomic weapons precludes any attack, as it has for two decades. Beneath the Korea lobby's rhetoric of security, one hears the muted whispers of narrow bureaucratic and private financial interests, not a true national interest.

The other Asian lobbies in the United States finally collapsed after the nationalist/communist military victories in China and Vietnam. The Korean lobby is different, not the least because war is unlikely on the peninsula. That puts the job of countering the pro-Park Chung Hee lobby where it belongs—on the agenda of all groups and individuals in the United States concerned with human rights and more sensible military and foreign policies.

11

**Moon's Sect Pushes
Pro-Seoul Activities**

Ann Crittenden

A number of individuals and organizations connected with the Reverend Sun Myung Moon, the wealthy Korean industrialist and evangelist, have intimate ties with and have received assistance from the South Korean government and the Korean Central Intelligence Agency, according to former Korean and American officials and former members of the Moon organization.

At the same time the fast-growing Moon-affiliated groups have devoted much of their efforts to building support for the South Korean government in the United States. These efforts have taken the form of intensive lobbying on Capitol Hill, attempts to influence prominent politicians, businessmen, and community leaders, the development of a dedicated group of followers from many countries who have pledged to fight in South Korea in the event of a war there, and elaborate public-relations campaigns attacking communism and linking South Korea to patriotic American themes.

The maintenance of a favorable image in the Unites States is essential to the South Korean government, which depends heavily on American political, financial, and military support. Since World War II, South Korea has received $12 billion in economic and military assistance from the United States, more than any other country except South Vietnam. Since 1971, South Korea, whose leaders continue to express fear of attack from North Korea, has received almost $2 billion in military aid alone. In addition the United States maintains 40,000 troops and hundreds

of nuclear weapons in South Korea, at a cost of $500 million to
$600 million a year, by Pentagon calculations.

In 1976, the American foreign-aid budget to South Korea was
$323 million in economic and military assistance, and the Carter
administration requested $431 million in various forms of
assistance for fiscal year 1977–78.

Congressman Donald M. Fraser, Democrat of Minnesota,
whose Subcommittee on International Organizations has been
investigating the operations of the Korean CIA in the United
States, is holding hearings on the Moon movement's political
activities here. According to Fraser, and to a spokesman of the
Justice Department, those activities are part of a broader picture
of widespread South Korean attempts to influence the American
political process.

It is open to interpretation whether these activities are legal
and whether some of the Moon groups have violated statutes
governing the political activities of tax-exempt organizations or
requiring registration as foreign agents. But enough evidence
exists to raise questions in the minds of a number of government
officials. "We have received information which strongly suggests
that certain persons and associations close to Sun Myung Moon
have had a cooperative relationship with the Korean Government
and Korean C.I.A.," Fraser says. "Our information shows a
pattern of activity that raises serious questions as to the nature
and purpose of Moon's various organizations."

According to an American customs official, for example, the
United States government has reason to believe that the South
Korean government may have provided Moon's associates with
the use of diplomatic channels to bring funds from Japan and
Korea into the United States. Also a former South Korean
diplomat has testified that Moon's closest companion in the
United States has used top-level Korean embassy communication
lines to send messages from the United States to Korea. A former
high State Department official has also testified that the Korean
government has assisted one of Moon's foundations in beaming
anticommunist broadcasts into Southeast Asia.

Moon's central organization in the United States is the Unification church (officially the Holy Spirit Association for the Unification of World Christianity). The church claims 30,000 members in the United States and ten times that number each in Japan and South Korea. The Unification church's theology is loosely based on the Christian acceptance of Jesus as the savior, with the Second Coming of Christ to be in Korea. Moon's followers believe that he is not only sinless but is actually the new messiah. He has neither explicitly confirmed nor denied his belief in this. The church maintains that with the second advent, mankind will become one united family, dedicated to the elimination of evil and the establishment of the kingdom of heaven.

Members of the church in the United States have also established the Freedom Leadership Foundation, which conducts political propaganda activities in Washington, and the Korean Cultural and Freedom Foundation, also in Washington, which is devoted to improving the image of South Korea in the United States. The leaders of both organizations are Unification Church members as are almost all the members of the Freedom Leadership Foundation, and both groups also have links with the South Korean government or its CIA. In addition Moon's organizations, including the church and the overtly political International Federation for Victory over Communism, have received financial support from such Japanese ultrarightists as Ryoichi Sasagawa and Yoshio Kodama, the power broker who has been implicated in the Lockheed scandals in Japan.

The exact nature of Moon's relationship with the authoritarian regime of President Park Chung Hee is still shrouded in mystery. By one hypothesis the Unification church began as an independent movement but was subsequently put to use by the Korean president and receives favors in return. By another hypothesis the Moon-related organizations, however they began, are now in effect direct tools of President Park, who controls every aspect of Korean public life, and are controlled or guided by Korean secret agents. Lieutenant Colonel Pak Bo Hi, Moon's translator and closest associate, maintains that "there is no common line between our movement and the office of the President of Korea." "In no case are they trying to use us or exploit us or are we trying to use them," he said.

American authorities seem inclined to take Pak at his word, for a number of reasons. According to several congressional staff members, Congress is particularly wary of seeming, by investigating his activities, to threaten Moon's right to religious expression under the Constitution's First Amendment. A spokesman for the Justice Department, which is responsible for enforcing a number of statutes requiring foreign agents to register as such, insists that the department has seen no evidence directly linking Moon or Pak to the Korean government. Yet a former senior government official alleges that such information did exist, in the form of an intelligence report that the State Department and the Justice Department's internal security division had in their possession in the early 1970s. This was said to have placed Pak at a meeting with President Park in which they discussed ways of financing one of Pak's projects.

At that time the internal security division under the direction of Robert C. Mardian, who was later convicted of conspiracy in connection with the Watergate coverup, dropped an investigation into some of Pak's activities on the ground that "competent evidence" was missing.

No Investigations Underway

Currently there are no official investigations of Moon-related political activities in this country, although various other aspects of South Korean activity in the United States are under Justice Department surveillance. According to Richard L. Thornburgh, assistant attorney general for the criminal division, the primary focus is on financial transactions between the South Korean government and Korean nationals in the United States and on the alledged bribery of two congressmen by Korean agents, although indictments in the bribery case are "a long way off," Thornburgh indicated.

The active political efforts of the Unification church in the

United States apparently date from 1969. At that time, according to several former members, Moon ordered Neil A. Salonen to found an anticommunist movement here similar to the church's extensive anticommunist programs in South Korea and Japan.

Salonen, who has been a leading member of the church since its arrival in this country in 1969, established the Freedom Leadership Foundation as a nonprofit educational corporation. Salonen is the president of the foundation and president of the Unification church in America as well. According to a statement Salonen made to the Internal Revenue Service in 1974, the foundation has no relation to the Unification church except that the two organizations have some members, offices, and directors in common. Allen Tate Wood, president of the foundation in 1970 and active in the church until 1974, maintains, however, that the foundation was entirely funded by the church and was made up almost completely church members—a statement supported by several other former Moon followers.

The secretary general of the Freedom Leadership Foundation, Dan Fefferman, confirms that it "has been carried out almost exclusively by church members." He says that currently the subsidy provided by the church amounts to less than one-half of the foundation's budget. As for Moon's relationship to the foundation, Fefferman says that the organization simply consults with him from time to time. Linda Anthenien of San Francisco, who was active in the church in northern California from 1968 through 1970, says that church members were expected to work for the foundation, although they were told never to mention their church affiliation while engaged in political activities.

Moreover "in order to better present itself as a religion and more effectively influence the institutions of this country," Anthenien says, the church changed its name in January 1971 from Unified Family to Unification church. Both Anthenien and Wood, who is now a student at Rutgers University, say they left the church when they became disillusioned with its emphasis on political and material ends rather than spiritual ones. One of the foundation's first projects was a biweekly anticommunist news-

letter, *The Rising Tide*, which is still published and circulated to
20,000 people. In the fall of 1969 and in 1970, the foundation conducted an intensive public-relations campaign against the
American movement opposed to the war in Vietnam and in support of the invasion of Cambodia. This campaign was conducted
partly through an organization formed by members called
American Youth for a Just Peace.

According to Wood, who helped direct these activities, eight
Unification church members and four nonmembers were
rewarded for their work with fifteen-day trips to South Vietnam
and Cambodia as guests of those countries.

Several of these people, including Wood, then went on to visit
the Moon organizations in Japan and South Korea, where they
were given a tour of the Korean CIA building and told by church
members in Seoul that the church wanted to "make friends" with
the intelligence agency. According to Wood, "The American
movement's strategy at that time was to make President Park feel
that Moon was his greatest ally, not a threat. Moon told us that
our whole goal in America was to identify Park's goals and then
serve them."

In 1973 and 1974, Moon organized a media campaign of support for the beleaguered President Richard M. Nixon, spending
$72,000 in the effort, according to church statements. Full-page
advertisements placed in American newspapers told Americans
that God had chosen Nixon to be president and that therefore
only God had the authority to dismiss him. In December 1973,
some 1,500 Moon followers were ordered to Washington from all
over the country to demonstrate against impeachment of the
president. Subsequently Mr. Moon was invited to a White House
prayer breakfast and to a private thirty-minute session with the
president. Wood states that Charles Colson, then a special assistant to the president, also influenced several private individuals to
make contributions of a few thousand dollars to American Youth
for a Just Peace.

Colson, who was also later convicted in the Watergate case,
confirmed this, noting that the Moonist "peace group had

cooperated with the youth people" in the White House in their support of the war effort. "So I recommended their cause to some friends who had been helping us," he said, stressing, however, that he did not know that the group had any ties with Moon. Fefferman denies that the foundation conducts any lobbying activites, although he confirms that the Unification church does have an active program on Capitol Hill to maintain a "liason with Congress."

Legislators Cultivated
According to an active church member who prefers to remain anonymous, this effort is conducted by fifty church members at a time, who visit Washington from all parts of the country. Each is given a list of members of Congress to cultivate, first by befriending and offering help to their staffs, and eventually by inviting the legislators to a suite in the Washington Hilton Hotel, where dinner, films, and a talk on Moon's religious and anticommunist views are presented.

The lobbying procedure, according to this woman and others, was first taught to church members by a group of Japanese Moonies who had had experience in lobbying in the Japanese Parliament. "We were told to be somewhat vague when dealing with the Capitol Hill contacts in order to protect our presence there, but we were to try to influence our contacts to support Moon and South Korea," says Ann Gordon, a northern California woman in her late twenties who left the church in October 1975 after being deprogrammed.

The Unification church's efforts to influence the American political process are not confined to Washington. In January and March 1976, two prominent members of the church, Daikan K. Ohnuki and Michael McDermott, attempted to see Laurance S. Rockefeller at his office at the Rockefeller Brothers Fund in New York. On both occasions they brought gifts.

According to Yorke Allen, Jr., the staff member who received them, Ohnuki commented that, in view of the possibility that Vice-President Rockefeller might become president of the United

States, he might find the services of the church useful. The offer and the gifts were politely rejected, according to Allen. Neither McDermott nor Ohnuki could be reached for comment.

Numerous other wealthy businessmen have been approached by the Moon organization throughout the country, and a series of elaborate banquets have been held in recent months in New York City and Washington, D.C., for prominent community and ethnic-group leaders. The banquets featured traditional Korean and American songs and dancing, and an inspirational, patriotic message. Several former members of the church say that they were taught that they should be willing to die for the movement and for South Korea. They said South Korea was portrayed in Moon's theology as the Adam country, to be saved by Lucifer, the United States, from Satan, or North Korean communism, which was termed the center of worldwide communism. "It was obvious that to die for South Korea would be the greatest thing you could do," says Gordon.

Last year, according to Gordon and others, fifty to a hundred American followers and hundreds of supporters of other nationalities were flown by Moon from the United States to South Korea where they participated in a mass rally and pledged to die on the front lines if war ever broke out between North and South Korea. Michael Runyon, official spokesman for the Unification church in America, has said that the church had no lobbying groups. "We have a ministry on Capitol Hill, we witness to Christ and try to awaken the Judeo-Christian conscience of members of Congress. We try to bring God into government." He denied that support for South Korea was tied in with this work. "It's a case of people coming together to fight a common foe," he said. "It's very important to the freedom-loving nations of Asia" to support South Korea.

Both the Unification church and the Freedom Leadership Foundation are tax exempt, the church because it is a religious organization and the foundation because it is registered as a non-profit educational organization. Section 501c3 of the Internal Revenue code says that organizations formed exclusively for religious, charitable, or educational purposes cannot maintain their tax-exempt status if they devote a "substantial" part of their activities to carrying on propaganda or otherwise attempting to influence legislation or if they intervene in any political campaign.

According to a spokesman for the Internal Revenue Service, the term *substantial* has never been precisely defined. The law in this area, he added, is "awfully cloudy." He refused to say whether the tax-exempt status of any of the Moon organizations was being investigated, noting that IRS policy forbids discussing the audit of any return. If Moon's political activity in the United States is hidden in shadows, his allegiance in South Korea is completely open. It has been apparent for several years that the multimillionaire industrialist, who has interests in gun factories, ginseng products and titanium, and pharmaceutical and stone works companies, and his cult both enjoy the special favor of the Park government.

The businesses have thrived despite strict government control of all foreign travel, foreign-exchange privileges, import licensing, and franchising. The South Korean government reportedly gave a Moon company the right to build a factory for the exclusive manufacture in South Korea of M16 rifles, under license from Colt Industries, as part of the American program of military assistance to South Korea. When asked about this contract, a spokesman for Colt confirmed that the rifle was being manufactured under license in South Korea but said that the terms of the agreement, at the insistence of the Korean government, forbade revealing the name of the Korean licensee. All Wood said was that when he was the head of the Unification church in Maryland in the early 1970s, Moon asked his group to sell shotguns door to door. One of the members then told him that she did not think that would be well received in this country, Wood said.

Although a South Korea presidential decree forbids all public political demonstrations, Moon-related groups have held a number of giant rallies, including a gathering of 1.2 million people in Seoul in 1975. Moon also operates, through the Unification church–controlled International Federation for Victory over Communism, an anticommunist indoctrination school for Korean government employees, although in South Korea the CIA is explicitly in charge of "internal propaganda and anti-Communist indoctrination."

Diplomatic Channels Used

It has been confirmed that individuals in the Unification church in the United States are able to bring money into the United States through diplomatic channels. Sank Ik Choi, a leading organizer and fundraiser for the church, told an American businessman recently that the organization was growing so fast and spending so much money in the United States that it had to bring funds in from abroad, some through diplomatic means.

According to a former embassy official, Jai Hyon Lee, at least three American secretaries in the South Korean embassy were hired in the early 1970s upon the recommendation of the Freedom Leadership Foundation, of which Moon is "founder and chairman of the board." Lee has testified that the foundation furnished the names of prospective employees at the request of the embassy's CIA agents. Moon's most direct links with the South Korean regime seem to run through Colonel Pak, Moon's translator and constant traveling companion. Colonel Pak, who spent fourteen years in the Korean army, was a military attaché in Washington. He is also founder and head of the Korean Cultural and Freedom Foundation, a Washington-based nonprofit and tax-exempt organization. Its most prominent activities are sponsorship of the Little Angels of Korea, a children's dance troupe, and of the Children's Relief Fund for needy children in Southeast Asia. Colonel Pak maintains that there are no official ties between his cultural foundation and the Unification church, except that he is currently devoting full time to working for the church and that three members of the board of his foundation are church members.

But the Little Angels, who have performed as officially endorsed representatives of the Park government, were organized by Moon, at an expense of millions of dollars, he has said, to win influence among world leaders for his movement. And in 1972 Pak filed tax-exempt income-tax returns as president of both the cultural foundation and the Unification church of McLean, Virginia. On the foundation's 1973 tax-exemption form, he stated that the organization was not "related through common membership, governing bodies, trustees, officers etc. to any other exempt or non-exempt organization," although he himself headed the Virginia church, and roughly half the foundation's board at that time was made up of church members.

Robert Roland, a United Airlines pilot and acquaintance of Colonel Pak's during the colonel's Washington days, says that the colonel told him that as assistant military attaché at the South Korean embassy, his duties were to act as a liaison between Korean intelligence and the United States intelligence agencies. At that time Pak was already a devoted Moon follower and, according to Roland, was having problems with his superiors for spending so much time working for Mr. Moon. Pak concedes he knew Roland but says that the allegation of a Korean CIA link is "absolutely false, 1,000 percent wrong."

Backing from Ambassador
In 1964, Colonel Pak left government service to establish the cultural foundation, which he says was conceived by the late President Dwight D. Eisenhower and the late Yang You Chan, a former South Korean ambassador to the United States. When Colonel Pak resigned, Yang reportedly wrote to a number of top Korean officials to the effect that the colonel could be of greater service to his country by generating goodwill and friendship with the United States through the means of a private foundation.

The first honorary chairman of the cultural foundation was Kim Jong Pil, founder of the Korean CIA, an associate of Yoshio Kodama and, from 1971 until December 1975, prime minister of South Korea. Some six years after his departure from the Korean embassy, Pak still apparently had access to the embassy's highest communications channels, according to a statement by Jai Hyon

Lee, chief cultural and information officer of the embassy from 1970 until 1973, who defected to the United States in 1973 when he could no longer support the increasing authoritarianism of the Park government. In 1970 or 1971, the Korean ambassador, Kim Dong Jo, in Lee's presence, approved the sending of a message from Colonel Pak to Seoul through a cable channel that went only to the president, the foreign minister, and the head of the Korean CIA.

A former American government official recently told the Fraser subcommittee in executive session that he had seen an intelligence report identifying Colonel Pak as one of a group of individuals, including President Park, attending a meeting in the presidential mansion in connection with raising money for a cultural foundation project, the Radio of Free Asia. Subsequently, according to this official, in October 1970, President Park sent out a letter on official Korean government stationery to at least 60,000 prominent Americans soliciting contributions for the radio project, whose Washington-produced anticommunist broadcasts were beamed to the communist nations of Asia.

The letter, which also stated that the South Korean government was leasing its broadcasting facilities to Radio of Free Asia, and the intelligence report prompted the State Department in December 1970 to ask the Justice Department to investigate whether the cultural foundation was indeed a private American organization or an agent of the Park government, and as such in violation of the Foreign Agents Registration Act, which requires all agents to register with the attorney general. The act, which imposes severe criminal sanctions for failure to comply, defines an "agent of a foreign principal" broadly to include any person who acts "at the order, request, or under the direction or control of a foreign principal or of a person any of whose activities are directly or indirectly supervised, directed, controlled, financed, or subsidized in whole or in major part by a foreign principal." It further defines as a foreign agent anyone who "engages within the United States in political activities for or in the interests of such foreign principal" or who "solicits, collects, disburses, or dispenses contributions, loans, money" for a foreign principal.

Persons engaged solely in religious pursuits are exempt from the registration requirement unless they engage in political activities, which include the dissemination of political propaganda or attempts to influence the formulation of American policy. In July 1971, in response to a State Department request, the Justice Department agreed that the evidence suggested that Radio of Free Asia was "acting under the direction of and control of the Korean Government," as the Justice Department memorandum put it, and an investigation was undertaken.

On March 16, 1972, the Justice Department advised the State Department that the "allegations could not be confirmed by competent evidence," and the case was dropped. Soon after the foundation discontinued the broadcasts from Seoul. According to a spokesman for the Justice Department, there have been no investigations of any persons or organizations connected with Moon since that incident for violations of the Foreign Agents Registration Act, and there are no reports in the files of the case directly linking Moon or Pak with President Park or any other South Korean government official.

The spokesman said he could shed no light on why the earlier investigation had been fruitless because virtually all the members of the internal security division at that time had since left the department. The Justice Department's concern about South Korean political maneuvering in the United States is currently focused not so much on Moon as on the activities of the Korean diplomatic community, which has allegedly been involved in attempts to influence American politicians and to intimidate and silence Korean émigrés who are critical of the Park regime. In summer 1974, for example, a member of the South Korean National Assembly offered, through John E. Nidecker, a presidential aide, to contribute to any congressional election campaign selected by the White House. The offer was refused, according to Nidecker, now a Washington consultant. Title 18, section 613, of the United States Criminal Code makes it a crime for any foreign national to contribute or promise to contribute to any candidate for political office in this country.

Jai Hyon Lee, a twenty-year veteran of the Korean civil service, who is now a professor of journalism at Western Illinois University, states that in the embassy in 1970 or 1971 he saw Ambassador Kim, who later became foreign minister, stuffing $100 bills into an attaché case. When asked where he was going, Kim said, "to the Capitol," according to Mr. Lee. In September 1975, the South Korean consulate in Los Angeles covertly organized a fund-raising dinner for Senator John V. Tunney, who had not been particularly sympathetic to Korean-aid bills in the past. According to a member of the California Democrat's staff, his office canceled the event when it found out the consulate was arranging it.

Chun Kang, in the consulate's cultural and information office, said that the consul general's secretary had made the arrangements for the dinner. But when asked about the affair, the secretary said that she had not arranged it, that she thought it had been arranged by the city, and that she did not remember a thing about it. Asked again, Mr. Kang said, "We don't remember who arranged it."

Key Activities in New York
Much of the Moon organization's current expenditures in this country are concentrated in New York City. The church spent more than $1 million, according to Pak, to prepare for its "God Bless America" rally in Yankee Stadium on June 1, 1976. The church also announced the purchase of the New Yorker Hotel in Manhattan for "more than $5 million." Colonel Pak confirmed that some of the money to buy the building had come from the overseas churches.

Last year Moon told Gordon that income from the worldwide churches and his many businesses amounted to $60 million. According to Pak and other Koreans here, the South Korean government now is as eager to prove that it has no connections with the Moon organization as the organization is eager to demonstrate that it is a purely spiritual movement. Pak was asked why the Korean government would take such a stance, particularly in view of the fact that, as the colonel himself conceded, the regime was pleased with the Moon movement's aggressive anticommunism. He indicated that the government did not want to antagonize the traditional Christian churches in Korea by identifying too closely with their rival. However, a former Korean embassy official, who asked to remain anonymous, said that the Korean government had been embarrassed by press hints of an affiliation between the Park regime and the church and had ordered the embassy staff to avoid overt contact with Moon associates. "It doesn't matter to Colonel Pak," he added. "He knows the ambassador is only a pygmy. He would rather deal with the president directly."

12

On the Civil Liberties
of Sect Members

Part 1   Charles C. Marson
                                    Margaret C. Crosby
                                    Alan L. Schlosser

Interest of Amicus

The American Civil Liberties Union of Northern California is the
regional affiliate of the American Civil Liberties Union, a nation-
wide, nonprofit, nonpartisan membership organization dedicated
exclusively to the defense and promotion of the guarantees of
individual liberty secured by the Constitution and Bill of Rights.
Since its inception, the ACLU has directed a substantial portion
of its litigation program toward protecting the liberties
guaranteed by the First Amendment to the United States Constitution.

The present petitions heavily implicate the First Amendment's
guarantees of freedom of religion and freedom of association. The
American Civil Liberties Union of Northern California therefore
submits this brief in the hope that it will substantially assist the
court in resolving the important constitutional issues raised by
these petitions.

Statement of Facts

Amicus hereby incorporates the factual summary set forth in
petitioners' memorandum of points and authorities in support of
their amended petition for a writ at pp. 3–16.

Argument I: The temporary conservatorship orders in the present case
violate petitioners' first amendment rights to freedom of religion and freedom
of association.

Brief of the American Civil Liberties Union of Northern California as *amicus curiae*
in support of the First Amendment Rights to Freedom of Religion and Freedom
of Association.

The petitioners before this court share a common characteristic: all five adults elected to become members of the Unification church. This affiliation—and this alone—triggered the conservatorship petitions and provided the basis for the conservatorship orders.

As the record reflects, the hearings explored the theological beliefs and daily routine of members of the Unification church. The tenets of this church may seem, to a majority of society, to petitioners' parents, or to the lower court, bizarre. The life-style adopted by members of the church—the central place of religion in their daily existence—may appear eccentric in a secular society. Nevertheless a conservatorship order may not be based on an assessment of the spiritual existence elected by these five adults. The state has no power to evaluate the wisdom of a person's religious or associational choice; and this is precisely what the court below accomplished in granting the conservatorship petitions. As the Supreme Court has stated:

The law knows no heresy, and is committed to the support of no dogma, the establishment of no sect. [Citation]. . . . Freedom of thought, which includes freedom of religious belief, is basic in a society of free men. *West Virginia State Board of Education* v. *Barnette,* 319 U.S. 624, 87 L.Ed. 1628, 63 S.Ct. 1178, 147 ALR 674. It embraces the right to maintain theories of life and of death and of the hereafter which are rank heresy to followers of the orthodox faith. Heresy trials are foreign to our Constitution. Men may believe what they cannot prove. They may not be put to the proof of their religious doctrines or beliefs. Religious experiences which are as real as life to some may be incomprehensible to others. Yet the fact that they may be beyond the ken of mortals does not mean that they can be made suspect before the law. *United States* v. *Ballard,* 322 U.S. 78, 86–87 (1943).

The conservatorship proceedings below required petitioners not only to justify their religious faith, but to prove, to the satisfaction of a secular authority, that by holding those beliefs they were not mentally incompetent. This, amicus submits, is a blatant violation of the First Amendment.[1]

Argument II: Use of the temporary conservatorship statute for mental deprogramming threatens the first amendment freedoms of all members of unconventional religious or political organization.

Although the conservatorship statute was designed as a benign, provisional remedy, a conservatorship proceeding is both long range and punitive in effect. The conservatorship hearing itself, regardless of its outcome, may be traumatic: an individual's personality and intellectual competence are subjected to extensive probe and public scrutiny.[2] Moreover the consequences of a conservatorship order are severe. A religious adherent placed under conservatorship is involuntarily confined, isolated from his spiritual community, separated from his friends, prohibited from practicing his religion, denied his right to travel, and precluded from hearing and advocating theological concepts. Finally, even after termination of the conservatorship period, the stigma of mental incompetence lingers.

If affiliation with an unconventional organization subjects an individual to this severe sanction, associational liberty is severely jeopardized. The proceedings below provide a striking illustration of this threat. The lower court consolidated the hearings on five adults—whose only common characteristics were their membership in the Unification church and their parents' disapproval of their chosen religion—and, without differentiating among them, placed them all under conservatorship. Surely, the message must have emerged that affiliation with the Unification church subjects an adult to an adjudication of mental incompetence, with a resulting stigma and deprivation of liberty. Present members must feel pressure to leave, and potential members must be discouraged from joining.[3] It is precisely this chilling effect on associational liberty that the courts have sought to avoid in protecting sensitive First Amendment rights. As the Supreme Court admonished in *N.A.A.C.P.* v. *Alabama,* 357 U.S. 449 (1958), even a benevolent state action not directed at destroying a legitimate organization might indirectly inhibit freedom of association: "In the domain of these indispensable liberties, whether of speech, press or association, the decisions of this Court recognize that abridgment of such rights, even though unintended, may inevitably follow from varied forms of governmental activity (357 U.S. at 461)."[4]

The threat to associational liberty is not limited to members of the Unification church. The conservatorship law has been used—or abused—to gain custody of members of other novel religious sects. Target groups to date include the Society for Krishna Consciousness and the Church of Scientology. Any "marginal"—*i.e.*, exotic by majoritarian standards—religious organization is in jeopardy. Moreover the use of the conservatorship law is not restricted to religious associations: the line is narrow between deprogramming religious dissidents and deprogramming political dissidents.

In short to join an unconventional organization—if one's parents disapprove—is to invite a conservatorship petition. To the less than hardy, affiliation with the unorthodox is a dangerous matter.

Conclusion

The conservatorship orders in the present case constitute a violation of the constitutional rights of petitioners and a collective indictment of the Unification church. If these orders are sustained, this court will sanction abuse of the conservatorship law for the intellectual deprogramming of dissenters in this country. The threat to religious and associational liberty is direct and frightening. Accordingly amicus urges this court to reverse the lower court and vacate the conservatorship orders issued below.

Dated: April 4, 1977

Notes

1. Amicus set forth the First Amendment prohibitions against placing religious adherents under conservatorships more fully in a brief submitted to the court below. Amicus respectfully directs this court's attention to the brief of the American Civil Liberties Union Foundation of Northern California, Inc., as amicus curiae in support of proposed conservatees filed in each of the following cases: *In the matter of Jacqueline Katz*, no. 216828; *In the matter of Barbara Lael*

Underwood, no. 217039; *In the matter of John F. Hovard, Jr.*, no. 217040; *In the matter of Leslie Brown*, no. 217041; and *In the matter of Janice L. Kaplan*, no. 217063.

2. The proceedings below illustrate this point. No fewer than two psychiatrists and two psychologists examined each of the petitioners. These four physicians testified at length regarding petitioners' personalities, intelligence, and sexuality to their parents, to the judge, to a packed courtroom, and to the press.

3. Cf. *Shelton* v. *Tucker*, 364 U.S. 479 (1960), where the Court noted that compulsory disclosure of a teacher's affiliations would cause an applicant to avoid membership in controversial organizations: "The pressure upon a teacher to avoid any ties which might displease those who control his professional destiny would be constant and heavy." 364 U.S. at 486.

4. Cf. *Bates* v. *Little Rock,* 361 U.S. 516, 523 (1960), where the Court stated: "Freedoms such as these [associational liberties] are protected not only against heavy-handed frontal attack, but also from being stifled by more subtle governmental interference." In reviewing governmental action both federal and California courts have been extremely sensitive toward potential inhibition of First Amendment rights. See, e.g., *Dombrowski* v. *Pfister,* 380 U.S. 479 (1965); *N.A.A.C.P.* v. *Button,* 371 U.S. 415 (1963); *Talley* v. *California,* 362 U.S. 60 (1960); *Sweezy* v. *New Hampshire,* 354 U.S. 234 (1957); *Dulaney* v. *Municipal Court,* 11 Cal. 3d 77 (1964); *In re Kay,* 1 Cal. 3d 930 (1970); *Huntley* v. *Public Utilities Commission,* 69 Cal. 2d 67 (1968); *Burton* v. *Municipal Court,* 68 Cal. 2d 684 (1968); *In re Berry,* 68 Cal. 2d. 137 (1968); *Alford* v. *Municipal Court,* 26 Cal. App. 3d 244 (1972).

This has been a very emotional case that's been going on in this court since March 9, and I know that all the parties who are in this courtroom are interested in what this court is going to do with the matter that has been heard these many days.

First of all, I want to thank the attorneys and those people who were in this courtroom, the petitioners and the objectors, for having conducted themselves in an orderly fashion during the very difficult days that we had here.

This case is not a criminal case, and I want to say that we have some bailiffs in the courtroom, and I want to say why. It's my observation from other times that sometimes we have a little problem in the courtroom, and I want to say that I do not expect that anything is going to happen when I make my decision, which I am about to do. I am sure that everything is going to go along smoothly, not only in the courtroom but finally as you leave the courtroom through the corridor. This is the American system of justice.

There are people who criticize the American system of justice. You know, to criticize is very easily destructive. Criticism is easily obtained from people who say this is wrong, that is wrong, but when you ask, How do I correct it and make it better? then it is very difficult because, in my humble opinion, and I am sure those attorneys who have practiced before the American judicial system over the many many years, both those attorneys in the courtroom and the others over the years, I would challenge anyone to show me a better judicial system in all the world than America has.

It is not perfect because it is tainted with the imperfections of human beings, judges included. That is the reason we have appellate courts, and that is good, because there is not one human being that is not subject to fallibility. We are all fallible, and we are all subject to erring, and that is the reason we have this great system. Sometimes people criticize it. It is slow, but justice must be that way.

And so today I am about to make a decision. One side will like it and the other side will dislike it. But I want to tell you that I have studied this case. I took voluminous notes. I lived with it, and the decision I am making now is a decision that I believe is correct. If I am in error the attorneys on either side have a right to take it up to a higher court, which I think they will, and I think it is only right that they should , because I am just a judge sitting in the superior court, and we have to test this case. It is unprecedented.

I have researched the law, and with the exception of very few instances, there is nothing to give me a guiding light showing me which way to go. So in my opinion it is a case of first impression, and I welcome any appeal from the decision of this court, because I feel that in this field of law it is necessary that we have higher judicial authority study it because it involves many, many facets of the law. It is not a simple case. As I said, we are talking about the very essence of life here: mother, father, and children. There is nothing closer in our civilization. This is the essence of civilization.

The family unit is a microcivilization. That is what it is. A great civilization is made of many, many great families, and that is what is before this court. It is not the regular run-of-the-mill case that involves some money or some kind of damage. It is the very essence of life. I have researched the law. I have studied the case. I have listened attentively to the witnesses and to the arguments, and I am about to make my decision. When I make the decision, I am going to read it as to each party in the action, that is, the five different matters that were consolidated, heard together. And so the decision is as follows:

The petition of Raymond Underwood for temporary letters of

conservatorship of the person of Barbara Underwood is hereby ordered granted.

The petition of Doctor Thomas A. Brown for the temporary letters of conservatorship of the person of Leslie Brown is hereby ordered granted.

The petition of John F. Hovard for the temporary letters of conservatorship of the person of John F. Hovard, Jr., is hereby ordered granted.

The petition of Beatrice Kaplan for temporary letters of conservatorship of the person of Janice L. Kaplan is hereby ordered granted.

The petition of Carl L. and Louise A. Katz for the temporary letters of conservatorship of the person of Jacqueline E. Katz is hereby ordered granted.

All letters of conservatorship above ordered are for a period of thirty days, commencing on Monday, March 28, 1977. That is the order of this court.

Mr. Goorjian: Your Honor, you have already given us the period of time to go up on appeal. I assume that they are not under any restraint through Monday? I believe my days are wrong. Am I correct as to that?

The Court: The thirty-day period commences, as I indicated, on Monday, March 28, 1977. If there is some argument now that either side wants to propose to the court on when the parents will be entitled to take their children into their custody, you can argue that point right now.

Mr. Goorjian: May I make a showing, your Honor?

The Court: Very well.

Mr. Goorjian: As you are aware, I represent the five children, and I should request within your order which you just announced that certain restrictions be placed. I would request that as part of this order in light of the testimony that came in that the parents not be allowed during these thirty days to turn the five children over to any deprogrammers.

Mr. Underwood—what he wanted was thirty days for his daughter, Barbara, to get away from everybody. And I think that could be contained in your order. There should be a restriction in that order that the parents are allowed to take their son or daughter wherever they want but that they are not to be turned over to the deprogrammers.

As a further request in this, over the period of these two weeks these five people have just become more than just clients. They are people who are very close to me. I request that they be allowed at any time during the thirty days to contact me, talk to me. I am not talking about talking with anybody from the Unification church but to me personally. And further, that I be allowed to contact them and talk to them to see if they are being mistreated over the thirty-day period of the temporary conservatorship.

I further request that during these—I am not even sure what date it is, I guess it is next Monday—that the five individuals not be treated as if they are in a conservatorship and have access at the very minimum to counsel, and what I really request is whoever they want to talk to.

And further, since we have had a lot of testimony in this case, that what is involved is the religious freedom or the religious beliefs of these five individuals, and they, as a matter of our United States Constitution, should have access to their religious tenets and be allowed to practice these religious tenets, and they should have access to the elders of their church at such time as is convenient to the elders and to the five persons involved, because if we have—if they are denied this, then they are being denied their right to exercise their freedom of religion, which is guaranteed under our Constitution.

What I am asking you for is a restraint in your order. Please do not turn them over to the wolves. That is what I am asking. That is what I am asking you.

I am asking that I have contact with them during the whole thirty-day period so that I can see from at least their veiwpoint as it now stands that they are not being mistreated and that they be allowed to exercise their freedom of religion during these thirty days.

And finally I specifically request that at the end of thirty days, no matter what document comes before this court, that this court order all of them to be back in this court so you can see them, Thank you, your Honor.

The Court: All right Mr. Shapiro.

Mr. Shapiro: Your Honor, may I just respond briefly? First, as far as the last suggestion of Mr. Goorjian, I wholeheartedly join in it, and I am sure every parent whom I represent is prepared to come back into this court with his child or her child on a date close to the thirty-day period as the court calendar provides. I think that they owe it to themselves and to you and to their children to come back and report to you as to what has happened during that thirty-day period, and we agree without reservations.

The second thing insofar as what Mr. Goorjian said: I would like to point out that these young people are presently being entrusted to their parents. I know of no greater love in any area of life, be it animal or man, which exceeds the love of a parent for a child. In many ways it exceeds the love of a husband toward a wife and vice versa. I know of no parent who willfully subjects his child to any pain or suffering except in rare instances of psychotic people who need medical help. And you have seen these people.

I would tell this court that two of these fathers have already sworn in independent areas to uphold the Constitution—and they are officers of the court—with the dignity and the justice that this court has shown in this case. That is the two lawyers. One of the parents is a doctor. I can conceive of no justification or suspicion that this doctor is going to subject his daughter whom he loves so much that he is prepared and has given his time and his evergy and his strength to try to help her. He is not going to hurt her. This is not to deprecate the other parents whom I have not identified, because I know their love is equally great, and I know that we have a tendency sometimes to think of professional people as unloving, but they are not.

I do think these parents can be entrusted to the care of these young people, and these young people can safely be entrusted to the care of their parents and conservators. I have full respect—as you have probably noticed from my conduct in this case—I have full respect for the wisdom of this court. And on behalf of the people whom I represent, we feel that no court could have granted us a more complete and fair and unrestricted hearing and given it more consisderation and come to a decision, without being pressured by the pressures that might have otherwise been operative. So we are deeply grateful for just the way you have conducted this trial.

We are prepared to accept whatever you say. If you want to trust the parents, I can assure you that the parents will live up to your faith. But if you feel that you want to add something either orally or in writing, we are prepared to go ahead and abide by the decision, whatever it is, whatever way it goes.

I think, however, that one of the things that is involved is that there has been so much trauma, so much emotion, that the quicker this matter is resolved, the better everybody will be. And I think that the order should take place; this should take effect now. I think that it should not be the matter of discussion any more.

The finality, which is the crux of judicial wisdom, should now be applied, and a date thirty days from Monday should be selected as the hearing date for a review as to what has happened; the letters, the temporary letters, will expire after the thirty-day period unless the court extends them or unless permanent letters are granted.

But I think that for the benefit of everybody, the children should become part of the conservatorship by making the letters at this time.

Thank you, Judge, again, on behalf of my clients, not just for the decision—I never thank a judge for his decision—but I want to thank you personally because I think I have had enough experience to know good administration of justice, to tell you that I think it has been an excellent job, well done. And I would tell you either way the course went, that I appreciate personally on behalf of my co-counsel, on behalf of my clients the way you have handled this case.

The Court: Is there anything further?

Mr. Goorjian: Only that Mr. Shapiro is much more eloquent than I, and I would enjoin in what he just said and just request that you do stay this matter for the four or five days indicated to allow us to review it. And I would request again that your order contain the restrictions with the reservations I requested.

The Court: The reason I made it effective on the twenty-eighth is to permit you to take any action you feel appropriate under the circumstances. That gives you until Monday; then the order goes into effect. But I am ordering the immediate turnover of the children to the parents at this time. But they are not to be taken any place out of the jurisdiction of this court until you have the opportunity to take the action you feel appropriate in the upper courts.

The rest is as follows: All right, I will permit the attorneys to contact their clients. That is their right. I am not going to curtail it. The conservatees will have the right to communicate with their lawyers during this period of time. The conservators are to be with the conservatees at all times. That is, the parents are to be with their children at all times here.

One of the reasons that I made this decision is I could see the love here of a parent for his child, and I do not even have to go beyond that. Even our laws of this state, the probate laws have all been set up—the laws of succession, children succeed to the estate of their parents if the parents die intestate. So the law looks at that binding thing between a parent and a child. It is never ending. No matter how old we are, it is there. And that was one of the things that influenced this court. And in this era—I am not saying what is going to happen in thirty days.

I am going to give you a date. I want to look at the case. I want to see that everything is carried out for the benefit of the conservatees and the conservators during this period of time.

So now we will give you the date when you are to return. Then we will make some further conditions on how this is to be carried out thirty days hence.

We said this matter would go into effect as to where the parents want to take them, out of the jurisdiction of this court, on March 28, 1977, and I have put a time on it. That will be at 5 P.M. I would ask counsel for the petitioner here to prepare a formal order on this . . .

Mr. Shapiro: —I will—

The Court: . . . in this accord and submit it to opposing counsel for approval as to form before the court formally signs it.

Now the thirty-day period would then—we have three days left in March, and then we go twenty-seven days into April, is that right?

Have we got a date there, Mr. Flanagan, around the twenty-seventh of April?

The Clerk: April 27 is open, your Honor.

The Court: Starting at what, 10:30?

The Clerk: 10:30, your Honor.

The Court: 10:30, that is the date when all parties in this action will be ordered without further notice to appear in this court unless there is some indication to the contrary that you need not appear, and that would be by formal order of the court. So that will be that portion of the order. We said April 27 at 10:30 A.M.?

The Clerk: Correct, your Honor.

The Court: All five parties are ordered to return to this court along with the conservators, the conservatees, and the conservators.

Now there was another request by Mr. Goorjian about religious practice. I have no objection, and it is entirely up to the conservatees, all these fine young people, to make their own decision on that.

However, I am leaving it entirely up to the parents. I cannot make unreasonable restrictions on the parents. They are in charge of their children. And these are adults, but as I said before, a child is a child even though the parent may be ninety and the child is sixty. They are still mother and child, father and child. The parents are still in charge, and they are to work for the benefit of their children. If the children want some religious exposure, they are to grant it to them as reasonable parents should, but I am not making any specific conditions that would in any way restrict the conservators in this instance.

Mr. Baker: Your Honor, on that one point, since the allegation has been that they want them to make a free decision, embodied in that is that they should be able to look at both sides, and I think they should be able to request religious material, the Bible and other things to compare. This should not just be a one-sided situation. I think that is what Mr. Goorjian was setting forth. If they want something on Buddha or Christian Scientists, they should be able to get reading material. I do not think they should be bombarded with just one side here, and I think the whole spectrum—and I do not think your Honor would be going afield afar if they want certain material—they are not going to jail. Even in jail they give them material, whatever they want to read—and I think that would be a reasonable request on their part, your Honor. If they want certain materials, certain books, they should be able to read that and obtain it.

The Court: All right.

Mr. Shapiro: I am sure, your Honor, no parent that I represent in this case or any other case would deny his child anything to read if that child, no matter what age, wanted it. I would have no . . .

Mr. Baker: —well—

Mr. Shapiro: . . . if these people—and I speak for these parents, because in many ways I can relate to them—and I am satisfied that without an order these parents will each and every one of them respect the wishes of their children to have anything they want to read, to study.

Mr. Baker: And will Mr. Shapiro stipulate to that?

Mr. Shapiro: I will stipulate on behalf of these people that they are going to protect these children with their lives as they have done with their time and money and with their principles, and I know that.

The Court: All right. That is a stipulation.

Mr. Baker: All right, we will accept that. Thank you.

The Court: Now what else is before the court? Is there anything else?

Mr. Goorjian: The other thing was that they not be turned over to deprogrammers, your Honor.

The Court: I am not making any restraints on that. It is within the conditions of the conservators to take whatever appropriate action they feel is in the best interests of their children, and I am not permitting any restraints. But I am making the one condition here that they are to be present with their children, either one parent or the other, or both, at all times, because I feel that the parent loves his offspring to such an extent that the parent would lay down his life for his child.

I am sure they would. That is a true parent. And I do not think they are going to permit their son or daughter—there is only one son here, but there are daughters here—that they would not put them in a position that they would not want to be in themselves.

At the outset, the court wishes to commend both defense counsel and the district attorney's office on their obviously assiduous labors in the preparation of their memoranda of law and legal arguments based thereon.

Under indictment number 2012/76, the grand jury accused the defendants, Angus Murphy and Iskcon, Inc., of acting in concert to commit the crimes of (1) attempted grand larceny in the first degree, in that on or about April 12, 1976, they did attempt to steal from Eli Shapiro property, namely, money by extortion, by instilling fear in Eli Shapiro that physical injury would be caused to his son, Edward Shapiro, in the future, and (2) the crime of unlawful imprisonment in the first degree, in that between May 1973 and September 7, 1976, they did restrain the afore-mentioned Edward Shapiro under circumstances that exposed the said Edward Shapiro to a risk of serious physical injury.

Under indictment number 2114/76, the Grand Jury indicted the defendants, Harold Conley, a/k/a Trai Das, and Iskcon, Inc., for the crime of unlawful imprisonment in the first degree, in that on or about and between August 3, 1976, and September 7, 1976, the said defendants while acting in concert did restrain one, Merylee Kreshour, under circumstances that exposed her to a risk of serious physical injury.

It is noted that the grand jury's initial investigation, which commenced on September 7, 1976, was on the complaint of Merylee Kreshour alleging that she was kidnapped—not by the named defendants herein—but rather by her mother, Edith Kreshour, and one Galen Kelly. The uncontradicted testimony adduced in respect thereto shows that Merylee Kreshour (who at the time was and to the present day remains a member of Iskcon, Inc.) was forcibly taken from a street in Queens County on August 3, 1976, by her mother and others and for a period of four days was subjected to a treatment referred to as "deprogramming." This treatment, the mother testified, was administered in order to liberate her daughter's mind and to restore her "free will." The mother testified further that her daughter was the victim of "mental kidnapping" by the defendant Iskcon, Inc. and that by physically taking her daughter into custody she was "rescuing her."

On September 8, 1976, the grand jury voted not to indict either Galen Kelly or Edith Kreshour and instructed the district attorney's office to continue its investigation into any alleged illegal activities of the said Iskcon, Inc.

Thereafter numerous witnesses, comprised of experts in the fields of psychiatry, medicine, social work, and religion and also parents and relatives of former members of the defendant corporation, as well as former members themselves, appeared and testified before the grand jury. As a result thereof, the grand jury returned the two instant indictments that are the subject of this motion.

The defendant Iskcon, Inc. is a nonprofit religious corporation, a legal entity by virtue of the issuance of a certificate of incorporation for the International Society for Krishna Consciousness pursuant to the Religious Corporations Law of the State of New York (Religious Corporations Law, Book 50). The defendant Harold Conley was the supervisor of women at the New York Temple for the International Society for Krishna Consciousness (Iskcon, Inc.). The defendant Angus Murphy was president of the New York Temple.

Merylee Kreshour became interested in the Hare Krishna cult during the summer of 1974 while working as a secretary before returning to college in September. After going to meetings she decided to join the organization and moved into the temple. Her average day started before 4 o'clock by praying, studying, meditating, and chanting until about 8:30 A.M. when breakfast was served. The chanting lasted two to three hours each day, consisting of repeating the Hare Krishna mantra meditation continuously. In order to keep track of the chanting, each time a chant is finished a bead is moved from a strand of 108 beads worn around the neck. After breakfast the day's activities began with Merylee leaving the temple to distribute Krishna literature, sell magazines, and solicit contributions. Lunch was served at 3:30 P.M. and consisted of fruit, vegetables, and juice. She had two meals a day and went to sleep at 7:30 P.M. The money she received from selling books and literature, as well as the donations, were turned over to the treasury of the organization, and in return she was provided food, clothing, and shelter.

Edward Shapiro became interested in the cult when he was in high school, and during the first year of college he became an active member. However he did not live in a temple because he is a diabetic, requiring daily insulin and a special diet, which does not conform to the religious beliefs of the Krishna organization. He ultimately left college and started living at a temple. On April 12, 1976, Edward returned from a pilgrimage to India. His father went to Kennedy Airport to greet him when he returned from India, and it was obvious to his father as a medical doctor that his son needed immediate medical attention. He wanted Edward to have a checkup, but his son said he would not talk to his father unless his father wrote out a check for $20,000 to the president of the New York temple, otherwise he would have nothing to do with his father.

Based on the aforestated facts, the defendants were charged, as heretofore recited, with the crime of unlawful imprisonment in the first degree, in that they restrained the said Merylee Kreshour and Edward Shapiro under circumstances that exposed them to a risk of serious physical injury and, further, the defendants, Angus Murphy and Iskcon, Inc., were charged with attempted grand larceny in the first degree.

In reference to the charge of unlawful imprisonment, section 135.10 of the penal law provides as follows: "A person is guilty of unlawful imprisonment in the first degree when he restrains another person under circumstances which expose the latter to a risk of serious physical injury."

The two elements of this crime are the restraint of another person, thereby exposing such person to a risk of serious physical injury. The term *restrain* is defined in section 135.00 of the penal law as restricting a person's movements intentionally and unlawfully in a manner as to interfere substantially with such person's liberty by moving him from one place to another, or by confining him either in the place where restriction commences or to a place to which he has been moved, without consent, and with knowledge that the restriction is unlawful. A person is so moved or confined "without consent" when it is accomplished by "(a) physical force, intimidation or deception or, (b) any means whatever, including acquiescence of the victim, if he is a child less than sixteen years old or an incompetent person and the parent, guardian or other person or institution having lawful control or custody of him has not acquiesced in the movement or confinement."

It is conceded by the people that no physical force was utilized by the defendants against Merylee Kreshour or Edward Shapiro, and, further, that the said two individuals entered the Hare Krishna movement voluntarily and submitted themselves to the regimen, rules, and regulations of said so-called Hare Krishna religion, and it is also conceded that the alleged victims were not in any way physically restrained from leaving the defendant organization. However it is posited by the people that the nature and quality of the consent of the two alleged victims must be examined as it is asserted by the people that such consent was obtained by deception, and by the device of intimidation, control, and the continued restraint was maintained over them. From this premise the people draw the conclusion that the two alleged victims were deceived or inveigled into submitting themselves "unknowingly to techniques intended to subject their will to that of the defendants . . ." and that same resulted in ". . . an evil consequence. . . ." The entire crux of the argument propounded by the people is that through "mind control," "brainwashing," and/or "manipulation of mental processes" the defendants destroyed the free will of the alleged victims, obtaining over the mind control to the point of absolute domination and thereby coming within the purview of the issue of unlawful imprisonment.

It appears to the court that the people rest their case on an erroneous minor premise to arrive at a fallacious conclusion. The record is devoid of one specific allegation of a misrepresentation or act of deception on the party of any defendant. Concededly both Merylee Kreshour and Edward Shapiro entered the Hare Krishna movement voluntarily where they remain to this day as devotees of that religion. There is not an iota of evidence even to suggest that false promises were made to either of them or to indicate any act or conduct on that part of the defendants that might be construed as deceptive.

As to the premise posed by the people that the religious rituals, daily activities, and teachings of the Hare Krishna religion constitute a form of intimidation to maintain restraint over the two alleged victims, the court finds not only no legal foundation or precedent for same but a concept that is fraught with danger in its potential for utilization in the suppression—if not outright destruction—of our citizens' right to pursue, join, and practice the religion of their choice, free from a government-created, -controlled, or -dominated religion, as such right is inviolately protected under the First Amendment to the Constitution of the United States and article 1, section 3 of the New York State Constitution.

It is at this juncture the court sounds the dire caveat to prosecutional agencies throughout the length and breadth of our great nation that all of the rights of all our people so dearly gained and provided for, under the Constitution of the United States and the constitutions of all states of our nation, shall be zealously protected to the full extent of the law. The entire and basic issue before this court is whether the two alleged victims in this case, and the defendants, will be allowed to practice the religion of their choice, and this must be answered with a resounding affirmation. The First Amendment to the United States Constitution prohibits the establishment of religion by our federal legislators. Neither congress nor the states may establish a religion or compel individuals to favor one religion over the other. This precept was set forth by the forefathers of our country in the most explicit and unequivocal language in the articles in addition to and in amendment of the Constitution of the United States. In Amendment I it is mandated that "Congress shall make no law respecting an establishment of religion, or prohibiting the free exercise thereof."

We are given further guidance by the provision of the constitution of the state of New York that confirms, enhances, and elaborates upon this cherished right. Article 1, section 3, provides:

The free exercise and enjoyment of religious profession and worship, without discrimination or preference, shall forever be allowed in this state to all mankind; and no person shall be rendered incompetent to be a witness on account of his opinion on matters of religious belief; but the liberty of conscience hereby secured shall not be so construed as to excuse acts of licentiousness, or justify practices inconsistent with the peace or safety of this state.

Our country is a pluralistic society in religion. The First Amendment of the Constitution of the United States lays the foundation of the full play and interplay of all faiths. The freedom of religion is not to be abridged because it is unconventional in its beliefs and practices, or because it is approved or disapproved of by the mainstream of society or more conventional religions. Without this proliferation and freedom to follow the dictates of ones own conscience in his search for and approach to God, the freedom of religion will be a meaningless right as provided for in the Constitution.

Any attempt, be it circuitous, direct, well intentioned or not, presents a clear and present danger to this most fundamental, basic, and eternally needed rights of our citizens—freedom of religion.

The Hare Krishna religion is a bona fide religion, with roots in India that go back thousands of years. It behooved Merylee Kreshour and Edward Shapiro to follow the tenets of that faith, and their inalienable right to do so will not be trammeled upon. The separation of church and state must be maintained. We are, and must remain, a nation of laws, not of men. The presentment and indictment by the grand jury herein was in direct and blatant violation of defendants' constitutional rights.

The giving up of one's worldly possessions, social contacts, and former way of life—and the court clearly recognizes and sympathizes with the resultant hurt, fear, and loneliness of loved ones left behind—is not a matter under the present facts to be subject to judicial scrutiny by way of the invocation of criminal prosecution. Other than showing that Merylee Kreshour, Edward Shapiro, and others subjected themselves to the discipline and regimentation of this particular legally licensed, religious group, whereby they are apparently seeking their individual self-chosen road to eternal salvation, there was not a scintilla of evidence presented to the grand jury to indicate the practice of fraud, deception, intimidation, or restraint, physical or otherwise, on the part of these defendants. Religious proselytizing and the recruitment of and maintenance of belief through a strict regimen, meditation, chanting, self-denial, and the communication of other religious teachings cannot under our laws—as presently enacted—be construed as criminal in nature and serve as a basis for a criminal indictment.

The court points out that the numerous and well-documented cases cited by the people do, in fact, show, and correctly so, that "physical restraint" need not be shown as a basis for prosecution herein, but that the unlawful restraint may be accomplished by "inveiglement" (former penal law, 1909) or by a "fraudulent misrepresentation" that could constitute "deception negating consent." Succinctly stated in one case a victim was induced to leave New York for Panama on the promise of a job as a governess when in fact while enroute the victim learned the job was with a house of prostitution (*People* v. *DeLeon*, 109 N.Y. 226). In another case, the complainants were induced to enter defendant's car upon the fraudulent representation that they were needed as babysitters, when in fact the defendant wanted to engage in indecent sexual advances (*State of North Carolina* v. *Gough*, 125 S.E.2d 118). A third case involves the inducement of the victim to enter a wooded area upon the representation they would search for squirrels, when in fact it was defendant's purpose to assault the complainant (*State of North Carolina* v. *Murphy*, 184 S.E.2d 845).

The further cases cited in the people's memorandum involve psychologically induced confessions, mental disease or defect, hypnosis to destroy a free will, intoxication, and coverture. However in every case cited the criminal intent was shown, by the proof adduced therein, of the defendants seeking to compel their victims to perform some illegal act and that same was accomplished by false representations. In the case at hand, neither of these elements is present.

The final thrust of the people's argument aims at the unlawful restraint of an individual who has been declared incompetent and, therefore, by law the consent of the parent or guardian must be obtained, as set forth in subdivision (1) of section 135.00 of the penal law. In the case of Edward Shapiro, a Massachusetts court issued an order appointing Mrs. Shapiro as conservator of his property. There is a serious issue as to whether under the United States Constitution full faith and credit would be given to our sister state's aforesaid order. This question is moot, however, in view of the court's finding that the order does not come within the purview of our statute—as same merely appoints a conservator of the property rather than a guardian of his person.

To sustain this indictment would open the so-called Pandora's box to a plethora of unjustified investigations, accusations, and prosecutions that would go on ad infinitum, to the detriment of the citizens of our state and placing in jeopardy our federal and state constitutions.

The concept of mind control or brainwashing is not a crime in and of itself. The fact that indoctrination and constant chanting may be used as a defense mechanism to ward off what another person is saying or doing is devastating, and it is equally devastating when used as a technique for brainwashing or mind control. It may even destroy healthy brain cells. It may also cause an inability to think, to be reasonable or logical. However this does not constitute a crime. Neither brainwashing nor mind control per se is a crime. It cannot be used as the basis for making out the elements of the crimes charged herein.

The court finds that as to both indictments, numbered 2012/76 and 2114/76, there is insufficient legal evidence to sustain the offenses charged or any lesser included offense.

Based on the foregoing, the motions to inspect the grand jury minutes and to dismiss the indictments on the ground of insufficient legal evidence are granted. The balance of these motions is denied as moot. The indictments are hereby dismissed.

Order entered accordingly.

The clerk of the court is directed to mail a copy of this decision and the order thereon to the attorneys for the defendants.

IV

The Psychology and
Sociology of
Sun Myung Moon

13

Moon Madness: C. Daniel Batson
Greed or Creed?

A psychological war is being waged for the control of the minds of thousands of young people, and psychologists are not even on the sidelines. The battlegrounds are the several "psychoreligious" cults that have appeared in recent years, promising joy and meaning while demanding total allegiance in return. Characteristic of these cults, and the largest among them, is the Reverend Sun Myung Moon's Unification church, which claims 500,000 to two million members worldwide, and a following of from 10,000 to 30,000 in the United States. Of these only about 2,000 to 10,000 could be considered full-time members. Most are between the ages of eighteen and thirty. While not yet large, the group has grown rapidly. A self-styled evangelist from South Korea, Reverend Moon began his ministry in the United States in 1970 with only a few hundred followers.

Moon's teachings are a complex potpourri of orthodox Christianity, dialectic philosophy, anticommunism, and apparent egomania, but his basic message is clear. "I am a thinker, and I am your brain"; "What I wish must be your wish"; "The whole of humanity is to be as one perfect person. . . . If too much stress is placed on individualism, then collective virtues are lost. . . . If an individual cannot recognize that he is responsible to the public he can never find a happy place where he can live in harmony with others"; "The family is the fundamental unit of society."

From C. Daniel Batson, "Moon Madness: Greed or Creed?" *APA Monitor* 1976, 1: 32–35. Copyright 1976 by the American Psychological Association. Reprinted by permission.

It is necessary to give one's of individual self into the collective self of "God's family on earth." Moon serves as the head of that family. His followers, as children, are expected to be appropriately subservient; he in turn cares for them with parental love. His family offers friendship and a sense of belonging; freedom from competition for grades, jobs, and success; and strict guidelines for appropriate behavior that absolve responsibility for deciding what to do about sex and drugs. Berkeley Rice (*Psychology Today*, January 1976) contends that "Moon's Family offers the security of perennial childhood." Converts call it a source of personal meaning, happiness, and "greatest joy."

Moon's followers are taught to be energetic and effective proselytizers who make contacts with young people on street corners or college campuses. The initial contact typically ends with an invitation to a meeting at the nearest Unification church center. At this meeting, and at subsequent meetings and dinners at the center, the potential convert is surrounded by the warmth and friendship of the family. Soon he or she is invited to participate in a weekend workshop. These highly structured workshops include long hours of theological discussion based on Moon's teachings. There is little time for sleep and no time for private reflection. In small groups potential converts are encouraged to bare their souls and are presented with testimonials about the joy, peace, purpose, and love to be found in the family.

Before the weekend is over, commitment to a week-long workshop is sought. About one-fourth of the weekend participants agree. At the long workshop, the tempo escalates; training becomes more rigorous and "hard sell," regimentation more severe. Bombarded, allowed little sleep, and cut off from family and former friends, the participants are pressured at the end of the week to commit themselves to full-time membership. About half agree to further involvement, although many do not become full-time members, which would require giving up job and/or school.

Full-time members move into a local commune or to the church's headquarters at Barrytown, New York. Most sever all

contacts with family and former friends; many give all possessions to the church. Full-time members devote themselves to
study, prayer, fellowship, solicitation of funds, and proselytizing.
Men and women are carefully segregated to prevent temptation.
The church supplies all the individual's needs, including food,
clothing, and medicine. Moon even makes the final decision
about marriage partners, often pairing individuals completely
unknown to each other.

Many parents and traditional church leaders cry "brainwashing!" or "mind control!" Attempting to fight fire with fire,
"deprogramming often involves hours of intense questioning and
challenging before the person breaks and renounces the church."
In the words of a successfully deprogrammed ex-member, "They
. . . showed me how the church had twisted the Bible around. I
finally opened my mind and admitted I was wrong. That was the
hardest thing to face." Those who do not break during deprogramming describe the process quite differently. Said one church
member, "You are forced to sit and listen and repeat what they
say. They'll keep you there for however long it takes. It's so
obvious to me who's wrong."

In February 1976, more than 14,000 persons from Kansas and
surrounding states petitioned Senator Robert Dole (R-Kan.) to
hold a meeting. They were concerned that cults such as the
Unification church were entrapping unsuspecting youths and
domineering them to the point that they were not only rejecting
community values but were actually becoming subversive to the
American government. When Senator Dole scheduled the
meeting, more than 300 people representing groups from all over
the country jammed a Senate caucus room in an effort to persuade government officials to investigate the Unification church
and similar cults.

The director of Citizens Engaged in Reuniting Families, Rabbi
Maurice Davis of White Plains, New York, stated, "The last time
I ever witnessed a movement that had these characteristics—with
a single authoritarian head, fanatical followers, absolute
unlimited funds, hatred for everyone on the outside and suspicion

against the rest—was the Nazi Youth Movement, and I tell you I am scared." A psychiatric social worker called the Moon movement one of the "extremely important mental health considerations of the time," claiming that she had seen more than 150 young people who had left the movement and that "50 percent were schizophrenic or had borderline psychosis," which she presumed resulted from their indoctrination. While opposition was directed primarily at the Unification church, interest was also expressed in destroying the 5,000 other cults said to exist in the United States. Opponents felt that all cults employed psychological brainwashing to recruit members.

For the most part mainstream psychology has treated the Unification church and the other psychoreligious cults with amused neglect. Such a reaction is perhaps understandable, for emotions are high on both sides, extreme and unfounded statements are frequent, and few people are asking for data. If they were, psychologists would be hard pressed to respond. Are people being brainwashed? By whom? The persuasion techniques used on both sides of the indoctrination-deprogramming issue are certainly manipulative. But what are the necessary conditions for brainwashing or mind control? To date psychological research has been limited to postdictive speculation based on the reports of those who have undergone brainwashing.

Psychological theory can, perhaps, suggest why some of the techniques employed by both proselytizers and deprogrammers work. One finds in Moon the strong father image Freud led us to expect in successful religious movements. Moon's followers frequently speak of the conflict-resolving and identity-forming qualities of their conversions. They claim that their new spiritual insight allows personal, social, and even universal integration and identity. Erik Erikson suggested that religion could do as much. The arduous initiation and continuous personal sacrifice probably arouse cognitive dissonance. This dissonance may be reduced by enhancing the value of the group and the faith. Acting on one's beliefs by proselytizing, soliciting, public prayer, and so forth, further solidifies commitment. Social reinforcers are carefully manipulated; both proselytizers and deprogrammers isolate their subject from outside social supports while lavishing support from the desired reference group. Ethnocentric, we-they thinking is fostered, and the motives of the outgroups are impugned.

While each of the above explanations fits, each is also postdictive. They involve rather glib armchiar psychologizing. The truth is that we know very little about the psychological dynamics of religious conversion or about the effects of religious commitment on thought and behavior. In spite of the immense importance of religion in the lives of millions of people, psychologists have tended to treat religion as a vestige of prescientific civilization soon to disappear and therefore not worthy of consideration. The general attitude of most psychologists toward religion might be summarized by the one-liner, "A man without religion is like a fish without a bicycle."

There are some signs that this attitude may be changing. A new division of the American Psychological Association was established in January, 1975. Psychologists Interested in Religious Issues (division 36). Over 500 psychologists have already indicated an interest in joining. This division has set as its task the definition of, and reflection upon, issues that lie at the intersection of religion and psychology. But research as well as reflection is needed. It is too soon to tell whether this division will be able to stimulate serious research on the psychological effects of religious commitment.

In his APA presidential address last August (*American Psychologist*, December 1975), Donald Campbell challenged psychology as a whole to be more open-minded in considering the social and psychological impact of religious moralizing. He suggested that psychologists' tendency to celebrate personal freedom and to see repression and inhibition of individual impulse as undesirable, guilt as neurotic, and dutiful allegiance to higher authority as enslavement is no more scientifically based than the religionists' preaching that the individual must submit to higher authority and that self-indulgence, pride, greed, and lust must be curbed. Indeed Campbell argued that religion has the data on its side. Employing a social-evolutionary analysis, he contended that the pervasiveness of religion in modern societies suggests that it has definite survival value for a culture.

Campbell's argument, admittedly speculative, points to a potential value conflict for any psychologist examining religion. As it has developed, psychology has tended to absolutize the individual and the individual's need, even right, for free expression of selfish survival instincts. In contrast, as is dramatically illustrated by the Moon quotations, religion tends to have a group focus. Religion teaches conformity, obedience, and submission of individual desire to a larger purpose. Campbell implies that psychology's neglect of, or outright hostility toward, religion may in fact result from the threats that religion poses to the psychologist's unexamined value presuppositions.

By ignoring religion, psychologists may be overlooking more than an important variable in human behavior. Religion, especially psychoreligious cults like the Unification church, may provide psychology with a context in which to study the psychological effects of totalitarian social control. Since the classic Rogers-Skinner debates and before, psychology has toyed with the dilemma of individual freedom versus social control. Intrigued by social engineering but worried about the psychological effects of a religious social structure, we wish for data. We would love to be able to interview, give questionnaires to, and observe the behavior of Frazier and his cohorts at Walden Two or the citizens of the People's Republic of China. But both are inaccessible, for different reasons. And ethical considerations prevent us from creating a mind-controlling social environment simply for research purposes.

Religion may provide the answer. The recent development of psychoreligious cults offers a good opportunity to study the psychological impact of a deindividualizing social system. Whether ethical or not, religious cults have been experimenting with life-changing social control for some time. Techniques such as those described by Donald Campbell in his *American Psychologist* article,

"Reforms as Experiments," could be used to provide data on the psychological effects of the experience. Virtually every religious group claims to improve the psychological state and behavior of followers. With some ingenuity it might be possible to examine the perceived happiness, behavior patterns, cognitive style, conformity to authority, and so forth displayed by cult members.

The conflict between personal freedom and social control is almost certainly one that will assume increasing importance in psychology in future years. Currently this battle of psychological values is being waged between converts to psychoreligious cults like the Unification church and their parents. The converts willingly surrender personal freedom for the security, purpose, and community of the church. They relinquish their minds and claim to have found the "greatest joy." Parents claim the right and responsibility to liberate them from this "joy," by deprogramming if necessary. Psychology has been provided with a living laboratory.

14

**The Pull of
Sun Moon**

Berkeley Rice

This Tuesday evening, June 26, 1976, God willing and perhaps helping, the Reverend Sun Myung Moon will join such illustrious ancestors as Babe Ruth, Joe Louis, Johnny Unitas, Pope Paul VI, and Billy Graham as a featured performer at Yankee Stadium. Over the past few weeks New Yorkers have grown accustomed to Moon's face smiling at them from thousands of leaflets handed out by cheerful young Moonies. The leaflets, posters, and radio and television ads invite everyone to attend Moon's Bicentennial God Bless America Festival. Moon hopes to draw 200,000 people to the stadium (even though it will hold only 60,000). Those who get in will be treated to a rousing revival meeting with classical fan dances by the Korean Folk Ballet, inspiring songs by Moon's New Hope Singers, and a lengthy, energetic speech in Korean by Moon. The leaders of Moon's Unification church say the rally will promote the spiritual significance of the bicentennial and help "restore confidence in the American dream." It will also celebrate the Second Coming of the millionaire evangelist who proclaims himself to be the new messiah.

In a country whose young tripped out on radical politics or drugs in the 1960's, religious cults seem to be the opiate of the 1970s. Several are prospering, but Sun Moon's Unification church is by far the hottest—and most controversial. It now claims 30,000 followers and 5,000 members, has fund-raising and recruiting centers at a hundred American cities and college campuses, and takes in more than $10 million a year in donations and sales from solicitations.

To many anguished parents who have lost their children to him, however, this new messiah is a spiritual fraud, a devil who enslaves young Americans by means of brainwashing and mind control. Parents have tried to rescue or kidnap their sons and daughters from his communes, but often the kids cannot be found or refuse to come home.

The Moon phenomenon, his Moonies, and the controversy they have caused are exemplified by the struggle of Mr. and Mrs. Elton Helander, of Guilford, Connecticut, who have been fighting the church since their daughter Wendy joined it two years ago at age eighteen. Until then Wendy has led a well-rounded and unremarkable life. She was pretty, healthy, and bright enough to complete high school in three and a half years, with time to spare for cheerleading, skiing, and sewing. "She had so much to offer," says her mother, "and her morals were so good. She was dead set against drugs and sex and anything like that." As a college freshman she seemed a bit "confused" to her mother, perhaps because she became interested in such exotic notions as meditation and Eastern philosophy. Wendy later described herself that fall as an idealist who was troubled by the suffering and violence in the world and was searching for a "meaningful life."

Approached by Moon's campus recruiters, Wendy attended a Unification weekend in Maine, where the members "radiated so much love, so much warmth" that she soon decided her search had ended. She called her mother breathlessly to ask if she had heard the "good news." "What good news?" asked Mrs. Helander. "That there is a new messiah on this earth," said Wendy. When she came home at Christmas, her mother found her troubled: "She cried a good deal of the time, and yet she was telling me how happy she was." About that time Wendy gave away many of her cherished possessions to fellow members of what she began calling "the family." She dropped out of college, joining the church as a full-time member.

"I never had any questions," she said later. "It all made sense." It did not make sense to her parents, and eventually they abducted her from a church center and had her deprogrammed by Ted Patrick, a man who specializes in such treatment, to cure her of Moon's spell. It did not work. She left home soon after, taking only a toothbrush, and returned to the fold. "I think the poor kid was afraid," said her mother. "They had her mind all along."

The Helanders brought suit against the Unification church, which refused even to produce Wendy in court, saying she would suffer a "trauma." At the trial her lawyer argued that Wendy had not been brainwashed and was not under the church's control. "Her big crime," he told the court, "has been believing what she chooses to believe." Both sides produced members or ex-members who testified about their independence or lack of it. Both sides produced psychiatrists who argued about the state of Wendy's mind. The judge finally dismissed the case, ruling that the parents had not proved the church had exercised "control or restraint over her person."

The trial left no one happy. Mrs. Helander said, "Our daughter is not our daughter any more." Wendy said she still loved her parents but no longer trusted them. She was right. Last fall, while visiting Wendy at a church training center, her parents took her for a walk near a back road. A car pulled up, and Wendy was shoved in and driven away. She was held captive for about three months, moved frequently to avoid detection, and continually deprogrammed. One of those who worked on her, however, was actually a Moonie. With his help they both escaped and returned to the church. The Helanders have not seen or heard from Wendy since, and the affair has left them emotionally and financially devastated. "We were such a quiet, happy family before this happened," says Mrs. Helander, "but it's ruined our lives." They have spent close to $40,000 on legal fees, deprogramming, and other costs and are heavily in debt. Yet they have not given up hope: "All we want for our daughter is her freedom. We've got to save her mind." Wendy does not want to be "saved" but still hopes for an eventual reconciliation if her parents are "ready to accept the fact that this is where I want to be."

In cases like Wendy's, it is not easy to tell the good guys from the bad. Do good guys kidnap? Or bad guys rescue? Or do both do both? Both sides claim to have truth, justice, and love on their side. Whoever is right, thousands of young Americans like Wendy have left their homes, schools, and jobs to join Moon's crusade. Hundreds of parents like the Helanders have formed a national organization to fight the church and free their children from its control. And the church in turn has counterattacked, trying to achieve respectability through community goodwill and political influence.

To improve its image, Sun Moon's church hired Burson-Marstellar, the same public relations firm that has done work for Exxon and General Motors. (The relationship has since ended, in part because the firm began to worry about how the account might affect its own image.) And it makes great efforts to win friends in Washington. Groups of Moonies walk the halls of Capitol Hill offering tea and flowers to congressmen and trying to engage them in chats about God and his purpose in America. With bipartisan agility Moon has had his picture taken (and used repeatedly in church publications) with such senators as Hubert Humphrey, Edward Kennedy, Strom Thurmond, and James Buckley. With the enthusiastic support of Congressman Richard Ichord, former chairman of the Internal Security Committee, Moon recently presented a speech, "God's Plan for America," in the House caucus room. (Perhaps the congressmen should listen. Moon once told a group of trainees, "If the United States continues its corruption, and we find among the Senators and Congressmen no one useful for our purposes, we can make Senators and Congressmen out of our members.")

The church operates a political affiliate in Washington, the Freedom Leadership Foundation, which lobbies for U.S. military and economic support for South Korea; hence some critics suspect that Moon's movement is directed or subsidized by the

South Korean CIA, a charge the church denies. It is interesting, however, that two of Moon's closest aides are former Korean army colonels who served as military attachés in the South Korean embassy in Washington. Indeed a House committee held hearings in July 1976 on possible attempts by South Korea to influence American politics through the Moon movement.

Because of complaints about the Unification church's interest in politics and its emphasis on fund raising, various federal, state, and local government agencies have begun questioning its claim to be a religious movement. The Internal Revenue Service has not taken action against it—on complaints about its $10 million income-tax exemption—but the U.S. Immigration Service has; it has ordered the deportation of 600 Moonies, mostly from Japan, for illegal soliciting. Their visas had been granted for "religious education and training," but the Immigration official in charge of the case subsequently found little evidence of formal religious education: "As nearly as we can determine, their 'training' consists of soliciting funds and selling some items."

As part of its campaign to gain respectability, the church has spawned several quasi-academic organizations ostensibly devoted to the search for world peace and freedom. Though they are said to be independent, these groups generally share the leadership of Sun Moon and other church officials. One group, the International Cultural Foundation, held its annual conference on "the unity of the sciences" in fall 1976 at New York's Waldorf Astoria, drawing several hundred scientists and scholars, including a few Nobel laureates. While anti-Moon parents picketed outside with placards comparing Moon to Hitler and Mussolini, the scholars debated "the standard of values in society." The letters of invitation—offering to pay all expenses, plus $3,000 for cochairmen—failed to mention that the affair was sponsored by the Unification church or that Sun Moon would give the opening address. When they learned of Moon's involvement, many of those invited—including Buckminster Fuller, Norman Cousins, and several others who had agreed to serve as advisers for the conference—withdrew.

Yet not everyone feels an aversion to Sun Moon. Many parents either approve of or do not mind their children's joining his cult. Some think it is better than drugs or drifting aimlessly around the country. Others look with favor upon it as a Christian youth movement. While church members accept Moon's theology as revealed truth, nonmembers generally find it a mind-boggling mixture of pentecostal Christianity, Eastern mysticism, anticommunism, pop psychology, and metaphysics. According to *Divine Principle*, Moon's book of revelations, God intended Adam and Eve to marry and have perfect children, thereby establishing the kingdom of heaven on earth. But Satan, embodied in the snake, seduced Eve, who in turn passed her impurity on to Adam, bringing about the Fall of Man. God then sent Jesus to redeem mankind from sin, but Jesus also bungled his mission and died before he could marry and father a new race of perfect children. The time has now come for a second Christ, who will finally fulfill God's original plan. The Unification church coyly refuses to identify the new messiah, but like Moon, he just happens to have been born in Korea in 1920.

As told by Moon, and embellished in successive accounts by his disciples, the story of his life presents impressive qualifications for the position of messiah. "From childhood I was clairvoyant," he once told a group of followers. "I could see through people, see their spirits." When he was twelve, he began praying for "extraordinary things" and must have caught God's attention. At sixteen, while he was praying on a mountainside on Easter morning, Jesus appeared to him in a vision and called upon him to carry out his unfinished task.

After further visionary chats with Moses, Buddha, and assorted biblical luminaries, Moon began preaching his own version of messianic Christianity. In 1954, self-ordained, he founded the Holy Spirit Association for the Unification of World Christianity. As his cult grew, Moon ran afoul of the civil and religious authorities, a pattern that continues to plague him in the United States. He was excommunicated by his own Presbyterian church and arrested various times by the police: for anticommunist activities, according to Moon; and on morals charges, according to his Korean critics, because of "purification" rites with female initiates.

Moon's church has thrived under the military dictatorship of South Korea's General Park Chung Hee. While the Park regime has suppressed, jailed, or exiled hundreds of critics, particularly among the clergy, it has formed a friendly association with the Unification church. Moon preaches anticommunism and holds mass rallies in support of the government; Park extends various forms of official support, sending senior civil servants and military officers to Unification "leadership seminars," for example. A man of many parts, Moon has managed to divert enough attention from spiritual affairs to build an industrial conglomerate in Korea with sales of $15 million a year, drawing in part on the voluntary labor of his Korean followers. Moon's factories produce heavy machinery, titanium, paint, pharmaceuticals, marble bases, shotguns, and ginseng tea.

Since moving to the United States in 1973, the short, stocky, moonfaced evangelist, now fifty-six, has settled with his wife, eight children, and a staff of thirty-five Moonies in a twenty-five-room mansion overlooking the Hudson River in Irvington, New York. When not looking after his religious and corporate affairs, he spends a good deal of time fishing on his fifty-foot cabin cruiser, New Hope. Church officials bristle at criticism of Moon's luxuries. "Why must a religious leader be an ascetic?" asks one. "Look at the pope," says another. "Followers of many religions honor their spiritual leader with physical comforts worthy of the dignity of his position. I trust Reverend Moon's relationship with God, so I do not object to his life-style."

Though Moon takes little part in the church's day-to-day operations and meets only occasionally with its leaders, he supposedly approves all major decisions himself. "What he says goes!" says a nonmember who has dealt with the movement's top officials. At his rare public appearances, Moon is usually introduced by Unification's president, Neil Salonen, thirty-one, a smooth speaker who tells audiences that the United States is going to hell because of crime, suicide, alcoholism, divorce, sex, drug abuse, college radicals, and communists. He says God has sent Moon to the United States to solve these problems and to "mobilize an ideological army of young people to unite the world in a new age of faith."

Because Moon addresses his American followers only in Korean, outsiders cannot appreciate his charisma. His speeches often run two hours or longer and are full of hellfire and Korean brimstone punctuated with kicks, karate chops, laughter, and tears. (One reporter calls the performance a "kung fu tantrum.") Through his translator, a former South Korean army colonel named Pak Bo Hi, Moon tells his audiences of the approaching Apocalypse and offers them one last chance for salvation: "You can be the citizens of the kingdom of heaven if you meet the coming messiah. He is your hope . . . and the only hope of America and this world."

In fall 1975, I observed Moon at a sunrise service at Belvedere, the church's magnificent $850,000 estate in Tarrytown, New York. By 6 A.M. Moon was speaking to about 500 young members who had come up by church buses from New York City. Shivering in the predawn chill, they listened, seemingly captivated. When Moon laughed, they smiled. When he yelled, they stared back in awed silence. When he finished, an associate led the audience in a fifteen-minute prayer in which he asked repeatedly if they were willing to sacrifice themselves for the church. To each question they responded in unison, "Yes, Father." I thought they meant God.

After the service Moon marched up to the top of the hill overlooking the Hudson, circled by a phalanx of husky bodyguards and followed by the members. There he stood on what members call "the Holy Rock." With the rising sun just shining on his head—a setting and timing obviously choreographed with considerable care—everyone sang a church hymn, "Shining Fatherland." Moon then gave a ten-minute prayer in Korean, during which I caught the phrase "Yankee Stadium" several times.

Later as Moon talked with church officials inside the mansion,

I noticed a Korean identified as Colonel Han—"He used to be with the embassy in Washington"—giving orders with military crispness. Another fellow, in a blue uniform, turned out to be Spiro, the captain of Moon's yacht. As Moon prepared to leave, his party moved with the precision of Secret Servicemen escorting the president. Moon's bodyguards communicated by means of tiny wrist transmitters and earphones, saluting him as he climbed into his black limousine. As he sped away, they jumped into another limousine and followed.

When I returned to the Holy Rock, I found about twenty Moonies kneeling around it, praying aloud, some sobbing with fervor. Some jerked spasmodically in spiritual transport, crying out, "Father, of Father, please help us." By then I was no longer sure whether they were praying to God or Moon. To understand such devotion, one must follow the process by which the Unification church recruits and trains its members. Wherever the clean-cut, smiling Moonies can find them—on city streets or college campuses—they engage young Americans in discussions of the state of the country or of their souls. Many Americans are anxious to talk. As one church official told me, "There are a lot of lonely people walking around."

The discussions always end with an invitation to attend an introductory lecture at the nearest Unification center. The recruiters rarely mention the church or Moon; they usually say they belong to a Christian youth group. At college campuses the movement recruits through such church-controlled groups as New Education Development or the Collegiate Association for the Research of Principles. Whatever the name, the lecture introduces potential recruits to the basics of Unification theology. After the lecture come invitations to other lectures and dinners at the local center. Along with dinner comes a diet of relentlessly hearty friendship from the brothers and sisters of what soon becomes "the family."

The next stop for potential converts is a weekend workshop at a secluded retreat. An exhausting and rigid schedule leaves little time for sleep and none for private reflection. Recruits get a daily dose of six to eight hours of mind-numbing theology based on Moon's *Divine Principle.* By the final lecture they learn that God has sent Sun Myung Moon to save the world in general and them in particular. The rest of the days are filled with group activities: discussions, calisthenics, meals, sports, and singing and praying, generally starting at dawn and lasting well past midnight. In the evenings the Moonies give testimony of how they have found peace, purpose, love, and joy in the family. Never left alone, recruits are encouraged to pour out their hearts to their new friends, who offer continuous attention and comfort. The weekend ends with a hard-sell pitch for commitment to the next stage in the conversion process, a week-long seminar devoted to more of the same. About one in four recruits makes the step.

In the Northeast the church's training headquarters is situated in upstate New York in Barrytown, on a 250-acre former Christian Brothers monastery purchased for $1.5 million. Indoctrination at Barrytown becomes more rigorous and life more spartan than that of the West Point cadets just down the river. The lecture, discussions, calisthenics, singing, and prayer last from dawn until past midnight. There is neither time nor opportunity for phoning or writing relatives or friends.

At the end of the week comes the pressure to join the movement as full-time members. The recruits reach this moment of decision worn out from lack of sleep, numbed by the endless lectures, cut off from family and friends, and softened up by the embracing warmth of the group. "It was like being taken care of," one ex-convert recalls. "The people were very friendly, and you really thought they did love you." Another ex-Moonie remembers how "everybody was reinforcing each other all the time, and you just began to feel high. After seven days of fatiguing your body and manipulating your mind, they hook you, and you stay on."

Many Moonies are ready for such commitment and need little pressure. "I've been looking for something like this for years," one told me. "It answers all the questions I was asking." An ex-Moonie who had spent eight months in the movement said: "I'll tell you what attracted me. I saw people who looked happy at a time when I felt lonely and desperate. I had no idea what to do with my life, and they had a purpose." About half of those who complete the week-long seminar join the movement. Some join as followers, remaining at their jobs or at school and working evenings or weekends on church projects. Some contribute part of their salaries. Those who join as full-time members either move into a local center or stay on at Barrytown for increasingly intense seminars lasting from three weeks to four months.

During their first few months in the movement, new members often get phone calls or letters from distraught parents and friends, urging them to drop out or at least to come home and talk it all over. One who refused told his parents: "At least I believe in something." Those who waver are often told that their parents or others who oppose the church are acting on behalf of Satan. An evening of intense prayer and guidance generally brings such wayward sheep back to the fold. A few do drop out but only after strenuous objections from their group leaders. Doubters are told that Satan has invaded their minds and that they will lose their souls if they leave the church.

Once they move in, new members often give what possessions they have to the church. They no longer need money anyway. The church takes care of all their daily needs, from toothpaste to trousers. Directors of the larger centers sometimes buy up cheap lots of nearly identical clothing for their resident members, thereby increasing the degree to which Moonies tend to look as though they were cloned rather than recruited.

For those afraid of the outside world, unwilling or unable to face the frustrations of living on their own, life in a Moonie commune offers a welcome refuge: no drugs, no drinks, no sex, no money, no problems, no choices, no decisions. From the team leaders' cheerful "rise and shine" at 5:30 to the last group songs and prayers at midnight, Moonies rarely have to think for themselves. Full of fervor they follow orders and perform their assigned chores with gusto. Those who observe Moonies closely often notice a glassy look that, combined with everlasting smiles, makes them resemble tripped-out freaks and gives rise to rumors that the church drugs them. Although some of the glassiness probably results from a lack of sleep, many Moonies really are on a high—but they are tripping out on faith and devotion, not drugs.

Most parents find that hard to believe. They also have trouble understanding the church's puritan attitudes toward sex, which govern every minute of its members' lives. During a tour of Barrytown with Michael Warder, a thirty-year-old Stanford graduate who serves as director of training, I asked why all activities there and at local church centers were so carefully segregated by sex. "That way, everyone feels more comfortable in their study and in their search for the truth," Warder replied. "As soon as they're mixed together, you find the boys and girls begin thinking about other things. We feel there's too much permissive sex and promiscuity today."

Even if they were in favor of sex, the Moonies would scarcely have time for it. They put in grueling dawn-to-dusk days recruiting and fund raising. They peddle candles, peanuts, dried flowers. Some work in pairs at street corners or shopping plazas; others go out in teams selling door to door in suburbs. They rarely mention the church or Sun Moon. They are polite but persistent. When asked what they are raising money for, they give vague or misleading answers like "Christian youth work" or "drug-abuse program."

Fund-raising leaders send their troops off in the morning with songs, prayers, and pep talks, encouraging competition among one another and with other teams. Stoked up like marine recruits for a bayonet drill, the Moonies hustle for the Lord with a fervor no profit motive could inspire. Those who fail to meet a respectable daily quota often spend the evening praying for God's help the following day. The average Moonie takes in about $50 to $200 a day; the more successful can make up to $500. Every penny is turned over to the team leader, who turns it over to the church.

Except for the spartan food, clothing, and shelter provided for its members, the church invests most of its funds in real estate. It owns property in many states, including more than $15 million worth in New York alone. In May 1976 Unification agreed to pay more than $5 million for the forty-two-story, 2,000-room New Yorker Hotel to use for its world headquarters. As an investor in real estate, the church has a significant advantage over commercial competitors: its religious status exempts it from property taxes, and most of the repairs, renovations, and maintenance on the buildings are performed free by willing Moonies (critics call it "slave labor").

The New York City Tax Commission is questioning the Unification church's right to its tax exemption, and other challenges are being made to its legitimacy as a religious movement. The New York State Board of Regents has held up recognition of the church's new seminary at Barrytown. The New York City Council of Chruches has rejected Unification's request for membership, in part because of Moon's claims that he is the new messiah and that Christ failed in his mission. "They call themselves a church," says one council leader, "but they do not act like one, particularly in the matter of individual freedom and the alleged incarceration of young people."

Under the leadership of Rabbi Maurice Davis of White Plains, the national organization that has been formed of parents who have lost their children tries to locate them through the network of ex-members. If the parents wish, the organization puts them in touch with professional deprogrammers, like Ted Patrick, who may try to rescue the children for fees that can run several thousand dollars. The deprogramming can be more brutal than any brainwashing the church may practice. Rabbi Davis warns parents that such attempts may be illegal and dangerous. "And if it doesn't work," he tells them, "you may lose your child." But for those like Wendy Helander's parents, who feel they have already lost their children, the warning seems meaningless.

Rabbi Davis and others who have studied the movement say that what happens to the young Moonies follows the classic pattern of brainwashing. They are isolated from past and outside contacts; worn down physically, mentally, and emotionally; surrounded with new instant comrades and a new authority figure; and finally programmed with new beliefs and pressured into total commitment. "I am your brain," Moon has told them. "What I wish must be your wish." But while total conversion to the church may require or cause the suspension of one's critical faculties and while one may well question the independence of a true convert's mind, no one has proved that the church holds its members against their will.

Perhaps the Unification church has been criticized unfairly for doing much of what established religions have been doing for years. For example, suppose I described a church that has amassed great wealth and property in this country through charitable donations and profitable investments; a church whose leader lives in splendor while young novitiates live in ascetic communes, cut off from family and friends, leading lives of absolute devotion to the church and absolute obedience to its authority. Would this description not fit the Catholic church as well as that of Sun Moon?

Unification's leaders distinguish their movement from other cults by stressing their concern about crime, drugs, alcohol, and other social ills. But none of the recruits I saw looked like ex-junkies, and most come from middle-class homes rather than crime-ridden ghettos. For all its talk about social problems, the church runs no programs aimed at solving them and devotes almost no effort to helping nonmembers. Most of its resources are directed inward, producing more money and more members, who in turn will recruit more members and raise more money. When I asked one church official how these efforts would benefit society, he replied, "We can change the world by changing men's hearts." When I countered that such a policy would solve society's problems only if everyone joined the movement, he smiled.

Obviously everyone is not joining the Unification church. Through a process of self-selection, Moon's movement seems to attract only youths already seeking some form of commitment. Many have been drifting from cults to communes for years, sampling the spiritual fare like diners at a smorgasbord. The church may be capitalizing on their loneliness, but it can hardly be blamed for their vulnerability.

While critics describe the movement as authoritarian, the church leaders prefer to call their approach "loving and parental." I think both descriptions may be accurate. To thousands of young Americans threatened or frustrated by the prospect of adulthood, Moon's family offers the security of perennial childhood. To lonely young people drifting thorugh cold, impersonal cities and schools, it offers instant friendship and communion, a sense of belonging. To those troubled by drugs, sex, or materialism, the church offers a drugless, sexless world of ascetic puritanism. To those hungering for truth and meaning in a complex world, it offers purpose and direction. In exchange for their labor and devotion, Moon gives them a life of love, joy, and inner peace, with no problems, no doubts, and no decisions. Critics call that exploitation, but the Moonies consider it a bargain.

15

**The Eclipse of
Sun Myung Moon**

Chris Welles

Sun Myung Moon's quizzical countenance is still being plastered on thousands of billboards. His speeches are still being reprinted in big newspaper ads. The media are still obsessed with his apparent power to "brainwash" thousands of young followers into blindly devoting their lives to him. An article entitled "How Sun Myung Moon Lures America's Children" in the September 1976 *McCall's* calls Moon's Unification church "by far the most successful of the religious cults that have become so prominent and perplexing a feature of the American '70's." In fact, however, a two-month investigation into the structure and finances of Moon's cult reveals that it is dying.

In contrast to official estimates of 30,000, the actual number of confirmed American members is only about 2,000. Moon's energetic campaign to recruit new members has been a dismal failure, and to the intense dismay of church officials, the Unification church has shown no membership growth since 1974. Despite a goal of 200,000, only about 25,000 people attended Moon's Yankee Stadium rally in June 1976, fewer than those who showed up for his Madison Square Garden rally in 1974. Most were curiosity seekers attracted by the free entertainment, and many left before Moon finished his hour-long speech. To ensure a respectable turnout at Moon's Washington Monument weekend rally scheduled for September 1976, the church spent $1.5 million on weeks of media ads, a fleet of a thousand buses to bring people in from surrounding states, and the promise of fireworks billed as "the most spectacular aerial display ever." But despite this effort church leaders had long since been forced to abandon Moon's onetime goal of 500,000 and a traffic jam that would completely tie up Washington. Also abandoned was a national tour of speeches and banquets once scheduled for fall 1976.

So abundant is the evidence of Moon's eclipse that one must wonder whether he ever had power and influence even remotely resembling that which has been widely attributed to him. According to James Gannon, who produced an NBC documentary on Moon, the Unification church is "a potential threat to our government and our way of life." That Sun Myung Moon could be a menace to anybody except the tiny number of young people unfortunate enough to have been caught up in his cause is, more than anything, a product of media exaggeration. Moon's political activities have been almost totally unsuccessful. Cadres of female lobbyists in Washington have had no discernible effect on the legislative process. In contrast to Moon's political zenith—a 1974 White House private audience with Richard Nixon occasioned by Moon's shrewd support of Nixon during the Watergate crisis— the Ford administration showed no interest in Moon. Senator Robert Dole, Ford's 1976 running mate, led a widely publicized anti-Moon meeting last February, and President Carter has continued his predecessor's indifference. As a result of press reports of Moon's ties with the Korean CIA and his brainwashing tactics, legislators who once willingly allowed themselves to be photographed with Moon now shun contact. Moreover the Unification Church is now being investigated by Congress, the Justice Department, the Labor Department, the Internal Revenue Service, the Federal Reserve Board, the comptroller of the currency, and the Federal Trade Commission. In addition the Immigration and Naturalization Service is moving to deport 700 foreign Moonies for visa violations.

Hearings by the House Subcommittee on International Organizations, which has been looking into Moon, were scheduled for September 1976, and for the first time the subcommittee has been granted subpoena power to conduct its inquiry. The realization of such long-promised plans as Sun Myung Moon University, to be built on church land near Tarrytown, New York, and a daily newspaper to be published in an old candy factory in Long Island City seems far away. Moon's theology—a dense blend of evangelical Christianity and Oriental shamanism that features a titanic, Armageddon-like battle between God and Satan, and Moon's eventual enthronement as the new messiah—has attracted negligible adherence or interest beyond hard-core church members.

In this litany of failure, however, there is a startling exception: despite its small membership, the Unification church seems to enjoy extensive financial resources. Attention has been focused on the church's multi-million-dollar holdings of real estate, including the former New Yorker Hotel, the former Columbia University Club, and 350 acres of land in and around Tarrytown. Most of this property, though, is heavily mortgaged. Much more significant is the church's surprisingly high income, perhaps as much as $25 million a year and maybe even higher. With seeming ease the church manages to support its members, conduct elaborate rallies and public-relations campaigns, employ high-priced legal assistance, and still enable Moon and his family to live in baronial splendor on a twenty-five-acre, $625,000 estate in Irvington, New York.

As an officially designated tax-exempt, nonprofit religious organization, the Unification church is under no requirement to release financial figures, not even to the IRS, and it guards such data closely. The best available evidence suggests, however, that even after meeting expenses, the church may be accumulating excess cash running into many millions of dollars a year. Where this money comes from and where it goes has become the major area of speculation among Moon watchers and investigators. Money and power tend to flow together. If one can determine how and why the money moves, the answers to just what Moon is up to, who (if anyone) controls him, why his church is declining, and whether his plans to revive it will succeed come sharply into focus.

Where Does the Money Come from?
The Overseas Connection

Various hypotheses suggest that Moon is obtaining his financing from overseas sources, principally his Korean business empire, the Korean CIA, and powerful Japanese ultrarightist businessmen. Upon examination, though, none of these theories holds up. Moon's Korean businesses are simply too small. Moon, his church, and various church members own or control five Korean companies, notably II Hwa Pharmaceutical Company, which makes ginseng tea, and Ton II Industry Company, which, curiously for a church concern, makes rifles, air rifles, and components for M16 rifles. In 1975 these concerns had reported sales of $15.5 million and profits on only $2 million. Together they have 2,200 employees, mostly church members, and a net worth under $10 million. They could not begin to supply important financing for Moon's church in the United States.

Suspicions of contributions from the Korean CIA derive mainly from Moon's vigorous support of the despotic Park Chung Hee regime in South Korea and from vague KCIA associations of some Moon supporters, such as chief translator and confidant Colonel Pak Bo Hi. Given the KCIA's pervasive power in Korea, the Unification church would have difficulty surviving without the approval of it and the Park regime. Park apparently permits Moon to operate as a quid pro quo for Moon's support of Park in the United States, whose military and economic aid is vital for the Park regime's own survival. Because of Moon's rather meager influence in the United States, though, Moon's support is hardly critical to Park. As a fanatical megalomaniac, in the view of many Americans, Moon is less a likely Park puppet than an embarrassment to Park, and Park has acted to distance himself from Moon. He recently rejected Moon's plans to build a large headquarters near Seoul. If anything, Moon may have to pay off the KCIA instead of the other way around.

Just as Moon has diligently strived to obtain Park's allegiance, so also has he worked to develop associations with ultrarightist Japanese businessmen. Because of their numerous business ties with Korea, they are anxious to be friendly with anyone who seems to enjoy Park Chung Hee's approval. Thus some of them have helped Moon. But as far as can be established, their aid has been only nominal. Further, Moon's philosophy has never been very successful in Buddhist and Shintoist Japan, where Christianity is not well established and Koreans are subject to considerable racial discrimination. Moon's Japanese church is incapable of acting as a prime financial source. There is really no need for it or any of the other alleged overseas connections to do so. The American Unification church produces more than enough money all by itself.

The American Connection

Though Sun Myung Moon's Unification church has been a political and spiritual failure in the United States, it has paradoxically proved a resounding financial success. Despite its spiritual pretensions, the church's chief energies are devoted to generating money and recruiting more members to generate more money. It has evolved less into a religious sect than into an enormously profitable tax-exempt panhandling business, one that thrives despite systematic misrepresentation to donors, illegal trespassing, and violation of solicitation and immigration laws.

The church's financial success did not come quickly or easily. Moon's decision to concentrate on the United States in pursuit of his lifelong quest for power and wealth through religion came after he had failed in that goal in Korea. Moon founded the Unification church in Seoul in 1954. But for many years he was just one of many self-proclaimed messiahs and cultists who flourish in Korea, and he managed initially to garner only a few hundred loyalists. Later, as the Korean economy recovered spectacularly from the ravages of the 1950s war, Moon after numerous failures managed to assemble a marginally profitable group of business concerns to finance his church and provide employment for its members. But even today his Korean membership, now in the thousands, is still drawn principally from the poorer classes.

It was apparently clear to Moon in the late 1950s that Korea lacked the potential to provide him with sufficient financial resources with which to construct a power base. Hoping that it might prove a more fertile battleground for the war against Satan, Moon in 1959 dispatched to the United States Young Oon Kim, an English-speaking former university professor and one of his most loyal converts. By 1970 Kim had assembled about 500 members organized as a rather loosely connected network of state satellites. The branches were self-supporting, often independently incorporated, and quite autonomous of the national headquarters. This system reflected the philosophy of Young Oon Kim and of W. Farley Jones, a young Princeton graduate whom Kim had recruited as national president. To Kim, an intellectual who some members feel has an even deeper grasp of Moon's *Divine Principle* than Moon himself, local autonomy engendered creativity and flexibility and permitted members to develop their own individuality.

Whatever its spiritual benefits, the early church was a financial disaster. Attracted to the sect as much for religious as for psychological reasons, few state leaders had much appetite for or interest in finances or bookkeeping. Typically spending more than they were able to take in, most were unable to meet demands from the national headquarters for regular tithes, at one point $70 per member per month. Many state groups fell deeply into debt and in some cases were left to flounder.

In late 1971 Sun Myung Moon himself came to the United States to take charge. He had become distressed over the poor progress of the American church, but he was even more concerned over his operations in Japan and Korea. In Japan the church faced insurmountable political, racial, and religious obstacles; in Korea he remained at the mercy of the Park government and the KCIA. In the United States, in contrast, the First Amendment guaranteed him freedom from government interference. Korea's long history as a friendly ally and the establishment of Christianity as the dominant religion suggested at least a predisposition of Americans to be sympathetic to his cause.

Within months after his arrival, Moon began making sweeping changes. He castigated Young Oon Kim and Farley Jones for their lax, overly permissive approach and replaced Farley Jones with Neil Salonen, a smoothly articulate, ambitious former Dale Carnegie group leader. Moon instituted a much more disciplined and tightly organized structure that replaced local autonomy with strong national control. The church's finances were centralized in Washington. States were sent elaborate directives on how to keep their books and were ordered to make regular reports to Washington.

The change in philosophy was quickly echoed by Moon's aides. "I used to think that to restore the world you needed love and truth," Kenneth Sudo, director of the church's Barrytown, New York, training center, remarked to an associate. Now I think you need money and manpower." To mobilize the manpower in order to produce the money, Moon and his advisers in 1972 developed what would become the instrument for the church's financial success: the mobile fund-raising team (MFT), a group of five to eight members who travel in a van and raise money by selling such products as candy and flowers. That the MFT was a powerfully lucrative device was spectacularly demonstrated in mid-1972. To make the $250,000 down payment for the purchase of the Belvedere property in Tarrytown, formerly the estate of Seagram's Samuel Bronfman, which was to serve as Moon's personal residence (it is now a training center), Moon organized the church's first nationally directed fund-raising drive. In just forty days several MFTs, assisted by state organizations, managed to sell some 200,000 candles produced by church candle factories. Manufactured at a cost of forty cents each, the candles were sold for two dollars. The states did well. But the return from the MFTs surpassed all expectations. A sufficiently instructed, motivated, and supplied MFT, after meeting expenses, could return to national headquarters profits of close to $100 per member per day.

The MFTs soon replaced the state groups as Moon's chief money-making mechanism. Yet important shifts in tactics were necessary to hone the MFTs to peak efficiency. The initial emphasis on candles and geraniums has given way to more salable and easily obtainable products such as flowers and candy. The church now buys millions of dollars' worth of roses and carnations. Costing as little as six cents each, the flowers are usually sold for a dollar. Boxes of mints purchased by the truckload from Delson Candy Company in Englewood, New Jersey, for thirty-seven cents each are sold for two dollars.

The MFTs have redirected their selling from private homes to shopping-center parking lots and most recently to such facilities as stores, office buildings, and factories. Factory night shifts are especially lucrative. Because of numerous arrests and fines for illegal solicitation, the church has been making token efforts to obtain permits, but it has done nothing to curb illegal trespassing, even on military bases. It merely avoids establishments that have strict rules against soliciting. Nor does the church bother about misrepresentation: MFT fund raisers seldom identify themselves as Unification church members. "If you take money from someone," says former Moonie Cynthia Slaughter, "you are laying the foundation for their restoration to the Kingdom of Heaven even if they do not know where the money is going."

To maintain high productivity, precise dollar goals are regularly established by national headquarters leaders. The extent to which they achieve those goals, MFT members are told, directly determines their standing within the church and their closeness to Moon. Other inducements include contests, with signed pictures of Moon as prizes. Most of the winners are women, who are much more productive fund raisers than men. Handling the volume of cash that MFTs and other fund raisers generate has been a problem. Petty thievery at the local level has been serious. To funnel the cash to national headquarters as quickly as possible, MFTs must now take the day's earnings to a local bank where it is wired to central church bank accounts (the main one is at Chemical Bank in New York City). And to keep MFT leaders honest, Japanese female members—whom Moon regards as the most scrupulously trustworthy and who are regularly used to spy on local groups—are assigned to MFTs to serve as bookkeepers or "team mothers."

Even allowing for some pilferage, the take from the MFTs is substantial. Some 800 MTS members are currently in the field. They work perhaps 300 days a year and average about $150 a day in sales. Most MFTs, whose members sleep in vans or out of doors and eat frugally, after paying expenses, including product cost, manage to send to New York about 60 percent of their gross income (and some have exceeded 90 percent). If these numbers are accurate, the Unification church's gross from the MFTs is well over $20 million a year. Subtracting a national budget of $12 million, the church may be accumulating a net of as much as $10 million a year.

In spite of these gains, the church from time to time has considered replacing street selling as the chief money-generating device with more formal businesses, such as those it owns in Korea. A few member-operated ventures have been organized. Though Moon has failed in his effort to make ginseng tea as popular in the United States as Coca-Cola, the church runs a ginseng store on Queens Boulevard. Some state organizations operate small retail facilities such as restaurant and gasoline stations. By far the largest group of legitimate concerns is operated by the Bay Area branch, which conducts a successful hotel-and-store-cleaning business. Yet since 1974, the church has done little to expand these business activities. One of the problems is that state members seldom possess the expertise to run a successful business. Moreover the church risks losing control of members who are engaged in their own businesses. "The Unification church," says former Moonie Allen Tate Wood, "thrives on the army psychology of the faceless automaton who sacrifices every ounce of his blood. If he gets into a really creative job, where he is working and competing with people not in the church, it is a very dangerous psychological situation for the church."

But the main reason that church officials have lost interest in legitimate businesses is that the profit is simply too low compared to that gained from selling flowers and candy. No ginseng-tea house, no laundromat, they know, can immediately begin generating $100 per day per employee with a negligible capital expenditure and a return on sales of 60 percent. Like any other businessman thirsting after a fast buck, Moon simply allocates his manpower resources where the money return is highest. Moon seems to figure that the more money he can grab away from Satan's world in a hurry, the better off God—and he—will be.

Where Does the Money Go?

Several possibilities for the disposition of the Unification church's burgeoning excess wealth present themselves: The first is real estate. Moon's numerous acquisitions of property have been the most visible of the church's assets. Church officials value its property holdings in the United States, mainly in and around New York City, San Francisco, and Los Angeles, at $24 million. The church's actual equity in real estate, though, is a good deal less, probably well under $10 million. The reason is that nearly all its properties are encumbered by a large amount of debt. In June 1976, for instance, the church paid $5.6 million for the New Yorker Hotel to serve as its "world mission" center. Equitable Life Assurance Society now holds a mortgage from the church for $3.6 million. When Moon paid $1.2 million in 1975 for the former Columbia University Club in New York City for his national headquarters, he put up only $300,000 in cash. He borrowed the rest from the club's former owners, the trustees of Columbia University, who almost rejected the loan because of the church's highly leveraged condition.

Though Moon's church has become a substantial property owner, it is apparently unwilling to tie up in real estate any more than the smallest possbile amount of actual cash. The official explanation is, of course, spiritual. "It's a blessing to someone if we're in debt to them," says a former Moonie. "It means they are connected up to the Messiah." Another explanation is that borrowing reduces exposure to loss if something should go wrong.

Another possibility for using the money is corporate investments. Ever since reports of the church's wealth first appeared in the press, the church predictably has been besieged by bankers and businessmen anxious to involve it in deals. It has, however, rejected nearly all such solicitations. Shortly after he joined the church, Melvin Orchard, a Salt Lake City businessman, became close to Moon and tried to interest him in backing a chain of dry-cleaning shops housed in prefabricated Fiberglas structures that Orchard was privately promoting. The plan was vigorously opposed by Takeru Kamiyama, a thirty-three-year-old Japanese member who is the church's chief financial adviser. Though Kamiyama felt the idea was self-interested, he was apparently mainly upset over Orchard's attempt to ingratiate himself with Moon, which seemed a violation of the church's tight hierarchical structure. At the top are Koreans and Japanese. At the bottom are Americans, whom Koreans do not really trust. Even American-church head Neil Salonen is little more than a figure-head (which has caused a bitter rivalry between him and Kamiyama). Moon sided with Kamiyama, and Orchard is now back in Utah.

Moon and such close Korean aides as Pak Bo Hi and Han Sang Kook are investigating numerous other ways to invest the church's excess cash. The church already own Christian Bernard of Paris, a small jewelry concern, which has a Fifth Avenue showroom. Moon is eager to get into the martial-arts and shipping businesses. Recently Moon personally discussed the purchase of Baker's Fisheries, a New Jersey-coast fishing concern.

Moon's major known corporate investment to date has been in banking. As early as 1974, he began discussing with senior members the advantages of owning or controlling a bank. It could serve as a repository of church funds, a mechanism for loaning money to church enterprises, and a means of shifting money from country to country, perhaps in ways that outsiders might find very difficult to trace. In June 1977, it became publicly known that Moon and twenty-two of his associates had spent $1,232,000 the previous fall to acquire 51 percent of the stock of a newly formed Washington, D.C., institution catering to Asian-Americans, the Diplomat National Bank. Technically, the 51 percent ownership could permit the Moonie shareholders to dominate Diplomat's board of directors and dictate bank policy. Since the bank opened for business in December 1976, church members have become depositors in Diplomat, and one Moon-affiliated group, Pak Bo Hi's Korean Cultural and Freedom Foundation, which is a large depositor, has been granted a $100,000 loan by the bank.

The circumstances under which the Moon associates acquired their Diplomat stock are shrouded in some mystery. They claim to have made their purchases independently with their own money, though none received salary from the church, and the church's plan to buy into a bank has been well known among members for nearly two years. Also unclear is the role of syndicated columnist Jack Anderson, who is chairman of Diplomat's executive committee, a member of the board, and a founder, and for whom revelation of the Moonies' involvement has caused no small amount of chagrin. Anderson claims to have had no knowledge of the Moon shareholders until recently, though he admits a close personal and business relationship with Jhoon Rhee, a Korean karate-school owner who is also on Diplomat's board and who has long been involved with Moon. To impress Park Chung Hee, Moon himself has worked to associate himself with Anderson and has provided Anderson information favorable to the Park government. In contrast to wide press criticism of the Park regime, Anderson's columns have been generally favorable. But Anderson, who initially may have been naive about Moon's intentions, maintains that he and other Diplomat executives are determined to prevent any attempt by Moon to influence bank policy. Diplomat is even looking for ways to cancel the Moonie shares. The Federal Reserve Board, meanwhile, is investigating possible violations of the banking laws that require prior federal approval of bank takeovers.

If my analysis so far is accurate—that the Unification church is generating millions of dollars a year more than it spends and that it is investing only a modest amount of the excess in real estate or corporate ventures, there appears to be only one other likely recipient: Moon, the presumed messiah. "Christians think that the Messiah must be poor and miserable," says a Unification church training manual. "He did not come for this. Messiah must be the richest. Only He is qualified to have dominion over things. Otherwise, neither God nor the Messiah can be happy."

Moon claimed in a recent interview that "God knows nothing belongs to me, not even a penny for my own savings." Yet Moon did manage to scrape together $80,000 for Diplomat stock. And in 1974 over a third of the MFTs were organized as a specially selected group of "Father's MFTs," which are said to channel money directly to Moon for his own personal needs. Even taking into account Moon's rather lavish living habits—in distinct contrast to those of his followers—Moon might be enjoying a personal surplus of $7 million to $8 million a year. Moon is reported to have told a group of MFT leaders in 1973 that he had $13 million in his own bank account. In 1976 he wrote a $175,000 personal check to help the church make a real-estate payment. Under the tax law, incidentally, religious organizations are exempt from taxes only so long as "no part of the net earnings . . . inures to the benefit of any private shareholder or individual." Whatever the case, somebody within the church is putting a lot of money away someplace. And considering the pressure on the MFTs to produce, he or she is doing it as quickly as possible.

How Long Will the Money Keep Coming In?

The key to the Unification church's continuation as "one of the major growth industries in the U.S.," as Moon attorney David Carliner puts it, is recruitment. Just to stay even, the church must continuously bring in new members. But it is now constantly losing members. The arduous deprogramming often necessary to wrest devout Moon converts from the divine principle has gotten much publicity, but many Moonies also simply walk away from the church because they are worn out by the spartan routine and frustrated and dispirited by the church's obsession with private gain instead of public betterment.

From the beginning church membership goals have gone unmet. In his book, *Doomsday Cult,* John Lofland reported that in the late 1950s Moon decreed that the church must assemble 144,000 converts by 1967, a time when his followers would become "rulers of a restored, eternal, and perfect Garden of Eden." Even today, ten years after the deadline, the church's worldwide full-time membership is only a fraction of that goal. Moon representation in most of the 120 countries where he claims to have branches consists of just a three-man missionary team supported by the parent church. But at least during the 1960s and early 1970s, church membership continued to expand. About the time of the Madison Square Garden rally in September, 1974, however, membership in the U.S. church peaked at 2,000. The immediate difficulty lay with the state organizations, which along with such Moon fronts as the Collegiate Association for the Research of Principles, had the primary responsibility for recruiting. But the states had fallen into disarray. Their autonomy had been taken away. Their best fund raisers has been usurped by the national MFTs. Their financial distress, despite Moon's bookkeeping instructions, had deepened.

It was true that the San Francisco Bay Area branch of the church remained a big new-member producer. Yet members produced by the California branch of the church have too often been professional cult freaks who lack the capacity to sustain a long-term spiritual commitment. Officials in the national headquarters were particularly worried over the plateauing of membership because of the bicentennial Yankee Stadium rally planned for June 1976. Moon had proclaimed an attendance goal of 200,000, which he felt would be necessary to perpetuate the public impression that the Unification church was "probably the fastest-growing faith in the world," as the *Washington Star* once put it. The officials knew they needed a dramatic increase in hard-core members to pass out tickets and entice people to come. In a speech in February 1975 to a group of members, Neil Salonen declared an "emergency measure of war" to bring in 20,000 new members.

To meet the goal, Moon and his advisers revived a then-moribund program called "pioneering witnessing." Under the revised version, which went into operation early in 1976, a member undergoes a 120-day training program at Barrytown. The pioneer is then sent to the field, where, as a devout witness to Moon's revelations, he or she is expected to bring into the movement three "spiritual children" a month. Not long after the first pioneers began witnessing (street proselytization,) it was clear the program was not working. Only a few were able to bring in even one spiritual child a month, and most could not recruit any. "Street-speaking" by themselves in unfamiliar places and unable to convince anyone to listen, the pioneers found themselves wrenched by self-doubts. They had been indoctrinated to believe there could never be anything wrong with Moon, the divine principle, or the Unification church. The problem, they believed, must lie within themselves: they were unworthy, they lacked sufficient faith, they had become possessed by Satan. They were lost without the church's most powerful psychological force: group reinformcement, the constant presence of other members to provide reassurance and support, which had proved so important to the MFTs' success. Moon and his aides have recently admitted to groups of members that the pioneer program has been a failure.

Moon can take some satisfaction from the fact that the MFTs still seem to be producing. Says former Moonie pioneer Alison Gardner, "It is much easier to get a few bucks from people than take away their life." But they also may soon begin to falter. Rises and falls in our fast-moving, fad-ridden, media-conscious. American society can be alarmingly swift, and Moon is beginning to be beset with a powerful downward momentum. Criticism in the press of his movement is growing. As the church's image darkens, government agencies investigating the church, which may have been fearful of being accused of religious persecution if they acted, may now feel free to move against it. This momentum may fatally affect Moon's vital alliance with the Park government. Park's support of Moon depends on Park's perception of Moon's influence in the United States, especially Washington. Whatever official sanction or restraint Moon may enjoy in official Washington depends in large part on Moon's perceived influence in South Korea. "Moon is in a precarious position," says former Moonie Gary Scharff. "Park won't want to commit himself to Moon if he feels Moon is going to be rejected by the American people. Park may be wondering why Moon did not do better in Yankee Stadium. If Park steps back, Moon will have a harder time declaring to the American people that he has Korea on his side. If he cannot maintain his connections, his power base will crumble."

If it does, the Unification church will gradually fade from view, the mortgagees will repossess their real estate, his members will return to college or their parents, Moon will repair to wherever his gleanings from Satan's world have been stored and gather around him the few survivors among the faithful. He once told a group of members that he had bought an island off Korea where he would retire and start his own country if the world rejected him. It will not exactly be the millennium for Sun Myung Moon. But at least it will be a living.

16

Science, Sin, and Sponsorship

Irving Louis Horowitz

For the fifth time in as many years, the International Conference on the Unity of the Sciences met in November 1976 to discuss the "Search for Absolute Values." That they did so in comparative luxury, at the Washington-Hilton Hotel in Washington, D.C., and one year earlier, at the Waldorf-Astoria Hotel in New York, is hardly unusual. The holding of scholarly conferences in affluent surroundings has long been viewed as a perquisite of the intellectual class. What is unusual is the wildly eclectic representation of academic stars from all fields and all nations. Stranger still is the man who sponsors these annual gatherings: Founder and keynoter, Reverend Sun Myung Moon, spiritual leader of the Unification church. The sponsor garnered several hundred scholars to attend the 1976 conference. On the basis of past performance, they had every right to have high expectations.

The chairman of the meeting was Nobel laureate Sir John Eccles; the four section committee chairmen were Frederick Sontag, representing philosophy; Morton A. Kaplan, representing social science; Kenneth Mellanby, for the biological sciences; and Eugene P. Wigner, Nobel laureate and keynoter for the physical science section. The list of group chairmen and American and international advisers read like a who's who of the scholarly world, or of a section of that world. There are such eminent figures in social science as Daniel Lerner of MIT, Harold Lasswell of Yale University, and Dan V. Segre of Hebrew University. The philosophic talent was no less in evidence; it included Richard L. Rubenstein, Sir Karl Popper, Mikel Dufrenne, and

Geoffrey Parrinder. Then there were eminent figures from the world of literature, such as Arthur Koestler, followed in quick succession by Paul A. Weiss from biology, Ulf von Euler from medicine, and Gerhard Herzberg and Willis Lamb, both Nobel laureates in physics. This is by all odds a distinguished list of scholars and thinkers.

However one organizes the list, the participants seemed to be bonded more by dislikes than by likes: there were absolutists and relativists, monists and pluralists, democrats and autocrats, Europeans and Americans. But what these august figures had in common other than their presumed shared interest in the search for absolute values was probably a shared animosity for what they might call the communist menace.

By self-definition, the topic of the conference was what absolute values exist in science and society. This choice of subject in turn was predicated on the notion that there is harmony among the sciences and therefore presumably value in the world of society. But the cacophony of sounds bellowed by the publication of past volumes of the Moon conferences indicates that what each participant represented was of less concern to the sponsors than the legitimation provided to the Unification church by their attendance at such a church-sponsored conference.

The emphasis on the interrelation of values, religions, and problems of absolute values as they arise in history, art, literature, and science was undoubtedly intended to be an intellectual prop to the Unification church position that the twentieth century offers the ultimate showdown between America (and South Korea), which is based on religious universalism, and the Soviet Union (and North Korea), which is based on Godless communism. This theory sounds like such a crude throwback to an earlier era that one hesitates to employ the rhetoric of even the most primitive "cold warriors." But no matter how the conference is portrayed, it clearly represented the last hurrah of academic anticommunism of an older generation of intellectual warriors.

Their ideological commitment to the "free world" concept

rather than the funding they received to attend this conference explained the participation of most of these people. However, like the Platonic world they seek to reproduce in the twentieth century, the conference participants were divided into three categories: eminent people for whom "all expenses are paid for travel, hotel, and official meals"; prominent persons holding positions of leadership outside of the academic community, who must "pay their travel expenses" but for whom "hotel expenses and official meals are paid"; and the promising young neophytes who "must pay their own travel and hotel" but for whom "official meals will be paid." What snapped the austere majesty of this Platonic triad was a fourth category of people who were considered so important, organizationally or intellectually, that they received considerable honoraria for their participation.

The papers produced were the sort of puffery that people write when they go far beyond their fields of professional competence. Nonetheless the quality of persons, no less than the size of the gathering, would indicate a shared and wide-ranging perception of the breakdown of values in a relativistic universe. In that sense the Fifth International Conference of the Sciences was a vanguard thrust into backwardness, representing in its most blatant form the larger conservative reaction to functionalism in social science and relativism in physical science.

This was a conference with a difference. ICUS was not a get-together; not simply a group with a shared set of concerns for practical problems affecting people across many disciplines and professions. It was a conference based on a powerful a priori belief that only the wall of the absolute could stem the tide of totalitarian pragmatism.

There is an obvious analogy between the style of work the Reverend Moon employed in assembling his intellectuals for these conferences and the wooing of academics by South Korea generally. In an article published in *Christianity and Crisis*, Frank Baldwin documented the nature and existence of the Korean lobby. As the case of California Congressman Robert Leggett exemplifies, the techniques employed to ensure support were quite unusual. Indeed, the use of a spectrum of academics sometimes unwittingly and at other times even against their express will—as in the cases of Herman Kahn of the Hudson Institute, Franz Michael of the University of Washington, and Andrew Nahm of Western Michigan University—indicates that the approach taken by the Republic of South Korea and that taken by the Reverend Moon are close and the interpenetration keen.

The *New York Times* reports that the Unification church did have access to the representative of Korea's Embassy Communication Systems and diplomatic pouch, and the people linked to the Diplomat National Bank in Washington, D.C. reveal a strong correlation and connection between the Korea lobby and the Unification church. It should be added, however, that as the Reverend Moon established his American base, and the source of his funding became increasingly diverse, his linkages to the Korean government appeared to decrease.

The Moon people learned their lessons well: for every religious movement there must be a civil ideology, and for every zealot involved in street collections, there must be a corresponding man of words to provide a sense of balance as well as intellectual gloss to the street action. The intellectuals who attended this conference may be in search of absolutes, but these absolutists were also in search of intellectuals. On that common ground they met in the International Conference on the Unity of the Sciences.

After a decade of painful ethical and intellectual struggle concerning the proper relationship of science with government patrons and sponsors, a carefully embroidered consensus has emerged. The foundation of that consensus is simple: science in its various forms has both explicit and implicit values. Furthermore whatever interactions occur between science and politics, at the forefront is a sense of the importance of maintaining the relationship so that no cooptation or elimination of one by the other takes place. No one has ever doubted the autonomy of the political system, but many have disputed the autonomy of science.

Social scientists developed different strategies for handling questions of federal and administrative patronage. At one extreme they denied that any such relationship was permissible; at the other they asserted that the relationship was a prerequisite for social research and a perquisite of scientific investigators.[1] But there was a broad spectrum between these two polarities. Where one drew a line became the name of the game: to testify or not testify before congressional committees, to accept or reject foundation support, to distinguish between pure and applied research and theoretical and mission-oriented research. If no firm consensus was reached, at least a sense of the problem of values became acute. Perhaps at their most healthily introspective, social scientists thought carefully about who they were working for; they considered the ends of research and not just the subject matter being worked on.

To be sure, radical critique of value-free research sometimes had bizarre conservative outcomes. Nearly all professional associations, primarily to safeguard their own standing in the financial and university communities, rushed to create procedural rules, committees of ethics, and review boards that, if taken seriously, would have resulted in a near total suspension of all innovative research. Risk-taking research, in the behavioral sciences at least, did relinquish the field to safe and unquestioned lines of inquiry. On the other hand few scholars adhered to such rules, so they had the benefit of consciousness raising among social scientists who had failed to receive such training as graduate students.

But for every turn there is a twist. Scientists, including social scientists, have a problem in trying to decide how to respond to a religious or quasi-religious organization such as that headed by the Reverend Sun Myung Moon and his Unification church. The Fifth International Conference on the Unity of Sciences is a case in point.[2] What we do not know, and what the sponsors clearly are not about to reveal, are the numbers of academics contacted (including myself) who refused to participate. From an informal sample, I know that leading scholars such as Seymour Martin Lipset, Amitai Etzioni, and Elise Boulding in sociology; Ernest

Nagel and Abraham Edel in philosophy; Kenneth Boulding in economics; and Saul Mendlovitz in law and international relations, declined their invitations. Perhaps to reach the level of 360 participants, ten times that number had to be contacted; a ten percent response rate to a direct mail marketing effort is considered to be excellent. Whatever the case, the issue remains: What are the rules for participation in conferences put together by such organizational affiliations?

Without wishing to dwell excessively upon the sins of the Reverend Moon, one must at least mention secular activities of sponsors that might call into question one's participation.

One might simply write off the Reverend Moon as a bad joke and declare, as Undershaft does to George Bernard Shaw's Major Barbara, "What price salvation now?" when she finds out that all of her good works have been financially underwritten by the munitions manufacturer who capitalized on World War I. Attention might be drawn to the Nobel Peace Prize and the fact that Alfred Nobel derived his fortune from chemical manufacturing interests that were primarily turned to war-making activities at the turn of the twentieth century.

At some point in the genealogy of money, nothing becomes more absurd than a categorical denial that size of an offering is unconnected to the degree of participation. One does have to distinguish between the sources of funding and how funds are used. The late Mohandas K. Gandhi was told by a group of peasants who were his colleagues in the Congress party that he had erred in accepting money for party activities from landlords. They were repelled by the idea that the revolution was barely won, and English colonialists had hardly left Indian shores, before native landlords seemed to be marching in. Gandhi's reply was simply that "money is never dirty—only people." It was a neat response, but the issue remains: What is the proper relationship between private donor and scientific recipient, since what is often transacted is not simply funds, but services?

The situation remains ethically obscure if not downright cloudy. It would be a fatuous injustice to those who have decided to participate in this international conference simply to condemn them for ethical error and demand that they repent. Yet there are issues that add up to a preponderant set of reasons not to participate in the activities of this conference and to scrutinize its sponsorship. With all due respect to those who continue to believe that money is never dirty but people sometimes are, I should like to argue that the questions raised extend far beyond the expenditure of funds or the cleanliness of the holy rollers and sinners who are conference sponsors.

Decisions concerning participation hinge on empirical information. Thus it is important to outline what is generally known, beyond dispute, about the Reverend Sun Myung Moon, his ideological offerings, and the organization of the Unification church. I will eschew discussion of the church's recruitment and conversion techniques. Much has been written about the subject from sociological[3] and psychological[4] viewpoints. Beyond that it can always be argued that all techniques of conversion and persuasion involve emotional appeals and irrational claims.[5] In this respect the Reverend Moon's church cannot be faulted as different or more pernicious than totalitarian movements in general.[6] There remain a series of relatively well established organizational linkages and ideological statements that have much more to do with the sociology of mass movements than with any religious force. At this level questions of participation do arise, even if they are at marginal points of interaction.

The Reverend Sun Myung Moon has conceded several crucial points. First, he is engaged in arms production in South Korean tool factories. A *New York Times* article claims that 10 percent of the production in his factories is dedicated to armaments.[7] Second, his industrial conglomerate in South Korea has sales of $15 million annually and engages in the manufacture of everything from heavy machinery to small arms. Third, in the wake of the Watergate scandal, Reverend Moon organized a media campaign of support for the then beleaguered President Richard M. Nixon, including full-page advertisements placed in American newspapers, telling Americans that "God has chosen Mr. Nixon to be President and, therefore, only God has the authority to dismiss him." Fourth, through the person of Lieutenant Colonel Pak Bo Hi, Moon's translator and closest associate, there seems to be a clear line running to President Park Chung Hee at one end and the Korean CIA at the other. While Moon's relationships and that of his church to both the Korean presidency and its intelligence-gathering community is shrouded in mystery, there seems little question that a church operating within a dictatorship of the South Korean variety could not exist, much less expand rapidly, without official sanction.

The Reverend Moon operates much more than the Unification church in the United States. Through political mechanisms such as the Freedom Leadership Foundation, he lobbies for U.S. military and economic support to South Korea. His American Youth for a Just Peace was a crucial conduit aiding right-wing Republicans during the final years of the Nixon administration. The International Cultural Foundation represents the Reverend Moon's penetration of the intellectual community. These support foundations, like the Unification church itself, are tax exempt and are declared adjuncts to religious institutions registered as nonprofit, educational organizations. In this fashion the Reverend Moon has been able to acquire considerable assets, estimated at more than $20 million in the United States alone. His financial resources have permitted his organization to engage in congressional lobbying and other forms of political activity that possibly are beyond the legal limits of a tax-exempt status.

Moon's ideology is organized around the theme of crude, unadorned anticommunism. Among the key points made by the Reverend Moon in a rare interview given to *Newsweek* is that messianic salvationism is central: "The Unification Church is not another denomination. It is a movement to save the world."[8] The three headaches that God presumably has commanded the Reverend Moon to cure are "moral corruption, division within Christianity, and communism as the primary evil force in the world." Moon considers his movement dedicated to reverse all three satanic tendencies.

The Reverend Moon is clearheaded enough not to claim directly that he is the messiah. He does, however, say that he is "just following God's instructions." Why he has been chosen from among all living creatures is wrapped up with the peculiar nature of Korea, which he refers to as "a lineup between the heavenly world and the Satanic world in Panmunjom. We must make a showdown in Korea. Korea's victory, particularly against Communism, is not Korea's alone. I came to America to bring it back to the scene of the struggle. America has been retreating from responsibility; that has happened in Vietnam. America will decide the world's destiny."

In true messianic fashion Moon claims to have been "ordered to act as were many prophets in history." Beyond that he assures his flock that he is "in daily communication with God." The admixture of theology and politics is so close that even to attempt to segregate them is hardly possible. Yet by choosing slogans such as "God Bless America" as the basic text for his keynote speech at Yankee Stadium festival in June 1976, and by identifying God's goal in history with American triumphalism, he leaves hardly any doubt of his political message.

Moon's Yankee Stadium statement on June 26 was dominated by such phrases as, "It is my firm belief that the United States of America was indeed conceived in God's image. It is apparent that this unique creation of America is a creation of God." Moon's linkage of America and God becomes so close that the mere hint that one could survive without the other becomes questionable: "If America wants to keep the blessing of God as the leading nation of the world, it must form a partnership with God. Do you have God in your homes? Do you truly have God in your church? Do you have God in your society and nation? God is the cement. With God, America will stay together like concrete. But if God leaves, she will be like sand. When the flood comes, all will be washed away."[9]

The Moon movement is certainly worth studying. Indeed calls for further research have been made. Calls for studies of psychoreligious cults like Moon's as a means of examining the psychological impact of all de-individualizing social systems have been heeded. In the work of pioneering social researchers, the Moon movement has received a fair, and at times even a highly sympathetic, treatment. But a scientific analysis of movements is clearly not the same as participation by these same scientists in a movement. That is the issue to which we must ultimately return.

As everyone within Western culture influenced by twentieth-century trends and philosophies must realize, the phrase "unity of science," which was used by the International Conference, far from means a search for absolute values; it was the organizing premise of the positivism and empiricism of the Vienna Circle that, in the presence of Carnap, Schlick, Wittgenstein, and Neurath, among others, brought philosophical thinking screaming and kicking into the scientific and analytic era, making it aware of Riemann's geometry, Einstein's physics, and even Marx's sociology. Above all "unity of science" meant linking the content of experience, whether it be on a physical or psychological level, with the structure of the world. To conduct a frontal assault on the experimental and relativist bases of science through expropriation of the phrase "unity of sciences" for an international conference that has as central to it agenda a search for absolute values, must be registered as grim humor. The scientific participants in this conference have forgotten that science, like ideology and theology, remains a fundamental standpoint to be fought for no less assiduously than the searchers for absolutes fight for theirs.

U.S. News and World Report indicates that at present "anywhere from one million to three million Americans, mostly in their twenties or late teens, are involved in 200 to 1,000 [religious] cults." One of the largest and most controversial of these religious cults is the Unification church of Sun Myung Moon. The group claims 30,000 adherents in the United States, who average twenty-four years of age.[10] If one believes, as some religious scholars apparently do, that these groups represent a healthy way to cure or avoid drug problems or are an effective way to overcome antisocial behavior, then participation in a conference sponsored by the Reverend Moon might be in order. But to take the view that there is an absolute gap between fact and value which permits conference participation, whatever the nature or source or purpose of the sponsorship, represents an abdication of moral decision making that presumably is linked ultimately to some sort of empirical moorings. Turning a moral blind eye is a risky business, particularly when participation might legitimate activites that one considers questionable, if not downright absurd.

By embarking on a search for absolute values, using total truth as an organizational premise, one will do exactly what is expected, namely, arrive at absolute values in religion, philosophy, or social science and the humanities, and hence foreclose on the most important question: whether the search is worth undertaking. Perhaps an analogy, that much-maligned form of reasoning, is in order. If one were asked to attend a conference in the Soviet Union on the theme of American imperialism and how to rid the world of it, would it not be reasonable to assume that it would be extremely difficult under such sponsorship and circumstances to inquire into the nature of Soviet expansionism and how to eliminate it? It is not that America is without imperialism; it is rather that framing the problem in such exclusionary terms falsifies the results. Similarly there may indeed be absolute values common to all of the social sciences. But at the very least, a parallel inquiry should be made into the relative values common to the social sciences.

As an example, take one of the subjects covered within the sociological panel of ICUS:V: the cause and prevention of crime in modern society. It might very well be that the absolute prevention of crime is impossible without entirely stagnating society; crime, like industrial growth itself, may be typical of modern societies. But framing problems in sloganeering terms that satisfy the search for the idea of the absolute raises serious doubts about the scientific nature of an endeavor.

All participation in conferences, lectures, seminars, and so forth involves an implicit laying on of hands. Participation represents an ongoing legitimation process. When publishers advertise their wares in scholarly journals, they endow those journals with something of value. When academics speak before political and public forums, they similarly are transmitting their institutional attachments, in addition to their personal beliefs. This is so whatever disclaimers are made that the scholar is speaking only in his or her own name. For example, in the preliminary announcement of the International Congress, the name of the institutional affiliation of the chairman of each panel was printed as large as that of the individual chairman. It would be the height of folly to imagine that sponsors of this conference did not see the value of this legitimating device. Indeed one might well argue that legitimation is all that the Unification Church sponsors expect to gain, and that individual contributions and papers are really not at stake or being questioned. Therefore one does have the obligation to inquire, What is being legitimized?

When I became aware of the sponsorship and nature of this conference, I registered my unwillingness to participate with Michael Young Warder, who was listed as secretary-general for the Conference. But his primary responsibility is to serve as director of the Moonie Training Center at Barrytown, New York, which has been the object of so many parental complaints that authoritarian psychological techniques are employed to gain adherence and converts. In this connection Warder's remarks in the *New York Times Magazine* about why the sexes are segregated offers a most curious insight into his views on absolutes in ethics.[11] He says that "by sexual segregation everyone feels more comfortable in their study and in their search for truth. As soon as they are mixed together, we find the boys and the girls begin thinking of other things. We feel there is too much sex and promiscuity today." But the address given for Warder for this conference was a post office box number in New York City. His relationship to the Moon group was not indicated on any information I received.

In response to my letter bringing to his attention that the founder of the ICUS is the Reverend Sun Myung Moon and asking for some clarification of the Reverend Moon's role, Warder simply informed me that freedom of speech would be maintained and that the Reverend Moon's participation would be restricted to giving an initial convocation of the gathering.[12] It would seem coincidental that in the opening letter of invitation, the first paragraph did not mention the Reverend Moon but rather Sir John Eccles, a Nobel laureate, who served as chairman of the conference at the Washington-Hilton Hotel. Only by the most careful perusal does one come upon the name of Reverend Moon, since his name does not appear on the preliminary agenda. He is listed only on one of the sheets concerning the organization of the ICUS meetings and is there simply as founder. Interestingly too, of all participants, he alone is not provided with any category of interests or any place or institution. Presumably the whole world and all of its artifacts is home for the reverend.

As a social scientist I did take the liberty of contacting those members of the U.S. and international advisory boards who were most closely linked to the social and behavioral sciences. The responses I received represent a moral panpoly of American scholarship. Frederick Sontag, professor of philosophy at Pomona College, represented the dominant thinking of those who replied:

Since I have been consulted about the formation of the Vth ICUS and the questions to be discussed, as well as those invited to participate, I can say that Rev. Moon's role is that of sponsor. Those organizing the conference have had every assistance but also every liberty to structure the conference according to the topics selected by those involved. I have myself seen no way in which the conference is as such linked to the Rev. S. M. Moon's own religious doctrine. I think perhaps the best answer I can give is that I know of no agenda except the questions and topics announced by the group charged with planning the conference, and I know of no formal discussions planned except those generated by the invited papers.[13]

The Distinguished Professor of International Relations at the University of Chicago, Morton A. Kaplan, expressed sincere appreciation for my concerns and those of others but indicated his own experience as follows: "I participated last year as a Section Chairman and also as a Committee Chairman. In no respect was there any effort by Mr. Moon to control the intellectual content of the conference apart from his own ten-minute Sponsor's presentation. I see no reason to believe that this will change and hope very much that you will be able to participate."[14]

The distinguished Nobel Prize physicist at Princeton University, Eugene P. Wigner, assured me that "Reverend Moon did not try to influence the substance of the last meeting, the one I attended . . . Reverend Moon in his opening speech said that everyone should give his opinion as clearly as he can and should not feel influenced." As if to lend weight to this, Professor Wigner, long known as a strong anticommunist, noted that "frankly, I do not put much weight on the sponsorship of the conferences I attend. In fact, I have attended conferences sponsored by communist governments."[15]

The distinguished biologist at Rockefeller University, Paul A. Weiss, also thought the previous meeting of ICUS was "quite constructive and wholly unprejudiced." However, he also indicated a philosophical appreciation for what this conference was about. In this instance at lease one could respect the decision to participate since Weiss's reasoning seems to rest on a positive intellectual judgment of the effort, sympathetic to the intent of the Unification church conference.

In fact, being increasingly concerned about the fractionation of human thinking, even in science, I see no objection to continuing the exercise as long as it shows no political or sectarian influence. Having had, for more than half a century, research support from various foundations and organizations, I have never investigated the sources of their income. However, having enjoyed the faith of others in trusting the honesty and unselfishness of *my own* decisions, I greatly honor the virtue of the expressions of others diverging from my judgement.[16]

From a personal point of view, perhaps the most interesting letter came from a friend and colleague, Daniel Lerner, currently in residence at the East-West Center in Hawaii, who headed up a sociological wing of the conference. His letter raised serious questions about sponsorship as such and therefore deserves to be presented in full. He noted:

I have not withdrawn my support as a participant in the Fifth ICUS because I am quite used to the idea of crooks and cranks supporting worthy causes. After all, there was nothing very saintly about Messrs. Carnegie, Ford and Rockefeller. My only point of principle is that the financial sponsor does not tamper with the product in any way. In my four years of experience with the ICUS programs, I have never found the sinister hand of Moon visible in any degree. My role in their past seminars and conferences has been exactly what it would be if I were participating in a session of the AAAS or APSA. I respect your decision to withdraw, just as I understand Marty Lipset's strong objections to participation by any of his friends. I share his antipathy for Moon, who may be both a crank and a crook. However, I feel that ICUS provides a valuable scientific meeting of minds and I shall continue to participate in it until there is some hard evidence that Moon is using (or abusing) it for his own devious purposes.[17]

At one level we are dealing with matters of degree and not simply absolute rights and wrongs. How crooked and how cranky the sponsor is cannot be ignored. Surely one cannot simply assert that because someone is cranky or crooked that this provides participatory license. If a conference held on crime as an American way of life were sponsored by the Mafia, one can imagine a perfectly reasonable series of essays by top-flight scholars; but I hardly imagine that the crookedness or crankiness of the sponsors would be entirely irrelevant to the output.

At another level we must confront matters of principle. There may be occasions when support from the Carnegie, Ford, or Rockefeller foundations should be scrutinized. It is by no means axiomatic that the more powerful the sponsor, the more automatic the participation. But even more, to draw the analogy between the ICUS and participation in a session of the American Association for the Advancement of Science or the American Political Science Association entirely misses the point. The latter are *our* associations. They are wholly, or at least in considerable measure, governed by laws and norms made by ourselves as professional scientists. They represent a consensus of professional opinion as to the current situation in any scientific endeavor.

Nothing could be more lacking in Professor Lerner's analogy than to claim that this is the case in respect to the ICUS. Precisely the absence of professional leverage beyond one's own personal predilections seems to be the missing ingredient in Moon's conference. Advisory boards hardly qualify as more than window dressing. I doubt seriously that any of them would claim that their advisory role permits, much less encourages, a wider organizational role. Such a role may simply provide legitimacy rather than insure decision-making leverage. I also doubt that any of these esteemed gentlemen would even want such a role, given the sponsorship of this organization. Therefore simply to view ICUS as one more professional association is at best a misperception and at worst misanthropic. Further, and not incidentally, the AAAS or the APSA has never offered a scholar "all expenses paid for travel, hotel and meals" to present a paper. This is, for the most part, his or her responsibility or that of the university or the agency wishing the results of a project to be shared colleagially. The generosity of the sponsors is in no small part a source of this widespread interest in the Reverend Moon and his scientific concerns. Fiscal support, even of a modest variety, remains a relatively attractive form of inducement for those raised in the earlier tradition of genteel academic poverty.

In a political context quite distinct from the present, Harold Orlans properly noted a decade ago that the basic source of ethical problems involving research sponsors and investigators has to do with funding. "Money is not a free good, available for any scholarly purpose, and those with funds to dispense do so for purposes and under conditions of their own choosing. This is inevitable and it is fruitless to lament it." Orlans urges us not to confuse politics and morality at the risk of demeaning both. It might be argued that in concrete circumstances, fine-line distinctions can be easily blurred. Yet his conclusion is hardly subject to such doubt: "If you disagree with the objectives of an agency, do not decry the morality of its staff but try to change their objectives and, in the interim, do not take their money."[18] This should be far easier to accomplish in circumstances clearly not subject to major fiscal pressures to conform.

It might be argued that accepting travel fares, hospitality, and accoutrements does not constitute money in the big research grant sense of the term. True enough. But this should also make it easier for scholars to say no. The same rule of thumb with respect to funding might apply to the ICUS meeting. What is not permissible on intellectual grounds is to decry the objectives of the Moon forces and yet participate in its affairs. I have no wish to be argumentative with any of the sponsors or participants. Certainly they thought long and hard before coming to their decisions to participate. But it does seem that the basis of academic participation and legitimation deserves to be thought through by those who affirm their right to participate, no less than those who choose not to do so.

I am not alone in having the feeling that the Reverend Moon's role in this conference was, to put it mildly, carefully screened, if not entirely muted. Marshall McLuhan, director of the Centre for Culture and Technology, has indicated to me that he too, until receipt of my letter of inquiry to Mr. Warder, was unaware of the Moon sponsorship, although he is listed as a member of the International Advisory Board: "I am very grateful to you for revealing the sponsorship of the Fifth International Conference on the Unity of the Sciences. The 'Moon' name had not surfaced in the initial invitations, so far as I can recall. In the light of the dubious Reverend Moon's activities, I shall be glad to withdraw my endorsement."[19] That a feeling of unease has settled in even among the advisory board of the Moon-sponsored ICUS meetings was reflected by Seymour S. Kety, chief of the department of pyschiatry at Massachusetts General Hospital. His letter to Sir John Eccles makes it clear that Marshall McLuhan's reconsideration is not an isolated event:

Although I declined the invitation and honorarium to serve as a Committee Chairman for the Fifth International Conference on the Unity of the Sciences, I agreed to have my name listed as one of the American advisors. I did this because of my respect for John Eccles and others on the International and American Advisory Board whom I know as outstanding scientists and defenders of the dignity and political freedom of human beings. I was also motivated by the theme of the next conference "The Search for Absolute Values: Harmony among the Sciences," and by the generally salutary recollection of my participation in a previous conference which was marked by an entirely free exchange of ideas among scientists.

Since that time I have seen a number of articles in the public press regarding the Unification Church and its founder with which the International Cultural Foundation is associated, which have been a cause of great concern to me. Serious charges have been made regarding the motivation and policies of the church and its founder which I have neither the time, the means, nor the disposition to attempt to evaluate. Yet my continued appearance as an American advisor implies that I support the International Cultural Foundation in spite of these charges. This I cannot in good conscience do and I must therefore ask you to remove my name from the list of American advisors in subsequent mailings and publications.[20]

The persistence of the Reverend Moon's associates, well known to anyone who has been accosted on the streets by their followers, extends to the higher reaches as well. Despite his earlier refusals to participate, Saul Mendlovitz, director of the Institute for World Order, continues to be plagued by invitations. His response, too, indicates the wide scope of opposition that built up to the conference and the ideological force it represents.

I must confess that I am somewhat surprised that you continue to persist in these invitations. You will recall, no doubt, that when you were organizing the 1974 conference, that despite offers of relatively high amounts of remuneration and accommodations for my family, I was unwilling to participate in that conference. My reason for not doing so was based as I then told you on my net judgment that Reverend Moon's activities represented forms of religious, social and political action which I find repugnant. In fact I shared these thoughts with Professors Richard Falk and Elise Boulding both of whom then, you will undoubtedly recall, saw fit to distribute letters on their unwillingness to participate in the conference based on their negative assessment of Reverend

Moon and his organizational activities. So, once again, I would like to respectfully decline participation in this event sponsored by the International Cultural Foundation which promotes the work of Reverend Moon.[21]

For those who believe that the search for absolute values is the central preoccupation for scientists and social scientists in an age of fragmentation, this conference might have made good sense. But those who believed that the conference was sponsored and administered by cranks, crooks, and perhaps even criminals and nevertheless participated should have acknowledged that they made their decision on criteria having little to do with the presumed open-ended intellectual foundations of this affair. The courageous and self-critical letter from Elise Boulding, professor of sociology at the University of Colorado, explained her acceptance and her later rejection of an invitation to participate in the Fourth International Conference on the Unity of Science. Her letter reminds us all that ideas have consequences and more, that people are consequential. The *traihson* of intellectuals has its limits.

When I accepted a co-convener role with Kenneth Boulding for one of the Conference Sections, it was on the strength of the Conference purposes and other known participants. The published proceedings of the previous years' Conference and the roster of persons committed to participating in 1975 include persons for whom I have the highest respect. It seemed at the time we agreed to participate like a fine opportunity for world-minded scholars to further the common enterprise of creating a world community we are all concerned about. It did not seem inappropriate to me that an evangelical sect might choose to fund such a conference. I now have further understanding about the nature and activities of the sect, and no longer feel that it is an appropriate sponsor for an international scholars conference. The moral purposes of the Unification Church, of the Holy Spirit Association for the Unification of World Christianity, are obscure to say the least. I am in particular concerned over the following points:

1. At a time when a number of leading Christians of South Korea are in jail because of their opposition to the Park govern-

ment, Rev. Moon not only enjoys friendly relations with the government, but apparently operates an anti-communist training school for government employees. 2. Rev. Moon publicly opposed the impeachment of President Nixon and announced that he ruled by divine right. 3. His anti-communist activities and religious activities seem to be closely intertwined and they are supported by a variety of funding operations which have triggered an Immigration Service investigation, but brought no clarity about his mode of working. The list of business, religious, scholarly and cultural organizations through which he works have no explicable relation to one another. 4. His teachings include elements of demonism and spritual welfare of his disciples, and destructive of family values and the spirit of community service.[22]

One of the most serendipitous aspects of the Moon-ICUS conference was its calling attention to the failure of nerve of one professional association after another and the failure of one esteemed scientist after another to inquire about the larger meanings of his research and what such activities signify. Ultimately this professional failure accounts for the Moon group's success. Still we run the risk of a failure of rationality itself, an inability, if not a downright unwillingness, to inquire as to when one ought to participate with those who would presume to rule the universe. Until the scientific community as a whole, and in its parts, candidly addresses itself to its own role in contributing to authoritarian agencies and sponsors, it will not be able to claim to being the force for liberation that is such a constant theme in the literature of science.

All events have the potential for irony; the 1976 ICUS conference was no exception. The Washington-Hilton was overrun by thousands of foot-stomping, fiddle-playing dancers attending the annual Square Dance Cotillion. These sturdy citizens— women and girls dressed in short gingham dresses with puffed sleeves and crinolines, and men and boys in western-style shirts and neckerchiefs — enjoyed life, danced around the clock, and blessedly at times drowned out the ICUS proceedings. They also served as a useful reminder that plain people still gather at their own expense to have fun and establish human communion without the sanctions of carefully drilled pseudotheological divines. God not only lives; he sometimes uses his flock to mock and make merry. God bless America.

References*

1. Irving Louis Horowitz and James Everett Katz, *Social Science and Public Policy in the United States* (New York: Praeger Publishers, 1975).

2. Michael Young Warder to Irving Louis Horowitz, March 27, 1976.

3. John Lofland, *Doomsday Cult: A Study of Conversion, Proselytization and Maintenance of Faith* (Englewood Cliffs, N.J.: Prentice Hall, 1966).

4. Berkeley Rice, "Messiah from Korea: Honor Thy Father Moon," *Psychology Today* 9, (January 1976): 36–47.

5. Berkeley Rice, "The Pull of Sun Moon," *New York Times Magazine*, May 30, 1976, 18–25.

6. Daniel Batson, "Moon Madness: Greed or Creed," *Monitor* 1 (June 1976): 32–33.

7. Ann Crittenden, "Moon's Sect Pushes Pro-Seoul Activities," *New York Times*, May 25, 1976, pp. 15, 16.

8. Kenneth L. Woodward, et al., "Life with Father Moon," *Newsweek*, June 14, 1976, pp. 60–66.

9. Sun Myung Moon, "God's Hope for America," *New York Times*, June 3, 1976, p. 42.

10. "Religious Cults: Newest Magnet for Youth," *U.S. News and World Report*, June 14, 1976, 52–54.

11. Rice, "Pull of Sun Moon," p. 24.

12. Michael Young Warder to Irving Louis Horowitz, April 30, 1976.

13. Frederick Sontag to Irving Louis Horowitz, May 5, 1976.

14. Morton A. Kaplan to Irving Louis Horowitz, May 3, 1976.

15. Eugene P. Wigner to Irving Louis Horowitz, May 10, 1976.

16. Paul A. Weiss to Irving Louis Horowitz, June 3, 1976.

17. Daniel Lerner to Irving Louis Horowitz, June 8, 1976.

18. Harold Orlans, "Ethical Problems in the Relations of Research Sponsors and Investigators," in *Ethics, Politics, and Social Research*, ed. Gideon Sjoberg, (Cambridge, Mass.: Schenkman Publishing Co., 1967), pp. 3–24.

19. Marshall McLuhan to Irving Louis Horowitz, June 7, 1976.

20. Seymour S. Kety to Sir John Eccles, June 17, 1976 (copy sent to Irving Louis Horowitz from Kety).

21. Saul H. Mendlovitz to Michael Young Warder, August 5, 1976. (copy sent to Irving Louis Horowitz from Mendlovitz).

22. Elise Boulding to Irving Louis Horowitz, August 8, 1975.

* I would like to thank all of the people whose correspondence is herein cited for permission to reprint their remarks in my article.

Contributors

Dick Anthony
Department of Psychology
University of North Carolina
Chapel Hill, North Carolina

Frank Baldwin
Director of Japanese Studies
Tsukuba University
Tokyo, Japan

C. Daniel Batson
Department of Psychology
University of Kansas
Lawrence, Kansas

Ann Crittenden
The New York Times
New York, New York

Margaret C. Crosby
Civil Liberties Union of
Northern California
San Francisco, California

Agnes Cunningham
Professor of Patrology
Mundelein Seminary
Chicago, Illinois

Thomas E. Curtis
Department of Psychiatry
School of Medicine
University of North Carolina
Chapel Hill, North Carolina

Madeline Doucas
Department of Psychology
University of North Carolina
Chapel Hill, North Carolina

Barbara W. Hargrove
Department of the Sociology
of Religion
Yale Divinity School
New Haven, Connecticut

William L. Hendricks
National Council of the
Churches of Christ
in the U.S.A.
Commission on Faith
and Order
New York, New York

Irving Louis Horowitz
Department of Sociology
and Political Science
Rutgers University
New Brunswick, New Jersey

Jorge Lara-Baud
National Council of the
Churches of Christ
in the U.S.A.
Commission on Faith
and Order
New York, New York

John J. Leahy
Superior Court of the
State of New York and
the Community of Queens
New York, New York

Jai Hyon Lee
College of Arts and Sciences
(Journalism)
Western Illinois University
Macomb, Illinois

Marianne Lester
The Times Magazine
Washington, D.C.

Charles C. Marson
Civil Liberties Union of
Northern California
San Francisco, California

Sun Myung Moon
The Unification Church
New York, New York

J. Robert Nelson
National Council of the
Churches of Christ
in the U.S.A.
Commission on Faith
and Order
New York, New York

Berkeley D. Rice
Psychology Today
New York, New York

Thomas Robbins
Department of Sociology
Queens College–CUNY
New York, New York

A. James Rudin
Interreligious Affairs
Department
The American Jewish
Committee
New York, New York

Alan L. Schlosser
Civil Liberties Union of
Northern California
San Francisco, California

Frederick Sontag
Department of Philosophy
Pomona College
Clarement, California

Marc H. Tannenbaum
Director
Interreligious Affairs
Department
The American Jewish
Committee
New York, New York

S. Lee Vavuris
Superior Court of the State
of California in and for the
City and County of
San Francisco
San Francisco, California

Chris Welles
Writer
New York, New York

Name Index

Addabbo, Joseph, 164
Albert, Carl, 164–65, 167
Allen, Yorke, Jr., 183–84
American Psychologist, 224
Anderson, Jack, 168, 254
Anthenien, Linda, 181

Baldwin, Frank, 263
Barnett, A. Doak, 169
Beckmann, George, 169
Bellah, Robert, xiii, 47–48, 51, 60, 69
Bonker, Don L. 132
Boulding, Elise, 266, 279
Boulding, Kenneth, 266, 279
Bronfman, Samuel, 249
Brown, Leslie, 200
Brown, Thomas A., 200
Brzezinski, Zbigniew, 169
Buckley, James, 230
Bulletin of Concerned Scholars, 125

Campbell, Donald, 223–24
Carliner, David, 255
Carnap, Rudolf, 270
Carnegie, Andrew, 275
Carter, Jimmy, 244
Chennault, Anna Chan, 163
Chesire, Maxine, 131, 164
Chicago Sun-Times, 132
Chin Hwan Row, 132, 165
Chong-sik Lee, 170
Christ, xvi passim
Christian Beliefs and Anti-Semitism
  (Charles Glock and Rodney
  Stark), 93
Christianity and Crisis, 263
Christian Science Monitor, 124, 127
Chung Gam Nok, 112

Chun Kang, 190
Coleman, John, 48
Colson, Charles, 182–83
Conley, Harold, 208–9
Coolidge, J. T., 171
Cousins, Norman, 231
Crittenden, Ann, 167

Davis, Maurice, 221, 239
Divine Principle, 29, 35–37, 40, 52, 64,
  77–79, 81–85, 103–8, 111–18, 156,
  232, 236, 248
Dole, Robert, 156, 221, 244
Dong-A Ilbo, The, 124
Dong Won Shin, 124
Doomsday Cult (John Lofland), 92, 256
Dufrenne, Mikel, 261

Eccles, John, 261, 273, 278
Edel, Abraham, 266
Einstein, Albert, 270
Eisenhower, Dwight D., 187
Erikson, Erik, 222
Etzioni, Amitai, 266

Fairbank, John K., 172–73
Falk, Richard, 279
Fefferman, Dan, 181, 183
Fenn, Richard, 50, 60, 67–69
Ford, Betty, 165
Ford, Gerald, 133, 165, 244
Ford, Henry, 275
Fraser, Donald, 157, 161, 178, 188
Freud, Sigmund, 222
Fulbright, William, 166
Fuller, Buckminster, 231

Gallagher, Cornelius, 165

Gandhi, Mohandas K., 266
Gannon, James, 126, 244
Gardner, Alison, 257
Glock, Charles, 93
Gordon, Ann, 156, 183–84, 190
Goshko, John, 133
Graham, Billy, 75, 227

Hahm Pyung Choon, 161
Halloran, Richard, 127
Hammarskjold, Dag, 61
Han Sang Kook, 253
Han Sang Lee, 123
Helander, Elton, 228–30, 239
Helander, Wendy, 228–30, 239
Henderson, Gregory, 122, 127
Hendricks, William L., 82
Herzberg, Gerhard, 262
Hilsman, Roger, 169
Hippolytus (Saint), 79
Hitler, Adolf, 79, 231
Hovard, John F., 200
Hovard, John F., Jr., 200
Howe, James W., 165
Howe, Nancy, 165
Hughes, John, 124
Humphrey, Hubert H., 230

Ichord, Richard, 230

Jai Hyon Lee, 157, 168, 186–88, 190
Jensen, Dave, 149–51, 159
Jensen, Marvin, 149–50, 154–55
Jensen, Penny, 149–50, 154
John Chrysostom (Saint), 79–80
Johnson, Lyndon B., 163
John the Baptist (Saint), 64, 110
Jones, W. Farley, 248–49
Justin (Saint), 79

Kahn, Herman, 169, 264
Kamiyama, Takeru, 253
Kaplan, Beatrice, 200
Kaplan, Janice L., 200
Kaplan, Morton A., 261, 274
Katz, Carl L., 200
Katz, Jacqueline E., 200
Katz, Louise A., 200
Kelly, Galen, 208–9
Kennedy, Edward, 230
Kennedy, John F., 61, 66

Kerr, Michael E., 127–28
Kety, Seymour S., 277
Kim Dae Jung, 125, 167
Kim Dong Jo, 163, 188, 190
Kim Jong Pil, 187
Kissinger, Henry A., 133, 136
Kodama, Yoshio, 179, 187
Koestler, Arthur, 262
Kondracke, Morton, 132
Korea Journal, 123–24
Korff, Baruch, 55
Kornhauser, William, 50
Kreshour, Edith, 208–9
Kreshour, Merylee, 208–12, 214
Kwang Neun Hahn, 168

Lamb, Willis, 262
Lara-Braud, Jorge, 82
Lasswell, Harold, 261
LeBar, James L., 82
Leggett, Robert L., 164, 263
Lerner, Daniel, 261, 275–76
Levi, Edward H., 165
Lincoln, Abraham, 9
Lipset, Seymour Martin, 266, 275
Lofland, John, 92, 256
Louis, Joe, 227

McCall's, 243
McDermott, Michael, 183–84
McLuhan, Marshall, 277–78
Maharaj-ji (Guru), 56, 58
Mardian, Robert C., 180
Marx, Karl, 270
Meher Baba, 56
Mellanby, Kenneth, 261
Mendlovitz, Saul, 266, 278
Merton, Robert K., x
Mesta, Perle, 164
Michael, Franz, 264
Mijoo Dong-A, 124
Molière, Jean Baptiste, ix
Moltmann, Jurgen, 99
Morley, James, 170
Murphy, Angus, 208–10
Mussolini, Benito, 231

Nagel, Ernest, 266
Nahm, Andrew, 264
N.A.A.C.P. v. Alabama, 195
Neurath, Otto, 270

New Korea, 131
Newsweek, 268
News World, 95, 149, 151
New York Times, 92, 127, 129, 132, 167, 171, 264, 267
New York Times Magazine, 272
Nidecker, John E., 165, 189
Nixon, Richard M., 55, 61, 65, 69, 129, 132–33, 165–67, 182, 244, 268, 280
Nobel, Alfred, 266

Oberdorfer, Don, 127, 133
Ock Kim, 171
Ogle, George, 173
Ohnuki, Daikan K., 183–84
O'Neill, Thomas, Jr., 165
Orchard, Melvin, 253
Origen, 79
Orlans, Harold, 276

Pak Bo Hi, 41, 156–58, 179–80, 186–91, 234, 246, 253–54, 268
Park Chong Gyu, 168
Park Chung Hee, 41–42, 121–36, 150, 155, 157–58, 161–62, 166–70, 172, 174, 179–80, 182, 188–89, 233, 246–47, 254, 258, 264, 268
Parrinder, Geoffrey, 262
Patrick, Ted, 229, 239
Paul (Saint), xvi
Paul VI (Pope), 227
People v. *DeLeon,* 214
Peter (Saint), 108
Pond, Elizabeth, 124
Pontius Pilate, 99
Popper, Karl, 261
Pyong Choon Hahm, 124

Ranard, Donald L., 122, 132–33, 162
Rhee, Jhoon, 254
Rhee, T. C., 126
Rice, Berkeley, 220
Richards, Bill, 133
Riemann, Georg F. B., 270
Rise and Fall of Project Camelot, The (Irving Louis Horowitz), ix
Rising Tide, 167, 182
Robbins, Thomas, xiii
Rockefeller, John D., Jr., 275
Rockefeller, Laurance S., 183
Rockefeller, Nelson A., 183

Roland, Robert W., 158, 187
Rubenstein, Richard L., 261
Runyon, Michael, 184
Ruth, Babe, 227

Saar, John, 133
Salonen, Neil A., 157–58, 167, 181, 233, 249, 253, 257
Sank Ik Choi, 186
Sasagawa, Ryoichi, 179
Scalapino, Robert, 169–70
Scharff, Gary, 258
Schlick, Moritz, 270
Segre, Dan V., 261
Shapiro, Edward, 208, 210–12, 214–15
Shapiro, Eli, 208
Shaw, George Bernard, 266
Sinott, James, 173
Slaughter, Cynthia, 250
Sontag, Frederick, xiv, 261, 273
Stark, Rodney, 93
State of North Carolina v. *Gough,* 215
State of North Carolina v. *Murphy,* 215
Strauss, Anselm, ix
Sudo, Kenneth, 249
Sugwon Kang, 125, 169
Sulpicius Severus, 80
Sungjoo Han, 169
Sun Man Lim, 123
Sun Myung Moon, x passim
Szymanski, Albert, 48–49

Tertullian, 79
Thompson, Suzi Park, 164
Thornburgh, Richard L., 180
Thurmond, Strom, 230
Times Magazine, 150–53, 155, 157
Tonga Ilbo, 169
Tongsun Park, 165
Truman, Harry S., 27
Tunney, John V., 131, 190

Underwood, Barbara, 200
Underwood, Raymond, 199
Unitas, John, 227
United States v. *Ballard,* 194
U.S. News and World Report, 270

Vidich, Arthur, 62
Von Euler, Ulf, 262

Walzer, Michael, 69
Warder, Michael Young, 238, 272–73,
    277
Washington, George, 8
Washington Post, 127, 129, 131–33, 157,
    164–65
Washington Star, 257
Weiss, Paul A., 262, 274
West Virginia State Board of Education v.
    Barnette, 194
Wiggins, Charles E., 165
Wigner, Eugene P., 261, 274
Wilson, Bryan, 47
Wittgenstein, Ludwig, 270
Wolff, Lester, 164
Wood, Allen Tate, 157–58, 181–82,
    185, 251
Woon-ha Kim, 122
Worldview, 125
Would-Be Gentleman, The (Jean Baptiste
    Molière), ix

Yae-heun Choi, 132
Yang You Chan, 187
Young-baik Kim, 123
Young-dal Ohm, 132
Young Oon Kim, 248–49
Yung Hwan Kim, 132, 161, 164

Subject Index

Academia (U.S.): KCIA attempts at manipulation of, 125–26, 168–71; and Unification church, 261–82
American Civil Liberties Union (ACLU), 193
American Civil Liberties Union of Northern California, 193
American Psychological Association (APA), 223
Anti-Semitism, and Unification church, 75–85, 92–93, 114–15

Civics, vs. religion, xiii–xviii
Civil liberties, of Unification church members, 193–216
Civil religion: decline of in U.S., 48–53; definitions of, 48; themes in Unification church, 59–66; of Unification church, xiii–xviii, 47–73; in U.S., xiii–xviii, 47–73
Collegiate Association for Research on Principles (CARP), 52–53, 58–59
Congress (U.S.): and Korea lobby, 162–68; and Unification church, 183–86
Critique: of Unification church, 20–43, 88–97; of Unification church theology, 90–97, 103–18

Divine Principle, 103–18, 232; definition of, 105; doctrines, 107–12; presuppositions, 105–7, 113–17; purpose of, 104; review and critique of, 104–12; theological critique of, 112–17. *See also* Name Index

Fifth International Conference on the Unity of the Sciences (ICUS: V),

261–82; founder's address, 13–18. *See also* Sciences
Freedom Leadership Foundation (FLF), 167, 179, 181, 186, 230; tax-exempt status of, 184–85
Funding, of Unification church, 245–58. *See also* Profits; Sponsorship, and science

Human rights, and KCIA, 121–47

Jews, and Unification church, 75–85
Judaism, and Unification church, 75–85, 92–93

Korea. *See* South Korean regime
Korea lobby, xvii, 161–74, 263; and South Korean regime, 263–64; and Unification church, 161–74, 263–64; and U.S. Congress, 162–68. *See also* South Korean regime
Korean Central Intelligence Agency (KCIA): clandestine activities in U.S., 121–47; and human rights, 121–47; NBC report on, 126–27, 244; and Unification church, xvii, 230–31, 246; and U.S. academia, 168–71; and U.S. policy, 132–35. *See also* South Korean regime
Korean Cultural and Freedom Foundation (KCFF), 130–31, 179, 186
Korean Institute of International Studies (KIIS), 169
Korean Traders Association (KTA), 171–74

Lifestyle, in Unification church, 53–55, 153–55, 237–38

Messianism, of Unification church, 92–94, 269
Metaphysics, of Unification church, 47–118

National Broadcasting Corporation (NBC), report on KCIA, 126–27, 244

Philosophy, of Unification church, 56–59
Politics, of Unification church, 118–216
Power, of Unification church, 149–59
Profits, of Unification church, 149–59, 233. See also Funding
Psychologists Interested in Religious Issues, 223
Psychology, of Unification church, 219–82

Religion, vs. civics, xiii–xviii. See also Civil religion; Theology of Unification church

Sciences: autonomy, 264–65; harmony among, 13–18; and sponsorship, 261–82; and values, 13–18, 264–65. See also Fifth International Conference on the Unity of the Sciences (ICUS: V)
Sociology, of Unification church, 219–82
South Korean regime: and Korea lobby, 263–64; and Unification church, xvii, 177–91, 233, 263–64; and U.S. academia, 263–64; U.S. policy toward, 132–35. See also Korea lobby; Korean Central Intelligence Agency (KCIA)
Sponsorship, and science, 261–82. See also Funding

Tax exemption: of FLF, 184–85; of Unification church, 184–85, 231, 239, 245
Theology, of Unification church, 3–43, 56–57, 90–97, 103–18. See also Religion, vs. civics
Theory: psychological, 222–25; of Unification church, 3–43

Unification church, 87–100; activities in New York City, 190–91; and anti-Semitism, 75–85, 92–93, 114–15; appeal, 55–59, 227–41; characteristics of members of, 53; charges and responses of, 20–43; civil liberties of members of, 193–216; as civil religion, xiii–xviii, 47–73; critique of, 20–43, 88–97, 103–18; decline of, 159, 243–58; financial resources of, 245–58; greed vs. creed in, 219–25; and Jews, 75–85; and Judaism, 75–85, 92–93; and KCIA, xvii, 230–31, 246; and Korea lobby, 161–74, 263–64; lifestyle of, 53–55, 153–55, 237–38; messianism in, 92–94; metaphysics of, 47–118; philosophy of, 56–59; politics of, 118–226; power of, 149–59; profits of, 149–59, 233; psychology of, 219–82; recruiting and training for, 235–41; as social movement, xiii–xviii; sociology of, 219–82; and South Korean regime, xvii, 177–91, 233, 263–64; tax-exempt status of, 184–85, 231, 239, 245; theory and theology of, 3–43, 56–57, 90–97, 103–18; and U.S. academia, 261–82; vs. U.S. churches, 97–100; and U.S. Congress, 183–86; use of diplomatic channels by, 186–90. See also Divine Principle

Values: absolute, 13–18, 270–71; and science, 13–18, 264–65